W9-ATP-750

TEMPTING TROPICALS

Please excuse the

TEMPTING TROPICALS

175 IRRESISTIBLE INDOOR PLANTS

ELLEN ZACHOS

TIMBER PRESS

Photographs are by the author unless otherwise identified.
Frontispiece: An orchid case is suitable for growing more than just orchids.

Copyright © 2005 by Ellen Zachos. All rights reserved.

Published in 2005 by

Timber Press, Inc.
The Haseltine Building
133 S.W. Second Avenue, Suite 450
Portland, Oregon 97204-3527, U.S.A.
www.timberpress.com
For contact information for editorial, marketing, sales, and distribution
in the United Kingdom, see www.timberpress.com/uk

Printed in Singapore

Library of Congress Cataloging-in-Publication Data

Zachos, Ellen.
    Tempting tropicals : 175 irresistible indoor plants / Ellen Zachos.
        p. cm.
    Includes bibliographical references.
    ISBN 0-88192-732-5 (hardback)
    1. House plants. 2. Tropical plants. I. Title.

SB419.Z33 2005
635.9'523--dc22

A catalog record for this book is also available from the British Library.

I dedicate this book to my husband, Michael, who indulges my obsession with exceptional patience and good will.

For years Michael has helped me understand science, tirelessly explaining the difference between relative and absolute humidity, or building a model out of cat toys to show me how the tilt of the earth's axis affects the quality of light we receive.

In turn, he has learned a thing or two about horticulture.

I thank him for giving in to temptation.

CONTENTS

PREFACE

Expand Your Plant Palette

Many moons ago I played Tzeitel in *Fiddler on the Roof* at the Jupiter Dinner Theater in Jupiter, Florida. Instead of sending me opening night flowers, my friend Mark gave me a *Spathiphyllum*. Mark and I had been on the road together with *Les Miz*, and in every town we played, his temporary lodging instantly became a real home, with the simple addition of a few houseplants. I was horticulturally clueless, but greatly admired Mark's skills. He must have been convinced there was a gardener inside me somewhere and the gift of a plant was all that was needed to unleash her.

He was right. After the show closed, my husband and I made a tour of Florida, and my *Spathiphyllum* was lovingly bundled into the car with us. She then became my carry-on luggage, and once home in New York City, we rearranged our bedroom to accommodate her light needs. She and I grew closer with every bloom; the road to obsession was a short step away.

I admit, I proved fickle; I outgrew my *Spathiphyllum* in a few years. As my horticultural tastes grew more adventurous, I sought out exotic plant material wherever I went. Each new show in each new town was an opportunity to explore a new group of greenhouses and nurseries. I began to work with plants between acting jobs. Most out-of-work actors waited on table—I renovated greenhouses. And one day, when an acting job interfered with my horticultural activities, I realized the time had come to give up the stage and focus on what mattered most.

This book is the product of years of obsessive collecting and education. The world of tropical plants has been underappreciated, and I often had to search long and hard for information and plant sources. Now, however, more unusual plant material is available than ever before; it's the perfect time to expand your plant palette. With this book, I hope to spare you some searching by providing both an encyclopedia and a reference guide. We'll start by discussing what makes a houseplant a houseplant, then move on to the tools of the trade, including potting mixes, pots and mounts, watering, and feeding.

We'll investigate the temptation to play god (the sun god, that is) by altering the light and humidity of our growing environments. I'll introduce you to various plant pests and diseases, and we'll discuss a few extracurricular activities.

Tempting Tropicals includes detailed descriptions and photographs of 175 unusual houseplants (no *Spathiphyllum*!), as well as advice on how to propagate them and keep them healthy. Information on how these plants grow in nature, along with a description of their basic morphology, will help you learn how to give them the care they need to thrive in an indoor environment.

I want this to be your favorite plant book, the first book you turn to when you're shopping for a new plant or need to solve a problem. I hope you'll share my enthusiasm and this book will encourage the development of what can be a most wonderful obsession.

Acknowledgments

Very special thanks to John Keane, my personal editor-in-chief. I depend upon his extraordinary research skills, broad knowledge base, and seemingly endless good will. Nothing escapes his notice. Thanks also to my sister Elizabeth, who generously offered to read and edit despite the demands of family and work. Many thanks to Katherine Powiss, librarian at the Horticultural Society of New York. Her generous assistance made my research more pleasant and complete. And thanks to Neal Maillet for deciding to give it a go.

I am grateful to the following growers, nurseries, and suppliers: Shawn Derouen at Stokes Tropicals; Dennis Cathcart at Tropiflora; Bisser Georgiev at Herbert Englemann Nurseries; Gregory, Eric, Scott, Jeff, and Gail Keil at Otto Keil; Dennis Schraeder at Landcraft Environments; Jessica Atchison at Ball Horticultural; Coastal Cuttings of Lake Worth, FL; Charlie's Greenhouse Supply; and Charles Walton at the Smithers-Oasis Company.

1

What Is a Houseplant?

What is the difference between a tropical plant and a houseplant? Many people use the terms interchangeably, but they are not exactly the same thing. A houseplant is any plant you grow successfully in your home. A tropical plant is any plant that is native to the tropics (that part of the earth located between the Tropic of Cancer to the north and the Tropic of Capricorn to the south). Although tropical habitats are typically warmer, brighter, and more humid than temperate climates, the tropics include a wide range of growing environments. There is a significant overlap between houseplants and tropical plants, but they are not identical.

Plant Classification

If the plant has unique characteristics, it may be given a cultivar name to distinguish it from other plants of the same species or hybrid. A genus is a group of plants classified together because of common ancestry; it can be constructed by humans or naturally occurring. The genus name is always capitalized and either underlined or italicized. A species is a further division of a genus and is also a closely related group of plants. Its name is always lowercase and, again, either underlined or italicized. A hybrid is the offspring of two different genera or two species. An intergeneric hybrid is usually given an entirely new genus name, with a multiplication sign preceding that name: ×*Aporophyllum*. An interspecific hybrid

Opposite: Grouping plants in a conservatory creates a welcoming environment and elevates ambient humidity.

name may be expressed as a cross between its two parents (*Pinguicula ehlerserac* × *P. oblingoloba*) or with a multiplication sign preceding the specific epithet, especially if hybridization has occurred in the wild: *Abutilon* ×*hybridum*.

Cultivar names can be confusing. A cultivar is a single genetic representation of a species or hybrid. It is usually created by humans, and its name is enclosed in single quotation marks. A cultivar name is given to a plant that is special enough to deserve distinction. For example, a hybridizer may experiment with breeding and create a generation of *Phalaenopsis* hybrids. The hybrids are all from the same parents, but have slightly different genetic makeups. Some are more beautiful, fragrant, disease resistant, and/or long-lived than others, and the most distinctive are singled out and given a cultivar name so everyone will know it's special and be able to buy it easily.

That's how it's supposed to work. Unfortunately, some growers see the naming of different cultivars as a marketing tool for increasing sales. They will gratuitously

GENUS	SPECIES	HYBRID	CULTIVAR
A group of plants classified together based on common ancestry	A further division of a genus; a closely related group of plants	Offspring resulting from crossing two species; hybrids of species from different genera are sometimes possible	A single genetic representation of a species or hybrid
Always capitalized; either italicized or underlined	Always lowercase, italicized or underlined	Species name preceded by a multiplication sign or both parents' names separated by a multiplication sign	Set off in single quotation marks
Aspidistra	*elatior*		'Milkyway'
Abutilon		×*hybridum*	
Pinguicula	*ehlerserac*	× *P. oblingoloba*	

Plant nomenclature simplified

distribute cultivar names among very similar plants, hoping that avid collectors will need one of everything.

You'll have to do some homework here. If you know that *Asplenium antiquum* 'Victoria' has a more relaxed, open shape than *A. antiquum*, you can make an educated choice and purchase the cultivar you prefer. If you see two very similar plants labeled *Codiaeum variegatum* 'Morning Sun' and *C. variegatum* 'Dawn's Early Light', you should probably do a little more research. Perhaps the plants are significantly different in ways not immediately obvious. Or, perhaps a grower, building on the popularity of one cultivar, has decided to give an almost identical plant a similar cultivar name in order to cash in on a good thing.

The Tropics

The earth's axis is tilted about 23.5° from vertical as it rotates around the sun. As a result, temperate latitudes have seasons; the two hemispheres receive varying intensities of sunlight, depending on the season. In the tropics, the intensity of light is more uniform than in other latitudes, since the angle of the sun does not change much during the course of a year. In temperate zones, the angle of the winter sun is more oblique, while in summer the angle is more direct. A more direct angle results in more intense sunlight hitting the earth. In addition, day length in the tropics is essentially the same all year round, whereas in temperate climates a winter day may include only nine hours of sunlight and a summer day may be 15 hours long. In other words, summer light in temperate zones lasts longer and is much more intense than winter light in the same location, while tropical regions receive a more even amount of intense sunlight all year long. Because the sun is almost directly overhead year round in the tropics, temperatures do not vary as widely as they do in temperate regions.

Although differences in elevation, weather patterns, and geology result in varying ecologies in the tropics, including rain forests, grasslands, and deserts, all of these environments are frost free. Tropical plants, in general, are killed by a frost.

Tropical Plants

Most of our houseplants are also tropical plants. This makes perfect sense when you consider the growing conditions of their native habitats. There are no well-defined seasons in the tropics. Although certain times of year can be considered "rainy" or "dry" seasons, there are no temperature fluctuations such as those we associate with the traditional four seasons of temperate climates. Growing conditions in your home are similarly uniform.

Now consider the temperature of an average home. Our indoor temperatures are consistently warm, ranging from 65 to 75°F (18–24°C). A plant that requires a dormant period with temperatures below freezing will probably not grow well for us indoors, where the temperature rarely drops below 60°F (16°C). On the other hand, our in-home temperatures are well-suited to growing tropical plants, which cannot survive freezing temperatures.

Light is a more complicated issue (and will be dealt with at greater length in chapter 3). Not only do the tropics receive more hours of daylight, but the light itself is more intense than light we can give plants indoors. While artificial light can be used to increase the number of species we can grow successfully, many full-sun tropical plants may not thrive in the home. Direct sunlight outdoors can be 10 times stronger than the sunlight that shines through glass onto a south-facing window sill. Even greenhouse glass blocks a substantial amount of the sun's intensity through reflection and diffraction. Light is an important limiting factor when it comes to growing indoors.

For example, *Lantana camara* is native to tropical South America, where it grows in full sun. While household temperatures are appropriate for growing *L. camara*, this plant requires more intense light than most of us can give it in our homes, even in a south-facing window. When grown indoors, it will bloom for a short period of time, then stop flowering and become leggy, producing long internodes between increasingly smaller leaves.

Tropicals whose native habitats are shaded or receive dappled light are better choices for most indoor gardeners. *Piper ornatum* is native to Brazil, where it grows as a groundcover on the floor of the rain forest. The light that reaches this plant is dappled, and this low intensity light is easily replicated in the home. It is important to consider a plant's native habitat when choosing a plant for your interior collection.

Houseplants

While many houseplants are native to the tropics, there are also temperate plants well-suited to growing indoors. Sometimes the term *subtropical* is used to describe the warm regions adjacent to the true tropics. Light frosts occasionally occur in these areas, but they are rare. "Mediterranean" climates and citrus-growing regions of the United States are both considered subtropical.

Clivia miniata is native to South Africa, which is situated south of the tropics in a warm, but temperate, climate. While the top growth of *C. miniata* cannot survive freezing, its roots may survive a frost and produce new foliage. This plant blooms best when autumn temperatures drop to about 40˚F (4˚C). It is easy to reproduce this seasonal temperature drop by keeping the plant in an unheated guestroom or leaving it outdoors until temperatures drop to 40˚F (4˚C), then bringing it indoors. *Clivia miniata* makes an excellent, low maintenance houseplant, despite its temperate origins.

Obviously not all plants native to temperate climates are suitable as houseplants. Some require a prolonged period of cold dormancy while others simply do not adapt well to indoor growing conditions. Many familiar garden perennials, such as *Pulmonaria longifolia*, will not flourish as houseplants. While you might be able to give it adequate light in your home, it would be quite difficult to reproduce the garden conditions (high humidity, good air circulation, evenly moist, humus-rich soil) under which *P. longifolia* thrives.

Although the majority of houseplants are tropicals, I have included a few excellent subtropical plants in this book, simply because they are worth growing. Ultimately, what is most important is that a plant grows well indoors. Consider temperature, light, and any other idiosyncrasies of habitat before experimenting with a new plant species. And remember, the more you know about the way a plant grows in nature, the better your chances for successful indoor gardening.

2

Sustenance

Plants are enormously adaptable, and thank goodness for that. We ask them to grow without sunlight and they do. We try to grow them without soil, and they oblige. But without water there is no plant life, of that you can be sure. So let's talk about what every plant absolutely must have in order to survive—H_2O.

Watering a plant sounds simple, but in fact it is an art. Overwater and you kill the plant. Underwater and you kill the plant. The symptoms of both can look bafflingly similar. In essence, what happens is the same. When plants are watered too infrequently, their roots don't absorb enough water, and the plant shrivels and dies. When plants are watered too frequently, their roots never dry out the way they should. As a result, they rot, and the plant has no way to absorb water or nutrients. Its leaves start to look shriveled, and the plant eventually dies.

Watering is infinitely variable, and you must grasp several basic concepts to achieve competence in this area. Only by understanding how a plant uses water, as well as what affects the rate at which water is used, can you accommodate a plant's needs.

Although everyone knows that plants need water, not everyone understands how much they need or why the amount of water is important, so let's start there. Plants in the ground have a vast amount of earth through which they can extend their roots in search of water and nutrients. Plants in containers have a very limited amount of potting mix from which their roots can draw water and nutrition. The amount of potting mix in a container determines how much water can be retained. Water molecules adhere to soil particles, displacing air molecules that are present when the potting mix is dry. A plant needs both water and oxygen, so it's important to find the right balance in your watering schedule. You must allow the soil to dry out enough to provide the plant's roots with oxygen; keeping the soil consistently damp may make it impossible for the plant to breathe. (That being said, some plants have adapted to soggy soils and grow best in potting mixes that are consistently wet. This is an exception to the rule.)

Water enters a plant through its roots, travels up through the plant's vascular tissue to the leaves, and is eventually released to the air via transpiration, the giving off of water through stomata on the underside of plant leaves as a byproduct of photosynthesis. Water also leaves the plant's foliage through the process of osmosis, the passage of water from a region of high water density through a semipermeable membrane to a region of low water density. When humid air surrounds the plant, it slows the rate of osmosis. Conversely, drier air speeds the process.

It is extremely important to water a plant thoroughly each time you water it. Thorough watering means watering a plant until water runs out the drainage holes in the bottom of the pot. If a plant is bark-mounted, or potted in bark mix, thorough watering means soaking the entire plant (pot/mount and all) for 10 minutes or so in a bowl of water. If you water a plant incompletely, you encourage root growth only in the portion of soil that has been watered. This means that roots grow only through the portion of soil that receives moisture, instead of deeply and throughout the pot.

One of the primary functions of any root system is to provide anchorage for the plant. A plant with an underdeveloped root system is at a disadvantage because it will not have the ability to absorb adequate water and nutrients from the soil, and it will not be well anchored where it grows. If a root system is confined to the top few inches of a container, it is entirely possible for that plant to tip out of its pot. (I've seen it happen; it's not a pretty sight.)

Every plant requires this kind of complete watering, from the moisture-loving *Pinguicula* to the drought-tolerant *Dioscorea*, from the 2-inch pot to the 3-foot planter box. What varies is the optimal frequency of watering. This is determined by several variables: the physical structure of the plant; the temperature, light, and humidity levels of its environment; its stage of growth; the size and material of its container; and its potting medium.

Many plants experience a dramatic difference between dry and rainy seasons in their native habitats. To survive annual periods of drought, these plants may go dormant, thereby conserving resources. Some plants, if given adequate resources year-round, no longer experience dormancy when brought into cultivation. Others continue to require a dormant period.

The idea of dormancy may be initially intimidating but is both simple to handle and exciting to navigate. My first experience was inadvertent. After watching the foliage of several *Caladium* hybrids turn yellow and die, I dug up the tubers, intending to overwinter them in a pot of peat moss in my cellar. Despite my excellent intentions, the tubers sat in an open plastic bag on my potting bench all winter long. In April, I noticed new growth emerging from several tubers, which I promptly potted up and grew. Without really trying, I had brought my *Caladium* tubers through dormancy successfully. The point is that most plants will tell you when it's time for them to go dormant and when it's time for them to grow again. Watch for the signs and play along.

Physiology

At the beginning of this chapter, I wrote that plants are enormously adaptable, and nowhere is this more apparent than when looking at the numerous ways plants can store and retain water under dry conditions. Many desert plants have developed a specialized method of photosynthesis in order to conserve every possible water molecule. Some plants have developed an especially thick cuticle (a waxy layer covering the plant's epidermis) to slow their rate of transpiration. A cuticle creates a barrier between moisture in the plant foliage and the surrounding air. The foliage thus loses less water through transpiration, and the plant can go longer between waterings.

Look for visual cues about your plants' water needs. Members of the cactus family have modified foliage (spines) and specialized storage tissue that allows them to go for long periods of time without water. Succulent plants have fleshy leaves and stems that can store water. Other plants, while not classified as succulents, may have thick leaves and cuticles and are therefore relatively drought-tolerant. Many members of the genus *Hoya* fall into this category, as do many peperomias, and even *Phalaenopsis*. Conversely, plants with delicate, thin leaves and slim stems lose water more quickly through transpiration, making specimens like *Fittonia verschaffeltii* higher maintenance houseplants.

If your landscape involves underplanting trees and massing various species, be sure to group plants with similar watering needs. Don't underplant a large *Euphorbia tirucalli* with *Cissus discolor*. You may certainly combine desert and rainforest plants in the same landscape, but give them separate containers.

Environmental Influences

You've probably noticed that your plants require less frequent watering in winter. This is a function of reduced temperatures and shorter daylight hours. In early spring, most tropicals begin to grow more rapidly in response to longer daylight hours and warmer temperatures. As their growth rate increases, so does their need for water. Water + Light + Carbon Dioxide $\rightarrow$ Oxygen + Energy + Nutrients. This is photosynthesis, a plant's means of producing its own food. For the rate of photosynthesis to increase, a plant requires more water, more light, and more carbon dioxide. Therefore, plants require more water as they move into active growth.

Plants in north-facing windows require less frequent watering than those in south-facing windows. The lower light and temperature of northern exposures results in slower photosynthesis and transpiration. Higher temperatures and light levels increase a plant's need for water and nutrients, and when these nutritional demands are met, the plant is able to grow more rapidly under warm, bright conditions. If nutritional demands are not met, new growth will be thin, spindly, and pale. If this happens, cut back the weak new growth and adjust your watering and feeding schedule.

Many city apartments are too warm and dry for humans as well as plants. Have you ever woken up on a winter morning with a nose so dry you could hardly breathe? Your mucus membranes aren't the only things in need of rehydration. Warm, dry air increases the frequency with which you should water your houseplants. If you control your own thermostat, consider maintaining a nighttime temperature of 60 to 65°F (16 to 18°C) and a daytime temperature of 70°F (21°C). Your plants will require less frequent watering and will be less stressed by heat and dryness.

Arranging plants in groups is an excellent way to increase ambient humidity. The air in a fully landscaped interior is more humid than the air in a room with no plants.

As one plant loses water to transpiration, that moisture passes into the air immediately surrounding the plant's foliage. Other nearby plants benefit from the moist air and contribute to it as they, in turn, transpire. With numerous plants in a single area, the air becomes more humid. Each plant then loses less water to the surrounding air and requires less frequent watering. Increased humidity is healthier and more comfortable for plants, and also for the humans inhabiting your landscape.

You might consider raising ambient humidity by incorporating drywells into your interior landscape. A drywell is a tray or saucer of pebbles upon which your plants sit. Keep the pebbles covered with water, just up to the level of the bottom of the pots. As the water evaporates from underneath and around the pebbles, it humidifies the air around the plants, reducing their need for water.

If you're growing under artificial lights, be aware that this, too, increases your plants' need for water. The lights generate heat and dry out container soil, while increased light hours speed up photosynthesis and transpiration. The closer the lights are to the plant material, the more frequently you will need to water.

Active Growth

Most houseplants are in active growth from spring through fall. Active growth indicates a high rate of photosynthesis, which requires frequent watering to support it. Some plants, however, are in active growth when you least expect it. For example, while most houseplants require less frequent watering in January or February, that is exactly when *Clivia miniata* blooms, after a period of cool drought. Your clivia will need increased water at this time to support flowering. Your cue will be when you see the beginning of a bloom stalk.

Similarly, winter cacti grow best with a period of cool, dry dormancy in early fall, followed by a period of bloom in the winter. Once buds start to form on these epiphytic cacti, increase the frequency with which you water.

Container Choice

When creating an interior landscape, you will certainly give careful consideration to your containers. But did you know that the type of container you choose can affect the frequency with which you'll need to water? Both the size and the material of which the pot is constructed are significant.

The smaller the pot, the smaller the volume of soil and water it can hold. Therefore, a small pot needs watering more frequently, since its soil cannot accommodate as much water as a larger container. In addition, a pot made from a porous material such as clay or wood will lose water by evaporation through the container walls as well as through the soil surface. Containers made from nonporous materials such as plastic or metal will lose water through the soil surface only, and so will need less frequent watering. A porous terra cotta container becomes nonporous when covered with a waterproof glaze.

Container choice is primarily a matter of aesthetics, but there are practical considerations as well when planting large containers. Large trees or mixed plantings can be prohibitively heavy if potted in clay or wood. If you anticipate rearranging your landscape, the lighter weight of plastic or fiberglass containers is worth considering. Fortunately, there are attractive fiberglass pots on the market that resemble clay and cast cement. They are lightweight and nonporous, requiring less frequent watering than their clay counterparts. They are also easier to maintain, since minerals and salts leached from your water source do not accumulate on the pot rims.

If you choose to pot your plants in plastic for practical purposes, you may want to double-pot them in more attractive containers, such as art pottery or wicker cachepots. This is an excellent way to combine the practicality of a nonporous pot with the beauty of a unique container.

Potting Media

The composition of your potting medium also affects the frequency with which you water your plants. There are several things to consider. Garden soil is not recommended for potting houseplants because it is heavy and may contain harmful pathogens such as insects and fungi. Soil weight is an important concern, especially when landscaping with large containers. A half whiskey barrel full of wet soil is impossible for the average gardener to move. Also, garden soil dries out much more slowly than commercial potting mixes, and in a large nonporous container, garden soil could stay too wet too long, leading to poor oxygenation of the soil.

Many commercial potting mixes are actually soilless; these will be labeled "promix" or "professional potting mix" rather than "potting soil." They are lightweight and well-suited to growing tropicals. Peat moss is a common ingredient in soilless mixes and is used both for its light weight and its ability to retain water and nutrients. However, when peat moss dries out completely, it becomes hydrophobic, difficult to rewet. As a result, soilless mixes composed entirely of peat should not be allowed to get thoroughly dry. When shopping for a container mix, look for a combination of peat, perlite or vermiculite, bark, and a wetting agent, and check the proportions. Fafard makes several excellent mixes of varying weights, containing enough peat to keep them lightweight, but not so much that they become hydrophobic when dry. MetroMix 250 is appropriate for containers and comes in large bags (3 cubic feet). Promix BX is another good basic soilless mix. It comes in compressed bales of 4 cubic feet, from which you can make about 7 cubic feet of mix.

Prepared potting soil differs from ordinary garden soil in several ways. First, it is composed of sterilized, loamy soil, sand, perlite or vermiculite, and peat moss. The pH may have been adjusted for optimal growing, and both macro- and micronutrients are sometimes added. If you grow moisture-loving plants, consider using a soil-based potting mix. It will retain water longer than a soilless mix and drain more slowly, thus decreasing the frequency with which you need to water.

Certain plants require special potting mixes. As you learn more about how your favorite plants grow, you may decide to blend your own potting mixes. Creating a custom mix is simple. If you keep a few basic ingredients on hand, you'll be able to mix up exactly what you need. Start with the horticultural equivalent of a baking mix (not from scratch, but not ready-made, either). In other words, find a bagged mix you like and tinker with it, adding bark to make it drain more quickly, or steril-

POTTING MIX TYPE	BARK	PEAT MOSS	HORTICUL- TURAL CHARCOAL	PERLITE	STERILIZED SOIL	SAND
All purpose mix	3 parts	1 part		1 part		
General epiphyte mix	2 parts	2 parts	$1/2$ part	2 parts		
Cactus mix				1 part	1 part	1 part
Moisture- retentive mix		2 parts		$1/2$ part	2 parts	

Potting mix formulas

ized soil to make it retain water longer. Once you've got the feel of it, you can try composing a potting mix from scratch.

Epiphytes can be bark-mounted, mimicking the way they grow in nature. All of the epiphytes mentioned in this book will grow in containers, but you might enjoy mounting a specimen and learning how to grow it epiphytically. For instructions on how to do this, see chapter 10.

Fertilization

Fertilization in container growing is especially important to understand. Because the plant has a small volume of potting medium from which to draw nutrition, it is important that it be up to the task. Several components actually have no nutritional value whatsoever but are used for other reasons. Peat does not contribute nutrition to a potting mix, but it retains both water and nutrients well. Perlite does not contain nutrients, but is used to aerate the soil. Bark can also be used for aeration purposes, since the large size of the bark pieces creates a coarse mix. Both bark and soil contain organic material in various stages of decomposition. As organic matter decomposes, its nutrients become available to plant roots.

You should also remember that the more quickly a potting mix drains, the more rapidly its nutrients will leach from the mix. For this reason, you cannot rely solely on the nutrients in your mix and will ultimately have to feed your plants. Even the most nutrition-packed medium will eventually have its unconsumed nutrients leached by repeated waterings.

There are three primary types of fertilizers to consider: balanced, bloom-booster, and high nitrogen. A balanced fertilizer contains equal amounts of nitrogen, phosphates, and potash, and it encourages strong, all-around growth. The package is marked with three equal numbers (5-5-5 or 10-10-10, for example), which indicate the percentage of the fertilizer weight of each nutritional component. Nitrogen promotes healthy, green foliage; phosphates support root development and flower and fruit production; and potash is necessary for all-around health, as well as resistance to diseases and insects.

Some plants have special nutritional needs. For example, an epiphyte mounted on bark or potted in a bark mix requires extra nitrogen. Bark decomposes more slowly than soil, releasing less nitrogen to the plant's roots. In this case, use a fertilizer that has a higher first number, such as 30-10-10. If your plant isn't blooming the way you think it should, try feeding it with a "bloom-booster," that is, a fertilizer with a higher percentage of phosphates (and a formula with a higher middle number, like 5-10-5).

I think most people overfeed their plants, and I think most plant food labels encourage this overfeeding (after all, they're trying to sell plant food). As a general rule, use a balanced liquid fertilizer at half the recommended strength every other week during the growing season. For most of us the growing season begins in early spring and continues through early fall. If you notice buds forming, leaves emerging, or stems lengthening, the plant is in active growth.

Water-soluble fertilizers are easy to use. They can be added to water and given to your plant when you water. You can soak plants in a solution of fertilizer and water (especially good for epiphytes potted in bark-based mixes) or you can spray a fertilizer solution onto the leaves with a mister. This is called a *foliar feed*, and it is a quick, direct way of getting nutrients to your plant. If you choose a foliar feed, make sure you spray early in the day so any liquid left standing on the leaves has plenty of time to evaporate. Standing water at cooler night temperatures creates a breeding ground for plant diseases.

Time-release, granular plant foods are convenient, popular, and fine for many tropicals. As with water-soluble powders, different formulations of granules are available, providing either balanced nutrition or a specific concentration of nutrients. If, however, your plant is potted in bark, granules may fall through the spaces between bark pieces, so for these plants, use a solution rather than a granule. Check the package of any time-release fertilizer for recommended application intervals.

It is entirely possible to kill a plant with kindness; overfertilization can be deadly. A white crusty buildup on the edge of your pot or on the surface of the mix indicates that the fertilizer salts are not being fully flushed from the container. Too much fertilizer can burn the roots, which results in foliage damage and eventually can kill the plant. If you notice this type of buildup, stop fertilizing your plant and repot with fresh mix. With fertilization, it's better to err on the side of too little rather than too much.

Paraphernalia

Now that you fully understand everything that affects the frequency with which a plant needs to be watered and fed, it's time to consider how you will water your plants. What tools do you need?

There are several alternatives to the traditional watering can, and you can choose your tool according to your personal style. An indoor hose with a wand attachment can be hooked up to your sink with an inexpensive adapter. Hoses are lightweight and come in many lengths. Some are coiled, like telephone cords, and thus store easily. Wands may be used for watering or misting.

For watering hanging plants, you might consider a plastic squeeze bottle and tube combination. A rigid tube extends 2 to 3 feet from the top of the bottle, then curves down, making a "U" turn. Water can be squeezed from the bottle, through the tubing, to the soil surface, allowing you to water without taking hanging baskets down from their perches. If you water hanging plants in place, watch for spills. Consider holding a plastic wash basin under the plant to catch extra water, and tip the plant to pour out water left in the saucer.

A baster is an extremely useful utensil when performing your regular watering duties. Use it to suck up extra water from plant saucers. Overflowing water can ruin your floor or carpet, and a plant sitting in water is at risk for root rot. A simple, inexpensive baster can help you prevent both of these problems.

Finally, the traditional watering can is a handy tool. Any can should have a smooth flow of water; a long narrow spout will allow you to place the water exactly where you want it, without spilling or wetting foliage. Wider spouts deliver a greater volume of water more quickly than narrower spouts, so consider the size of the container you are watering when choosing a watering can.

Permanent plantings, such as walls of ferns or orchids, may be misted frequently instead of watered in the traditional manner, but I don't mean just a spritz from a mini-spray bottle. Consider a Herrmidifier humidifier aimed at the epiphytes. Hooked up to a hose, this humidifier can run constantly, and with a humidistat you can choose the relative humidity range best suited to your plants. A lighter duty alternative is a 4-gallon humidifier made by Vornado. It has a built-in humidistat and can operate for 24 to 32 hours between refills. You can keep it on a timer and run it while you're at work or asleep. For a thorough foliage soaking, use a 2- to 3-gallon pump sprayer containing water or a mixture of water and fertilizer. Or, use a misting head on your wand attachment to deliver a fine spray of water.

There are several chemicals in water that are actually harmful to certain plants. Many communities add fluoride to their water (approximately one-half to 1 part per million [ppm]) to reduce tooth decay. Unfortunately, some of our most common houseplants are easily damaged by fluoride, including *Chlorophytum* species, *Cordyline terminalis,* and many palms. *Maranta* species, *Spathiphyllum* species, and *Ctenanthe* species are also sensitive. The damage begins with grayish, watery lesions on foliage which eventually dies and turns tan or brown. This usually occurs at leaf tips and moves down the leaf. A general yellowing of the leaf may also result from fluoride damage.

Small amounts of fluoride occur naturally in some groundwater. A potting mix with a pH level higher than 6.5 will reduce the availability of fluoride to your plants, but if your water is heavily fluoridated, you may need to reconsider growing some of the more fluoride sensitive plants. Alternatively, you could use rainwater or distilled water to water sensitive specimens. Or, if your water is heavily

Chlorophytum amaniense shows fluoride damage on foliage.

This *Alsobia dianthiflora* has ring spot resulting from cold water damage.

fluoridated, consider installing an activated alumina, reverse osmosis, or distillation filter. These remove between 80 and 99 percent of the fluoride.

Chlorine is not present in treated tap water at concentrations high enough to damage plants. In fact, treated tap water includes chlorine at the rate of 1 ppm, while damage does not usually occur unless chlorine exceeds 70 ppm. Many growers let their tap water sit for 24 hours to allow the chlorine to escape, which is unnecessary. It does, however, provide the benefit of warming your tap water to room temperature.

In general, it's best to give your plants tepid or room temperature water. While some plants tolerate cold water on their roots, others react strongly and adversely. Cold water shocks roots, and over time this can stunt growth and weaken the general health of your plants, making them susceptible to disease. Be especially careful with gesneriads. Watering a gesneriad with cold water may result in cream-colored streaks and blotches on the foliage—this is called *ring spot*.

The key to successful watering and feeding is to correctly gauge how frequently you must deliver, not the amount you should give your plant. Each plant has its own optimal schedule, which you will establish by careful observation of the above criteria. A general rule of thumb for houseplants in containers less than 12 inches in diameter is that they need water when the top inch of soil feels dry to the touch. Stick your finger into the soil, and if it feels dry down to the first knuckle, it's time to water. Large trees and plants in containers more than 14 inches in diameter should be judged by a different standard. The top 2 to 3 inches of soil can feel dry to the touch before these plants require watering.

Over time, you will develop a feel for how often your plants need water. You can tell from across the room if a plant is thirsty or drowning by the color and turgor of its leaves, as well as by its feel. Don't be afraid to get your hands dirty—put them into the soil, test the moisture at different levels. Consistent care and attention on your part will always be essential to the health of your plants.

3

Let There Be Light

Although I've lived in New York City for many years, that sun-drenched apartment of real estate listings lore remains a fantasy. I long for a spacious loft with windows that stretch from ceiling to floor in four directions. Instead I have a studio apartment facing a brick wall. Fortunately, our home in Pennsylvania gets wonderful light, and I do most of my growing there. But I couldn't possibly spend even a few days a week in a place without plants; it wouldn't feel like home.

There have been great innovations and improvements in artificial light in the past 5 to 10 years, so even the complete absence of direct sunlight need not limit your interior landscape. If you have only north-facing windows but cannot rest until you've flowered *Hoya caudata*, consider augmenting your natural light.

Exposures Explained

Let's review the four basic exposures of light in your home. The brightest is usually a southern exposure. If it's unobstructed by trees or neighboring buildings, a southern window will probably get at least eight hours of direct sunlight per day. A western window gets afternoon sun. The amount depends on whether the view is clear or obstructed. Afternoon sun is usually warmer than morning sun.

An unobstructed eastern window receives morning light. This will be a cooler location than a western window but approximately equal in brightness, depending on neighboring obstructions. A northern window provides indirect light all day long. The brightness will depend on whether the window is blocked by anything outdoors.

In general, plants we grow for their flowers need more intense light to bloom. This means a southern, western, or eastern exposure. Plants grown for their foliage usually require less intense light.

Think about how these plants grow in nature. A plant whose native habitat is in full sun will need the brightest light you can give it indoors; a southern window will be best. An epiphyte, which lives in dappled light in nature, should probably be grown in an eastern or western window indoors. A tropical groundcover will not require intense sun; the indirect light of a northern exposure is adequate for healthy growth.

Skylights in a room increase available light and should be factored in, as should other variables such as awnings or eaves that might block light coming in a window. Reflective surfaces immediately outside a window (a body of water, a snow-covered lawn) will increase the light that enters through that window.

A greenhouse or conservatory room will get light from more than one direction because of its glass walls and roof. A freestanding greenhouse may get light from all four directions, as well as from directly overhead. A lean-to greenhouse will get light from at least one, and possibly three directions, plus overhead.

A conservatory room may be designed with either plants or people as a priority. If the room is primarily for human enjoyment, it may have been built with treated glass, which reduces the intensity of both visible and ultraviolet light. This glass makes the room more comfortable for people because it reduces heat buildup. A greenhouse with the thermostat set to 80°F (27°C) can easily reach 110°F (43°C) on a sunny, winter afternoon by virtue of the sun's radiation. This is something to factor in when making your plant choices or designing a conservatory room.

You can adjust your available light (to a certain extent) with sheer curtains or plant placement. If you don't want to hang curtains, you can move a plant away from the window, either to the side or deeper into the room, where the light that reaches it will be less intense.

Also, if you create layers in your interior landscape, you can provide varying light intensities. Tall trees in front of the windows will get direct sun, while small epiphytes hung from those trees receive dappled light. Floor specimens placed at a distance from the windows, or groundcovers used to underplant large specimen plants, will get indirect light.

How Plant Variegation Relates to Sunlight

Photosynthesis takes place in plant chloroplasts. Chloroplasts are plant organelles that produce several different plant pigments, such as chlorophyll *a* and *b*, carotene, and xanthophylls. All of these pigments contribute to photosynthesis, but chlorophyll *a* is the most important. A high chlorophyll content is marked by a deep green leaf color and denotes a great ability to photosynthesize.

A completely white leaf contains no pigments and cannot produce food. A plant with only white leaves would soon starve to death; a few white leaves on a plant may be supported by normal, pigmented leaves. Variegated foliage may be a combination of many colors: green, white, red, yellow, orange, purple, or silver. Variegated foliage contains less chlorophyll than solid green foliage and therefore has a lower photosynthetic capacity. In order to produce adequate food for healthy growth, a highly variegated plant requires more light to produce the same amount of food as a solid green-leaved plant. This is why highly variegated plants, such as *Codiaeum variegatum*, are recommended for high light situations.

If a highly variegated plant is grown in inadequate light, it may revert to a less intensely variegated leaf. In an effort to stay alive, a plant will produce more chloroplasts and consequently more chlorophyll. This chlorophyll masks the other, variously colored pigments.

While intense variegation is a desirable quality to many plant collectors, it's not something frequently found in nature. Lots of chlorophyll translates into lots of plant food. Plants less able to feed themselves are less likely to live long enough to successfully reproduce. This may be why plants in nature are not usually highly variegated. For example, the native species of *C. variegatum* bears little resemblance to the *C. variegatum* cultivars sold in most nurseries today. The straight species is considerably greener and less splashy than hybrids produced by humans. Hybridizers have manipulated recessive genes to selectively breed the highly variegated plants we grow in cultivation.

Characteristics of Light

There are several types of bulbs suitable for interior growing, and three characteristics of light to consider when you're deciding which bulb to use: color, intensity, and duration.

COLOR

The sun emits light in all colors of the visible spectrum: red, orange, yellow, green, blue, and violet. White light is a combination of all of these. However, not all colors of light are equally valuable to plants. Light in the blue and red ranges is most important for plant growth. Flowering plants require large amounts of orange and red light in order to bloom and set fruit, and light in the blue range promotes lush foliage.

INTENSITY

Light intensity is measured in several ways. Gardeners use the term *foot-candle*, which is defined as the "strength of light given off by 1 candle at a distance of 1 foot." (One foot-candle also equals 1 lumen per square foot.) Recently botanists have begun using another term, PAR, for photosynthetically available radiation, which is the amount of light available in the wavelengths necessary for photosynthesis. Light that seems bright to the human eye is not necessarily intense enough for optimum growth of tropical plants. Low light intensity may not kill a plant, but can result in weak growth with elongated internodes. Without adequate light, plants will not fruit or flower.

Consider that outdoors on a sunny day the light intensity of direct sunlight at noon can be many times stronger than the light that reaches a bright windowsill through a pane of glass. Don't panic. This does not mean it is impossible to grow plants indoors. Many wonderful tropicals are shade plants in their native habitats and do not require bright, direct sun. But some people assume that because a room

F-STOP	FOOT-CANDLES
2	100
2.8	200
4	370
5.6	750
8	1,500
11	2,800
16	5,000

Foot-candle calculation: With an SLR camera, set the film speed to ASA 25 and the shutter speed to 1/60th of a second. Focus on a sheet of white paper or cardboard in the area where you want to measure the light intensity. Foot-candles correspond roughly to the F-stop values shown in this table.

is full of light cast by incandescent or halogen bulbs, it is bright enough to grow a wide range of plants, and this is simply not the case.

DURATION

Duration refers to the number of hours of light a plant receives each day. If your landscape includes primarily foliage plants with a few blooming species, 14 hours a day is plenty. Other plants require longer exposure in order to flower and set fruit. Since artificial light doesn't exactly duplicate the color and intensity of sunlight, we compensate by giving plants additional hours of artificial light. The increased quantity compensates for reduced quality. While some plants will grow in constant light, many require some hours of darkness to flower and fruit. This is called *photoperiodism*. The amount of darkness required by a plant for optimal growth varies according to species.

Fluorescent Lights

Fluorescent lights are probably the most familiar types of grow-bulbs and are adequate for growing many foliage plants as well as supplementing natural light in a northern or eastern window. Bulbs and fixtures are inexpensive and require no special wiring or installation. They emit less heat than other types of bulbs and are therefore also recommended for use in terrariums and closed cases.

The type of fluorescent light used in commercial spaces (offices, stores) is usually produced by cool white bulbs. These emit a bluish light; they are inexpensive and easy to find. Warm white tubes emit more light in the red end of the spectrum. They are only slightly more expensive, and any good lighting store will carry them. Seeds can be started under cool or warm white bulbs, and many foliage plants can also be grown successfully under these lights.

There are also full-spectrum fluorescent tubes engineered to provide light in the wavelengths most useful to plants, those in the blue and orange-red ranges. To the human eye, the light given off by these bulbs is similar in color to that of the noonday sun. Aesthetically, it is quite pleasant. However, there is some controversy over whether these bulbs are worth the additional expense. Many growers believe that a combination of the less expensive cool and warm white tubes is equally effective; I use the full spectrum bulbs. If you are just beginning to experiment with growing under fluorescents, start with the less expensive bulbs and see how you do. If your plants grow well but you don't like the quality of the light itself, consider buying the full spectrum tubes.

Regular fluorescents and full spectrum bulbs are available in 24-inch and 48-inch lengths, which are the standard sizes for both grow-light and other fluorescent fixtures. Compact fluorescent bulbs can be used in individual spot or lamp fixtures. Full spectrum, high output fluorescent bulbs and fixtures are available from specialty supply catalogs, several of which are listed in "Resources."

Fluorescent lights are most efficient when used with curved reflectors that direct maximum light down toward the plants. You may decide to use fluorescent bulbs in a more finished, furniture-like fixture, but these will be less efficient, since they were not specifically designed to focus the reflected light on the growing area. Compact, free-standing models, perfect for growing on shelves or table tops, are also available. Fluorescent tubes should be replaced every 12 to 18 months, if they are being used approximately 14 hours each day.

It's a good idea to place plants with similar light needs under a single fixture, but it is also possible to vary the light intensity each plant gets by careful placement. The closer the plant is to the light tubes, the more intense the light it will receive.

Fluorescent lights in an adjustable tabletop fixture

Because fluorescent lights give off very little heat, plants can be placed close to the bulbs (3 to 4 inches) without risk of burning. Plants that grow best with more light can be raised closer to the tubes by placing them on overturned pots. In addition, plants receive less light when placed under the ends of the tubes than at the center. Plants requiring less intense light should be placed under the 3 inches of tube at either end of the fixture.

Incandescent Lights

Incandescent grow-bulbs are a less efficient means of artificial illumination, since much of their energy is given off as heat, rather than as visible light. They are not completely without merit, however. They emit an attractive white light, they can be used in many household fixtures, and they are adequate for certain low-light foliage plants. If a dark corner of your home calls for a large specimen plant, you might install an *Aspidistra elatior* or a *Tetrastigma voinierianum* under a single incandescent grow bulb. A 60-watt bulb at a distance of 2 feet will provide approximately 20 foot-candles of light. This is low intensity light, and plant growth will

Incandescent lights in a track light fixture

not be rampant, but certain species can be maintained under these conditions. Since incandescent bulbs are hot, be sure not to place the foliage too close to the light, or it may burn. A minimum distance of 18 to 24 inches is recommended.

Mercury Vapor Bulbs

Mercury vapor grow-bulbs emit a broader spectrum with considerably more power than incandescent grow-bulbs. They can be used in any incandescent flood-light-type lamp with a ceramic socket. They are self-ballasted, 150-watt bulbs, and are hotter than both incandescent and fluorescent lights, so be sure to keep your foliage at a safe distance from the fixture. If you need intense light but aren't ready to invest in a larger system, try a mercury vapor bulb.

High Intensity Discharge Lights

If you want to be able to grow anything and everything indoors, and your natural light is holding you back, you should consider high intensity discharge (HID) lights. These are the brightest lamps available and the most widely used by the commercial greenhouse industry. They can be installed anywhere in your home, garage, or greenhouse to supplement existing light or as the sole source of light for your plants. The fixtures themselves are somewhat bulky and plain, but they are wonderfully effective.

There are two subcategories of HID lamps, metal halide (MH) and high pressure sodium (HPS), each producing a different color of light. The color is determined by the specific blend of gasses contained in the ceramic or glass tube at the center of the bulb.

Both metal halide and high pressure sodium lights emit considerably more intense light than fluorescent or incandescent lamps. HID lights are twice as efficient as fluorescent lamps: one 400-watt halide system emits as much light as twenty 40-watt, 4-foot fluorescent tubes (800 watts, total). So, while the initial expense of an HID system is greater than that of a fluorescent setup, it will cost less money to run once it's in place.

All HID lights can run off regular 110-volt household current but require special fixtures with ballasts. A horizontally oriented ballast will run 25 percent cooler and therefore last longer than a vertically oriented ballast. Make sure all electrical equipment meets Underwriters Laboratories (UL) standards; a label on the fixture should state the product is "UL listed." In order for a product to have a UL Listing mark, it must pass dozens of tests, including tests for risk of fire and electrical shock and hazards. If you are ordering by telephone, be sure to ask the person taking your order if the product is UL listed.

METAL HALIDE (MH) BULBS

Metal halide bulbs give off light that is strongest at the blue end of the spectrum and looks most like natural sunlight. This light produces compact, leafy growth and is preferable when your light garden is an integral part of your home, since the light does not distort the colors of the plants (and people) it illuminates. Agrosun metal halides were engineered for agricultural use. They are color corrected and emit 15 percent more red-orange light than regular metal halides. Metal halide bulbs are less expensive than high pressure sodium (HPS) lamps, but need to be replaced more frequently, about once a year. If you are growing plants mainly for their foliage, this may be the best choice for you.

High intensity discharge (HID) lights: metal halide (MH) bulbs cast a bluish light.

HIGH PRESSURE SODIUM (HPS) BULBS

High pressure sodium bulbs last about twice as long as metal halide (MH) lamps but cost slightly more per bulb. They're preferred by greenhouse growers who use them to supplement daylight. High pressure sodium lamps emit a light strong at the red-orange end of the spectrum, thus promoting flowering and fruiting. However, they may also produce leggy plant growth unless used in conjunction with daylight or a MH system. If your goal is lots of bloom, use HPS lamps, but remember, their light has a strong red-orange cast and distorts the colors of everything

High intensity discharge (HID) lights: high pressure sodium (HPS) bulbs cast a yellow-orange light.

and everyone it illuminates. (My husband won't allow it in the living room!) New HPS bulbs with 25 to 30 percent more light in the blue spectrum are now available under the names Son Agro, Super Agro, and Hortilux. Using one of these bulbs means you may not need to supplement your HPS lamp with a MH light.

You can use a combination of HPS and MH lamps in a single location, but a MH bulb cannot be used in a HPS fixture, and vice versa. The ballast systems for the two types of bulbs are different. If you are using multiple fixtures, consider a combination of HPS and MH systems. If you have only one fixture, you may use a conversion bulb. A MH fixture can be fitted with a conversion bulb, which emits a sodium-type light; conversion bulbs are available in all sizes for halide fixtures. There is only one size conversion bulb for the reverse conversion: a 400-watt halide conversion bulb operates in a 400-watt sodium system. You can start growing under MH light, and when it's time to encourage bloom, switch to a conversion bulb that will give you sodium-type light, strong in the orange and red wavelengths.

Two additional pieces of equipment are important in setting up your light garden: the reflector and the light mover. As noted above, reflectors are an important consideration for everyone who gardens under artificial light. The most efficient are double parabolic reflectors, which direct all available light down toward the plants when properly placed. A flat reflector is less efficient since it reflects some light back onto the bulbs. Unpainted aluminum can reflect light unevenly, resulting in hot spots that may burn foliage, so look for a reflector painted white.

Not everyone wants or needs a light mover, but if you find yourself enjoying the wonderful world of HID light gardening, you might consider the next step. Light movers are useful machines that provide more bang for your illumination buck. They are most important for growers who are concerned about even light coverage and who have experienced light burn on the upper foliage in their garden.

There are two basic types of light movers: linear and circular. Both are mounted on the ceiling above your growing area and keep the attached lights in constant motion above your plants. Circular light movers are made for one or more lamps and rotate above your plants. A central hub holds one or more arms with lights attached; these arms rotate 360° around the hub. The multiple lamp option allows you to combine HPS and MH light, giving you lots of light in both the blue and orange-red ranges.

Linear light movers cover a rectangular space and move back and forth on a track installed above your plants. These can also accommodate one or more lights, giving you the opportunity to combine HPS and MH bulbs. You may choose to add a piece of equipment called a *smart box* or *stall box*. This pauses the light at either end of the rail so the plants in the middle do not receive disproportionately more light. If you grow in a rectangular area, this may be the best choice for you.

When you're choosing the wattage of your lamps, first determine how much space you need to illuminate. A light mover increases the square footage you can light with a single lamp, but as a rule, you'll want 20 to 40 watts per square foot of garden. Divide the wattage of your bulb by 20 (for example, 1000 ÷ 20 = 50), then divide the wattage of your bulb by 40 (1000 ÷ 40 = 25). This will give you the extremes of your light intensity range. With one 1000-watt system, you can light between 25 and 50 square feet of interior landscape, depending on the plants and their light requirements. You can adjust your setup as you observe how well your plants grow, and increase or decrease the intensity of the light accordingly. This can be done by shifting the placement of your plants or light fixture, but *not* by changing the bulb in your lamp to a bulb with more watts. Each lamp is designed for a specific wattage, and a 400-watt bulb cannot operate safely in a 250-watt system. (Before you install your new lights, make sure your household wiring is up to the task.)

For greenhouse growers where winter days are short, consider adding HID lights to keep plants in active growth during the winter months. A photosensor that will automatically turn on the lights on overcast days, or whenever light is low, can easily be added to your system. When combined with a timer, this is both efficient and practical.

If you're just beginning to experiment with artificial light, try the inexpensive fluorescent tubes and fixtures first. If you find the experience rewarding, you may decide to invest in an HID system, in which case you'll truly be able to push the edge of your landscaping envelope. With artificial light, especially HID lamps, you are limited only by your imagination.

4

It's the Humidity

During my showbiz years, whenever I arrived in a new city with a touring show I'd seek out a greenhouse to make myself feel at home. The high humidity of hothouse air embraced me as I walked through the door and helped me relax. I'd buy a few little green companions for my temporary home and settle in for the run of the show.

The air in a proper greenhouse makes your glasses fog up and turns your paperwork to mush. But oh, what it does for your tropical plants. Some tropical plants absolutely require the elevated humidity of a greenhouse (at least 50 percent relative humidity). But many will survive in average household humidity, about 20 to 25 percent relative humidity.

We've all heard the term *relative humidity*, but not everyone understands the concept, much less why it's relevant to plant growth. The amount of moisture air can hold is directly related to the temperature. Cold air holds less moisture than warm air before reaching the dew point, or the point at which moisture condenses out of the air in the form of water. Air at 50°F (10°C) with a relative humidity of 30 percent holds less moisture than air at 70°F (21°C) with relative humidity of 30 percent.

In winter, the relative humidity in our homes drops. We know that many plants suffer in drier air because they transpire more quickly, losing more water to the air that surrounds them. But why does the relative humidity in our homes drop in winter? Cold air is drier than warm air: it can't hold as much water vapor. As we heat the air it becomes capable of holding more moisture but in fact still holds the same amount of water vapor it did when it was colder. The result is that relative humidity decreases as we heat the air.

3 6646 00156 1156

If you don't have a greenhouse but would like to try growing high-humidity plants, there are several ways to elevate humidity levels in a small area of your home. Water is a byproduct of photosynthesis. It is given off as vapor through the plants' stomata; this is called *transpiration*. In especially humid environments, some plants exude water through specialized cells (called *hydathodes*) at their leaf tips in a process called *guttation*. Both transpiration and guttation raise the humidity of the air immediately surrounding the plants. Therefore, grouping plants can increase local humidity. As each plant releases water (as vapor or as liquid), the relative humidity of the air increases. This both reduces the frequency with which you need to water and provides a more "tropical" humidity level for your houseplants.

Try this simple experiment. Place a humidity gauge (a $10 item from a gardener's supply catalog) next to a single plant and record the humidity level over a 24-hour period. Then, group five or six plants together in the same spot, and take a new reading. Your second reading will be higher by about 10 percentage points, indicating a healthier environment for your plants. You probably won't create that fog-up-your-glasses greenhouse-quality humidity in your living room, but that isn't really what you're after. All you want to do is boost the humidity in a small area for the good of your plants.

Drywells

Another simple solution is to create drywells for your plants. A drywell is a tray or saucer of pebbles upon which your plants sit. Most of your plants are probably already on saucers, which catch the overflow of water. You can either add a layer of pebbles to individual plant saucers, or use a large cookie sheet with pebbles to hold several plants in a single spot. Keep the pebbles covered with water, just up to the level of the bottom of the pots. As the water evaporates from underneath and around the pebbles, it humidifies the air around the plants. A drywell is especially helpful when growing under artificial lights, since lights generate heat that dries out potting mix.

Not all plants can sit on drywells. Hanging plants or mounted epiphytes also appreciate a boost in humidity, but you'll have to get a little more creative—the occasional spritz from a spray bottle is not adequate. A heavy duty humidifier aimed at

To make a drywell, fill a saucer with pebbles and add water to the top of the pebbles.

Sit your plants on the drywell; top off the water every several days.

the plants will help, but it must be close to the plant material. Special models intended for growing plants have built-in humidistats, so you can choose the relative humidity range best for your plants.

Closed Cases

If you're committed to growing plants that require extremely high humidity (and there are plenty of these), you should consider Wardian cases and terrariums. The Wardian case is named after Dr. Nathanial Bagshaw Ward, a 19th century English amateur botanist. He kept moths in glass bottles to observe their life cycles. Inadvertently, he grew inside one bottle a rare fern that he'd been unable to grow in his garden. Dr. Ward understood that the bottle created a closed environment. Moisture vapor given off by the plant through transpiration condensed against the glass walls of the bottle and trickled back down into the soil.

Wardian cases can still be found in antique stores, although they tend to be pricey; modern versions are manufactured by companies like Orchidarium. (De-

A simple fish tank makes an excellent terrarium.

A mini-terrarium is the perfect size to hold a single *Episcia* hybrid, which requires high humidity.

A plastic tent creates a greenhouse atmosphere. This is especially useful for maintaining plants while you're away on vacation.

spite its name, the orchidarium is suitable for growing more than just orchids.) You may have visited a botanical garden and seen an elaborate orchid case furnished with fans and lights. All of these setups accomplish something very important: they create a highly humid atmosphere within the enclosure of the case. If this sounds tempting, you can put together your own case quickly and inexpensively with a simple aquarium. Smaller enclosed cases can be constructed from a range of clear bottles, jars, or dishes. This is an extensive topic, and the interested grower should consult any of the relevant titles included in the recommended reading section of this book.

While many plants grow well in average household humidity, some rain forest natives suffer from the dry air we breathe. If you understand how to manipulate the relative humidity surrounding your plants, you'll greatly increase the number of tropical species you can grow indoors.

5

Good Grooming

I'm not sure what it is about pruning that strikes fear in the hearts of normal human beings. Perhaps it's the sharpness of the tools involved, or maybe the remembered trauma of an early childhood haircut. Either way, pruning is a necessary skill for every gardener, and when approached gradually, it shouldn't be intimidating. Think of it as good grooming for your plants.

Pruning

The most elementary form of pruning is pinching, for which no special tools are required. If you've ever walked past a plant and pinched off a flower stalk or a pair of emerging leaves, you have, in essence, pruned a plant. Often, we do this to make the plant branch, grow more bushy and full. The plant's growth hormones are concentrated in the tip of the stem, and as long as the primary stem of the plant grows naturally, growth hormones elsewhere will be suppressed. When the dominant growing tip is removed, the growth hormones at lower nodes on the plant will often become active, causing branches to sprout lower down on the stem. What is a node? It's a growing point on a stem or branch. It can be marked by a bud scar, a bump, or a contrast in tissue color.

Not every plant responds to pinching, but many do. When a plant stem is soft and green, fingernails are the perfect tool for getting in close to the node and removing the dominant growing tip. This can be done if you'd like your plant to branch and grow into a fuller shape, and the technique can be practiced on side shoots as well as on the main stem. If you have a plant suffering from leggy growth because of low light levels, you may want to pinch back the unattractive growth before moving the plant into higher light where it will grow more fully.

If the plant stem feels woody and you can no longer easily make a cut with your fingernails, use pruners or snips. For small houseplants, a pair of micro-tip snips is perfect. The size of the blades allows you to get into tight angles and make clean, professional cuts. Using traditional pruners in very acute angles can be difficult; you can damage stem tissue with the scrape of a blade or by pushing the pruners into a space too small to accommodate them. So if you're working with delicate plants, buy a delicate pair of cutters.

For many houseplants, a regular pair of pruners is fine. Bypass pruners (one blade slices past the other, leaving a clean cut) are better than anvil pruners (two blades press together and meet in the middle, squishing the plant tissue near the cut). No matter which tool you use to prune, every cut should be made at about a 45° angle, just above a node. Stem tissue left in place above a node and below your cut will die back and bear witness to your lack of skill as a pruner. We call these nubs "coat hooks"; they are dead and bare, and the work of amateurs.

Pruning is a good way to rejuvenate a plant. If new foliage looks unhealthy, weak, small, or damaged, prune it off, correct the cultural problem, and wait for healthy new growth. For example, during your vacation a neighbor watered your plants. However, she inadvertently moved the plant up against a window, and several leaves suffered damage from the cold glass. Prune away the damaged leaves, move the plant back from the glass, and new growth should be perfectly normal. Or, your helpful neighbor watered well, but didn't notice that aphids had found the tender young leaves of your *Polyscias crispata*. Remove the aphids with soap and water, prune away the damaged leaves, and get on with your life.

Pruning can also help rejuvenate a crowded plant, one whose stems grow so closely together that interior foliage dies from lack of light. You may approach this in two ways. You can remove branches from the central stem that are growing in towards the center of the plant, much like you would prune a deciduous shrub in your outdoor garden. Or, you can cut a few center stems back to soil level to open up the middle of the plant.

Sometimes a plant outgrows its place, and it becomes a question of either finding it a new home or pruning it to fit the space. If a plant is an old favorite, it's preferable to cut it back and keep it in place. Start slowly and you won't do irreparable damage. You'll also avoid the psychological shock of seeing a large plant greatly reduced all at once.

Step back from the plant and look at its overall shape. Where exactly is it too big? Is it touching the ceiling? Is it nudging aside the artwork on the south wall of your living room? Is it draping onto the back of the couch? Start where it is most overgrown and remove about 10 percent of the offending branch. Work around the tree, removing approximately 10 percent from any part of the plant that is larger than you want it to be. Every now and then look at the shape of the tree, making sure your work is even and that you are happy with the overall form.

Ten percent is conservative, but by starting small you make the job less intimidating. You can always work around the tree a second time, whereas if you go too far with your first pruning experiment you may never pick up a pair of pruners again. And remember, always wield your tools with authority; avoid making a tentative cut. As the late, great Thalassa Cruso said in *Making Things Grow*, "Never mind if you don't feel at all confident—but do put on an act. To speak more plainly, don't dither." Plants can sense your fear.

Some plants, including many *Ficus, Euphorbia,* and *Hoya* species, exude a milky sap or latex when cut. When pruning plants that ooze, lay a drop cloth to catch drops that could ruin furniture or flooring. If you're only making a few cuts, a piece of wet paper towel pressed to the wound will staunch the flow.

Thick branches and tree trunks may be too large to cut with handheld pruners. A pair of loppers will cut through wood an inch to an inch and a half thick, and a folding handsaw with a sharp blade can handle anything thicker. Pruning limbs of this size on a houseplant is unusual, but may need to be done occasionally.

There are other types of cutting and pruning that are done for aesthetic reasons. Thin-leaved plants may brown around the edges as the result of over- or underwatering, dry air, or cold temperatures. With a pair of scissors, trim the damaged tissue from the leaf margin, preserving the original shape of the leaf. A pair of sharp scissors is the right tool for this job.

Dead-leafing is a form of grooming that can be accomplished with dexterous fingers. Brown or yellow leaves will not regain their original green color and should be removed in a timely manner. There is no point in allowing the plant to expend energy supporting a leaf that is doomed. That energy is best diverted to the strong and healthy growth of the plant.

Some people enjoy training their plants to grow in unusual shapes. I prefer the natural growth form of most plants, but if you'd like to try something different, a standard can be a worthwhile experiment.

A standard is a plant grown in a lollipop shape. A single, straight stem is pinched to encourage branching when it reaches the desired height. As it begins to branch, all leaves and side branches are removed from the stem to leave a bare trunk below the branching point. The top growth is allowed to grow to the desired size and can be sheared into any shape, usually a globe. To maintain this spherical shape, remove the occasional stray stem with a pair of snips or scissors.

Root Pruning

So much for shaping top growth. Now, can you say, "root pruning"? Please don't panic. Once you've mastered pruning stems and branches, pruning root growth is the natural next step. If a plant has outgrown its pot, but you don't want to move it to a bigger container, root pruning is an option. Knock the plant out of its pot to expose the root ball. Loosen the soil as best you can, and, just as you would with top growth, cut from all sides of the roots. If the plant has been in a large pot (greater than 12 inches in diameter), prune away approximately 2 inches all around the root ball. If the plant is in a smaller pot, prune away approximately 1 inch from all sides of the roots' mass. When the root ball has been appropriately reduced, put it back in the pot, and fill in around the edges with fresh soil, packing it in as firmly as possible. You may need a dowel or chopstick to do this.

After the root mass has been reduced, you will need to reduce the top growth proportionately. If you've reduced the roots by 10 percent, cut back the top growth by the same amount. The root system is responsible for pumping water and nutrients to the leaves and branches of the plant. Therefore, reducing the mass of the root ball reduces the extent to which the roots can deliver water and nutrients to the top growth. The original proportion of root mass to top growth should be maintained.

Training Vines

Many of my favorite houseplants are vines. Their growth habits make them versatile houseplants; they can be trained up and around windows, around topiary forms, or allowed to drape. It's up to you to decide how to best display your vines, and that will depend both on the plant you're growing and on the spot you have to fill.

First determine if your vine is a trailer or a climber. Trailers, like *Rhoicissus capensis*, *Aeschynanthus*, and *Rhipsalis*, are best grown in hanging baskets. They will cascade down, some branching, some nonbranching. Trailers may have thick stems that are not easily twisted around a form, or they may not produce aerial roots along the length of the stem. Without aerial roots, tendrils, or suction cups of some kind, a vine cannot climb on its own.

Slim vines without aerial roots, tendrils, or suction cups, like *Mandevilla* ×*amabilis* and *Stephanotis floribunda,* can be trained around a form. These plants need help getting started on their upward journey. It may be enough to weave them in, out, and around the form. Or, you may have to tie them onto the form at intervals along the vine.

Some vines, like most hoyas, dischidias, and *Vanilla planifolia*, produce aerial roots along their stems in humid conditions. In nature, these roots attach the vines to their host trees. The roots do not take nutrients from the tree; they merely anchor the epiphyte in place. In a greenhouse, vines with aerial roots will frequently attach themselves to walls, shelves, and beams. They also do well trained along an upright form such as a tripod or trellis.

Small-leaved vines such as *Hedera helix* and *Ficus pumila* can be worked in and out of a wire topiary form without difficulty. Both of these vines climb by virtue of small suction cups that form along the stem. In humid conditions they'll climb on their own, easily covering the wall of a terrarium or conservatory.

Some vines climb with the help of tendrils. *Passiflora violacea* and *Tetrastigma voinierianum* are both vines that attach themselves to trees, branches, or trellises by tendrils that wrap around the anchoring object. *Quisqualis indica* uses its hook-like spines to help it climb. If a tendril-climber ventures somewhere you don't want it, you can either untwine the tendrils or cut them without damaging the vine.

Some other plants classified as climbers, such as *Bougainvillea* hybrids and *Alla-*

manda cathartica, are woody enough to be allowed to grow as shrubs if kept pruned. They can also be tied to a trellis or other strong support, according to your planting plan.

Topiary forms are available in a myriad of shapes, from dinosaurs to simple geometrics. The base of a wire form is inserted into the potting soil, and the plant is trained up and around the form. Certain plants lend themselves to different types of topiary. A small-leaved creeper such as *Ficus pumila* is perfect to cover a moss-stuffed globe, whereas a vigorous vine such as *Passiflora caerulea* or *Hedera helix* will quickly cover a large pyramid. The vine must be twined in and out, around the form, as it grows. It's important to remove dead leaves from the interior of the topiary form, to keep the topiary healthy and looking neat.

It's normal for many plants to lose their lower leaves as they age. Of course, leggy plants can be rejuvenated by taking cuttings, but vines can also be given a new lease on life with a technique called "basketing." If you have a vine with long expanses of stem that has lost its foliage, twine the leafless stem around the inside of the pot's edge, then pin the stem to the soil at regular intervals. You can use a paperclip for this: straightened, cut in half, then bent into a "U" shape. The stem will root along its length and eventually send up growth from the newly rooted stem. Your plant will look as if it has been pruned, but you won't have to take cuttings.

Repotting

The most common error made in repotting plants is moving them into containers that are too large. Why is this dangerous? As we discussed, plant roots absorb both water and oxygen. In between waterings, the potting mix must dry out enough to provide the plant's roots with oxygen; keeping the soil consistently damp may make it impossible for the plant to breathe.

Think about how the potting mix dries out. Some moisture may be lost by evaporation through the pot's walls if the container is made of a porous material. Some evaporates through the surface of the potting mix. Most of it is absorbed by the plant's roots and transported through the vascular tissue to the leaves, where it is used in photosynthesis.

A plant's roots absorb water from the potting mix they penetrate. A large volume of potting mix without root penetration will remain wet; no roots can access its moisture for transport. As water is absorbed from the accessible potting mix, it is replaced (gradually, through diffusion) by the unused moisture in the surrounding, untapped potting mix. As a result, the root mass is kept moist much longer and does not get the oxygen it requires.

A plant with a 2-inch root ball potted in a 6-inch pot will be surrounded on all sides by 2 inches of wet potting mix. Very likely, this will lead to root rot and plant death. To avoid this, move your plant into a pot only one size bigger each time you repot. Pots are generally sold in 2-inch increments. The number refers to the interior diameter of the pot, and since most pots are of standard proportions, this is the only measurement you'll need to use. Specialty pots may have different proportions. A bulb pan is a shallow pot, about half the depth of a standard pot. An azalea pot is three-fourths the depth of a standard pot. However, if you are moving a plant from a small pot to a larger pot of the same design, you need only concern yourself with the diameter measurement. A plant whose root system has filled a 4-inch pot is ready to be moved into a 6-inch container.

When you look good, you feel good. Sometimes a light pruning is all it takes to make a plant look terrific, but sometimes a little more work is necessary. Whether your plant needs a simple haircut or an all-day spa treatment, it's up to you to administer the tender loving care.

6

Be Fruitful and Multiply

Plant propagation is making new plants from existing parent stock, and it's one of the most satisfying things a gardener can do. It's also a skill that's surprisingly easy to master.

There are many methods of propagation, all of which fit into two categories. Sexual propagation involves plants' reproductive parts such as seeds and spores. Asexual reproduction involves vegetative plant parts such as roots, stems, and leaves. Some plants can be propagated in several ways, both by seeds and by cuttings, so before beginning, find out which method is best for the plant you have in mind. Detailed information is available in propagation textbooks and plant encyclopedias, several of which I've listed in "Resources." In addition, each plant profile in chapter 9 includes propagation tips.

Sexual Propagation

Plants started from seed add variety to the gene pool, because cross-pollination creates new hybrids with new combinations of the parents' characteristics. Varieties may exhibit different characteristics such as double flowers, resistance to fungal diseases, or tolerance of cold, which gives growers interesting choices.

Many gardeners have started plants from seed at one time or another. It's the most familiar, and therefore least intimidating, propagation method. It is also an inexpensive way to increase your plant collection, and it's inspiring to watch a new plant grow from a tiny seed.

A seed contains a fertilized egg, which is the plant embryo. Seeds come in a wide range of sizes. Orchids can have 1,000,000 in a single ounce. The largest known seed is that of the double coconut palm (*Lodoicea maldivica*) which can weigh up to 50 pounds. While the double coconut palm is planted half in and half out of the ground, most seeds are planted at a depth equal to two or three times the height of the seed itself.

Regardless of the medium you choose for starting your seeds, it must be sterile in order to avoid dangerous pathogens, including the fungi which cause damping off diseases (these can kill newly sprouted seedlings in a matter of hours). This means that any mix containing soil must be sterilized either chemically, or by heat. There are plenty of sterile, commercial seed-starting mixes which are soilless; they contain peat and either vermiculite or perlite. These mixes are not only pathogen free, they are also lightweight and have excellent water retention.

The growing medium serves several purposes. It holds water, gives physical support to the root system, and provides darkness for the germinating seed. (While some seeds need light to germinate, most require darkness.) A fine-grained potting mix has numerous small pore spaces, allowing water to disperse quickly through the soil, resulting in even moisture levels. This is important for newly formed root hairs. As moisture is taken up by roots, that portion of soil is left dry and needs quick replenishment of water.

Some seeds require special treatment before they'll germinate. This is because the seeds have built-in protections to help them survive hostile environments. For example, *Ricinus communis* is native to southeast Africa, where a harsh dry season alternates with a rainy season. The seed coat of *R. communis* is shiny and hard and protects the seed from germinating prematurely under adverse conditions. In order to germinate, the seed coat must be soaked in water for 24 hours, or nicked (scraped or pierced by a sharp object) to allow water to penetrate the seed coat. If a seed began to grow during the dry season, when sufficient water was not available, it would surely die. If a seed coat has soaked in water for an entire day, this indicates to the seed that there is sufficient water available for healthy growth.

STARTING SEEDS
Choose a pot or flat large enough for your seeds and fill it with a soilless mix. Firm the mixture in with your fingers, but do not pack it solid; tamp down the soil to

about an inch below the lip of the pot. If you are using a flat, press the straight edge of a ruler into the soil, creating a groove where you can place your seed. If you are using a pot, you may poke holes into the potting mix with a skewer or pencil, but make sure not to make the holes too deep. Cover the seed to the appropriate depth, depending on the seed type. Check a propagation text or the seed packet to learn whether your seed requires light to germinate. If you can't find instructions, cover the seed to a depth of twice its height.

The next step is watering in. The seed must make good contact with the soil and be kept moist in order to germinate. You may water from either the top or the bottom, but be aware that uneven or careless watering can displace both seed and soil. If you water from above, use a watering can with a rose to break the flow of the water. Start and stop the stream of water against the side of the pot so the spray is fine and even. If you water from the bottom, fill the saucer with water and let the potting mix soak it up until it is evenly moist. This takes longer than watering from the top, but you are less likely to displace the seed.

For germination, the soil temperature should be approximately 70°F (21°C). On top of the refrigerator is one of the warmest places in the house, so you could put your pot or flat here. Or consider a propagation mat. These contain heating coils which warm the bottoms of pots placed upon them. It's an excellent way to improve your germination rate, especially if temperatures are cool. Be aware that the increased temperatures will cause the soil to dry out more quickly, and you will need to water the potting mix more frequently.

Once germination has occurred, seedlings can be removed from bottom heat and maintained at regular household temperatures. At this point light becomes important for plant growth, and your seedlings should be given indirect sun.

Ardisia crenata seedlings in a community pot

Initially, a seed will produce one or two cotyledons (seed leaves), depending on whether it is a monocot (one seed leaf) like a palm or grass, or a dicot (two seed leaves) like a cactus or hoya. These first leaves will not look like the plant's mature, true leaves. They were part of the embryo, enclosed within the seed coat, and they provide food for the developing plant while the root system and true leaves are forming. Your seedlings should be allowed to grow in their flat until they show their first set of true leaves. This indicates that the plants are ready for pricking out. *Pricking out* is the term for lifting a seedling out of its flat.

When it is time to move your seedlings to a new pot, remember, never hold a seedling by its stem. The plant can't grow a new stem; if you damage it, the seedling is doomed. Hold a seedling by its cotyledons or by its true leaves; a plant with healthy vascular tissue (an intact stem) can grow more leaves. Also, when re-potting a seedling, make sure you replant it at its original soil level. Burying the crown of the plant or exposing part of the root system can kill the seedling.

SPORES

Not all plants produce seeds. Ferns, many of which make excellent houseplants, produce spores, which can be treated in much the same way as seeds as far as propagation is concerned. Most of us know how to obtain seeds, but how to collect fern spores is not necessarily common knowledge. If you notice spores forming on the back of a fern frond, wait until they are ripe before harvesting. You can tell if a spore is ripe by tapping the fern frond. If a fine dust (spore) escapes into the air, the spore is ripe. Cut the frond and lay it spore-side down on a piece of paper overnight. The next morning, lift the frond, and the spore should remain on the paper.

A few additional supplies are needed for fern propagation because spores require slightly more careful handling than seeds. Have the following ready: 10 percent bleach solution, a clear plastic cup, paper toweling, a peat pellet, plastic wrap, an elastic band, a bucket, and water that has been boiled, then cooled to room temperature. Water that is too hot will steam the spore and kill it.

Rinse the plastic cup in the bleach solution and let it dry upside down on the paper towel. This will sterilize the cup (contamination can be a problem with fern propagation, hence the use of bleach solution and water that has been boiled).

Next, turn the cup over and place the peat pellet in the cup with the indent of the pellet facing up. Then, pour about an inch of water into the cup and cover the cup with plastic wrap, fixing it in place with the elastic band. Do this as quickly as possible to minimize exposure to airborne contaminants. Let the peat pellet sit for about an hour to absorb the water. If there is any standing water in the cup, pour it off.

To prepare the spore you must remove the chaff, which can also be a source of contamination. Place the spore on a piece of paper with a folded crease in the middle. Tilt the paper and gently tap it. The heavier chaff will fall down the crease and off the paper. Keep the spore in reserve.

Now, tap the chaff-free spore onto the saturated peat pellet. Re-cover the cup with the plastic wrap promptly, and label your spore. Place the cup where it will receive bright light but no direct sun. (Unlike most seeds, fern spores require light for germination.) Fluorescent grow lights can be used. The temperature should be between 60°F (21°C) and 70°F (16°C). High humidity is a must; 100% humidity is desirable. Keeping the cup covered with the plastic wrap will trap moisture inside and maintain elevated humidity.

If the peat pellet appears to be drying out, or if you don't see condensation on the plastic wrap, boil water, let it cool, and add a small amount to the bottom of the cup. You should see the beginning of growth within two to three weeks. It will appear as a green fuzz on the top of the peat pellet. Slowly, individual fern prothallii (the equivalent of a seedling for a vascular plant) will become visible. After about a month, you should be able to move a clump of prothallii to a small pot and grow it as a houseplant. The young fern must acclimate gradually to the drier air of your home. Otherwise, the transition from ultra-high humidity to normal household humidity can cause foliage damage. Poke a few holes in the plastic wrap covering the plastic cup and leave the prothallii like this for a few days. When you remove the prothallii from the cup and pot them up, place the pot on a drywell.

The spores of *Polypodium aureum* create a regular pattern on the back of a frond.

Asexual Propagation

You have many choices among asexual propagation methods. These range from simple division, to rooting cuttings, to air layering. There are several benefits to asexual propagation. You will get larger plants more quickly from vegetative propagation than from seed. And vegetative propagation will produce plants with exactly the same genotype as their parents. If you want to preserve certain characteristics of the parent stock, then the variation you get from seed-grown plants is not what you want. Vegetative propagation, on the other hand, replicates the genotype of the parent stock.

SEPARATION

The simplest type of vegetative propagation is separation. Some plants produce offshoots from the original plant. This can happen in several ways. *Saxifraga stolonifera* produces offshoots at the ends of stolons. A stolon is a modified shoot that grows from a plant. This shoot has nodes, from which flowers, new plants, or roots can form. Plantlets that form at the ends of stolons can be left on the mother plant to create an impressive, multigenerational specimen. They can be pinned to the soil with a bent paper clip, where they will root and form new plants. Or, they can be separated from the mother plant and potted up on their own. A plantlet that is allowed to root while still attached to the original plant will need no special care. A plantlet that is separated and potted up on its own will require higher humidity and more frequent watering while its root system develops.

Many bromeliads produce offshoots. However, they grow directly from the stem of the original plant, not at the end of stolons. Bromeliads are monocarpic, which means they flower once and then die. Before dying, a bromeliad produces new plantlets. These offshoots can be separated from the mother plant and potted up on their own once they have developed roots 1 to 2 inches long. Orchids also frequently produce plantlets on the stems of the original plant. Orchid offshoots are called *keikeis*, which means "babies" in Hawaiian. On sympodial orchids, keikeis grow from an existing cane or pseudobulb. On monopodial orchids, keikeis grow from bloom stalks. In either case, the keikei can be separated from the mother plant and potted in bark mix once its roots are at least an inch long.

DIVISION

Division is similar to separation but involves some sharp tools. However, if you mastered the pruning lessons in the preceding chapter, you're ready for this. Plants with more than a single clump or crown, such as alocasias, strelitzias, and anthuriums, are good candidates for division. Plants with a single growing point, such as a palm, ficus, or monopodial orchid, cannot be divided.

If a plant has outgrown its pot, why not try division? Knock the plant out of its pot and inspect it at soil level. How many individual crowns or growing points can you see? If there are two, this plant can be divided into two smaller plants. If you see six, you have choices: you can divide it into two, three, or more small pots. Make your decision based on how large you want the resulting plants to be. On your first try, keep it simple and split the plant in half.

You may be able to separate the two pieces with your hands, depending on the density of the root ball. Start at the top of the plant and hold the soil ball on either side. Tug gently at the two halves. If you can separate them a little bit, work your fingers into the crack, separating the roots gently. Then tug some more on the two pieces. Repeat the finger wiggling and pulling until you can separate the two parts of the root ball. It is inevitable that some roots will be broken, so don't worry. The root system of a plant can lose a few roots and still function. However, do be as gentle as possible without being tentative.

If the root ball is extremely dense and does not separate when subjected to manual tugging, you may have to pull out a sharp knife. Wield it like you know what you're doing and whistle a happy tune. Place the tip of the knife between the two growing points and cut down through the root mass, dividing the plant into two sections. Remove any severed root fragments.

Once the parts of your plant have been separated (either by hand or by knife) pot them up in containers of the appropriate size. It is important to develop a sense of the proper proportion of root ball size to pot size. In general, if a root ball is 3 inches in diameter, the pot should be about 5 inches in diameter. An inch of fresh soil around the circumference of the pot will allow for new growth. Hence, if you had an anthurium in a 10-inch pot and divide it into two sections with 4-inch root balls, put each in a 6-inch pot.

After potting up a division, you should remove some top growth. The root system has been shocked and can't efficiently provide water and nutrients to the plant's foliage until it recovers. Reducing the top growth by approximately 20 percent reduces the demand on the recuperating roots, which helps keep the existing foliage in good condition. Also, keep the plant out of direct sun and be particularly attentive to its humidity needs during this time. Usually after about two weeks, the plant will be ready to resume its original position. If you see new growth before that, congratulate yourself and move on. The more practiced and skilled you become at division, the less traumatic it will be for your plants. While some plants (like euphorbias) seem to suffer after even the most skillful division, others show few aftereffects when divided by an accomplished hand.

CUTTINGS

Many tropicals can be propagated by cuttings, which is an especially satisfying way to make more plants. Cuttings can be taken from stems, roots, or leaves, depending on which species you're propagating. In each case, watching new plants grow from pieces of the old is fascinating.

Propagation from cuttings is based on a plant's wound response to tissue injury. When plant tissue is cut, callous tissue forms. This is undifferentiated tissue and looks like warty, knotty growth. If you've ever rooted cuttings in water, you may have seen this kind of tissue develop on cut stems before new roots started to grow.

A word about rooting cuttings in water. Roots absorb oxygen and nutrients differently in water than they do in soil. Therefore, roots that grow in water may have a hard time adapting from water culture to soil culture. For this reason, I don't recommend rooting cuttings in water, then transferring them to potting mix. If you'd like to watch how roots grow, by all means, start a few cuttings in water. But don't be surprised if those cuttings don't prosper in soil. The roots may never be vigorous, and the plant may therefore always be weak and spindly.

Sometimes you have to make additional wounds to stimulate a strong rooting response. With a sharp knife or razor blade, scrape one or two sides of the stem to remove a little of the outer tissue. Don't go all the way around or you'll girdle the cutting and kill it.

Plants have polarity, which means they distinguish between up and down. The proximal end is the end closest to the crown of the plant and the distal end is the end of the cutting furthest from the crown. If you place the wrong end (the distal end) of a stem cutting in the rooting media, the cutting won't grow. To avoid this, standardize your method. If you always make your proximal cut straight and your distal cut slanted, you'll be able to tell the ends apart. You might not expect this to be a problem, but if you take several cuttings from a single stem it's possible to get confused.

Stem cuttings are the simplest to take. First, you will need a sterile potting medium. The medium must provide anchorage for the cutting, hold moisture, and drain quickly in order to provide air to the emerging roots. A sterile medium is guaranteed to be free from fungi and other pathogens.

Although it is not always necessary, applying rooting hormone can speed the rooting process. Plants produce hormones naturally, and auxin is the hormone that increases root production. By applying auxin to the cutting, the rooting process can be accelerated. In addition to auxin, rooting hormone contains cofactors, which plants require to root. Cofactors are stimuli that act as synergists to auxins. Cuttings that do not have cofactors available may be impossible to root and must be propagated in other ways.

Many tropicals root well from cuttings. Prepare several small plastic pots by filling them with a lightweight potting mix, usually a blend of peat and perlite. Firm the mixture with your fingers, and poke a hole in the mix for each cutting. If you're using 2-inch pots, one cutting per pot is fine. If you're using larger pots, give each cutting about 2 inches of space to grow.

Cuttings should be 4 to 6 inches long and include several nodes. Taking small cuttings reduces the potential for wilting and water loss by reducing the transpiration area. The more tender the leaf tissue, the smaller the cutting should be. If the surface area of the leaves is larger than 3 square inches, reduce it by trimming the leaves.

For the cleanest cuttings, use a sterilized razor blade and a piece of glass as a cutting board. Make your cut just above a pair of leaves, then remove the bottom pair of leaves from your cutting. This should leave one or two pairs of leaves at the top of the cutting. Dip the bottom of the stem in water, then in rooting hormone, being sure to cover both the bottom cut end and the wounds where the leaves have been removed. Tap off any excess hormone, and stick the cutting in the potting mix. Firm it into place and water the pot.

Cuttings don't have the ability to absorb water, and if they wilt, they're dead. So, during the rooting process you will have to provide elevated humidity while the root system forms. Small pots can be placed in individual zip-lock bags, blown full of air, then sealed. The air inside will be considerably more humid than that of the average home. A group of cuttings can be placed in a large dry cleaning bag, or in a plastic tent. Once your cuttings have rooted, you can reduce the humidity gradually while the roots begin to take up water.

Bottom heat can speed the rooting process for stem cuttings, especially when air temperatures are cool. Remember, however, that raising soil temperature causes the soil to dry out more quickly, so pay special attention to maintaining elevated humidity if you use a heat mat.

Check your cuttings after two weeks. Tug gently on the top of one; if it pulls out of the mix, firm it back in place and continue to wait. If you meet with some resistance, roots have started to grow. Continue to keep the cuttings in elevated humidity. When you see signs of new top growth, you can remove the cuttings from their shelter and treat them as individual plants. This can take anywhere from three to eight weeks, depending on the plant you are propagating.

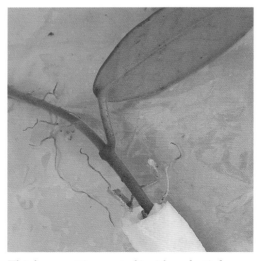

This hoya cutting rooted inside a plastic bag.

A new *Saintpaulia* grows from a single leaf cutting.

In the past, floral foam has been used to start cuttings. I prefer a new product called Natur-Plug, manufactured by the Smithers-Oasis company. It is a combination of peat, coconut fiber, and a hydrophilic polymer. The texture is excellent for rooting cuttings, and after the plug has been transplanted, it will eventually dissolve, unlike floral foam.

Some vining plants produce aerial roots along their stems in humid conditions. In nature, these roots hold the vine in place. In greenhouses you will often see these roots forming along a vine's stem, but in most homes, the ambient humidity is too low to encourage aerial root growth. If you can raise the humidity of your growing area and instigate the growth of aerial roots, you will be able to propagate the vine by pinning the rooted cutting to the soil.

To make a cutting with aerial root growth, take a cutting as you would for rooting in potting mix. However, wrap the cut end in a moist paper towel, and place the wrapped cutting in a large, clear zip-lock bag. Blow the bag full of air and place it in a warm, bright spot; direct sun is not necessary. Check the paper towel every few days to make sure it remains moist. If it has dried out, rewet the towel and reseal the bag.

Within two to three weeks, you will find that roots have grown not only under the paper towel, but also along the stem. Unwrap the towel as best you can. It is not necessary to remove every piece of paper towel before potting up the cutting. You may either plant the cut end in potting mix or pin the length of the vine along the surface of the mix with bent paper clips. As with any newly rooted cutting, humidity should be adjusted gradually from the high humidity of the propagation chamber to the lower humidity of your home.

Some tropicals can be propagated from leaf cuttings; plants in the *Begonia* ×*rex-cultorum* group, saintpaulias, and sansevierias are all excellent candidates. For example, a single leaf from *Saintpaulia ionantha* can be removed from the mother plant, the end of its petiole dipped in rooting hormone, and the leaf stem potted up in lightweight potting mix. Elevate humidity while the cutting roots, and within four to six weeks, a new plant will grow from the base of a single leaf.

To propagate *Begonia* ×*rex-cultorum*, remove a single leaf from the plant. Cut away the midrib and remove it. Cut the remainder of the leaf into wedges, making sure that each piece contains a major vein. Dip the bottom edge of the leaf in water, then rooting hormone, and place it on edge in the mix. Bury it only as deep as necessary to make the cutting stand on edge. New plants will grow from the edge of the cutting. Or, turn the entire leaf over and make several cuts across the major veins of the leaf. Then pin the leaf right side up on top of potting mix using bent paperclips. Make sure the cuts make good contact with the potting mix. New plants will grow from these points.

A single *Sansevieria* leaf can produce many new plants. Cut a single leaf into 1-inch sections, making sure to distinguish the proximal and distal ends of your cuttings. Let the *Sansevieria* cuttings heal for a day or so before planting. All succulent cuttings must be allowed to heal before being planted; otherwise, they may rot, not root. Dip the proximal end of the cutting into rooting hormone, then place it upright in a soilless potting mix. Plant the cutting only as deep as you must to get the leaf to stand on edge. Firm it in place and treat it as you would a stem cutting.

Because *Sansevieria* foliage is succulent, you may think maintaining high humidity is not as important as it is for a tender-leaved plant. But this is not the case. *Sansevieria* cuttings are slow to produce new growth and must be kept humid during this time.

It is important to note that not all sansevierias come true from cuttings. For example, *Sansevieria trifasciata* 'Bantel's Sensation' is a chimera, a plant variety created by chemically treating its meristem, which in this case is the terminal end of the underground rhizome. A leaf cutting from this plant will form a new rhizome, and since this rhizome has not been chemically treated, the plant will revert to its original species. The only way to propagate a chimera is by dividing the original plant, thus including a piece of the treated meristem.

Tuberous plants with a dormancy period, such as caladiums and colocasias, may be propagated before active growth begins in spring. Use a sharp knife to cut a large tuber into several pieces. Make sure each piece includes at least one growing eye, which may look like a small bump or indent. Dust the cut edge of the tuber with a fungicide and pot it up on its own.

AIR-LAYERING

Air-layering is a more complicated propagation method, but it's not difficult if you work deliberately and follow directions. Air-layering is the best way to propagate larger, woody tropical plants with thick, inflexible stems such as ficus or dieffen-bachia. If a plant has grown leggy and has large expanses of stem with no foliage, air layering is an excellent way to rejuvenate the plant.

Choose the site for your cut—this is where the new roots will grow. Remove any leaves from this area. Using a sharp knife, cut one-half to one-third of the way through the stem tissue with an upward slant. Cutting through a node gives you a better wound response, but is physically harder to accomplish, so don't worry if you can't manage it.

Once you have made the cut, do not let go of the stem or it may snap. Dip a toothpick or a small dowel in hormone powder and poke it into the wound. Then, push something inside the wound to keep the wound open. For example, you can leave the toothpick or dowel in the wound, or push moist, long-grained sphagnum moss into the cut. Then, wrap the stem with more moist sphagnum moss, and cover it with a layer of plastic. Plastic wrap is too thin, but a plastic sandwich bag cut into a flat sheet is about right. With clear plastic, you can watch for root growth and condensation. However, blocking light encourages root growth, so use two layers of plastic, black on top of clear. You can remove the black plastic periodically to check on the progress of your experiment, without losing moisture. Seal the bottom and the top of the clear plastic with tape and tie the black plastic in place with twist ties.

Check the wound weekly, making sure the sphagnum moss remains moist (re-wet if necessary). Roots should be visible within six to eight weeks. Once the new roots are about 2 inches long, you can sever the top portion from the original plant and pot it up in a container of the appropriate size. New growth may start from the cut on the parent plant.

There are so many ways to make new plants: germinating seeds and spores, root-ing cuttings of leaf or stem tissue, air-layering. I suggest you try all of them. Go forth and multiply.

7

Plant Pests

There are a handful of insect (and noninsect) pests that will snack on your house-plants, given the opportunity. However, if you're vigilant, you can keep damage to a minimum. It's impossible to avoid insects entirely, but a few sound cultural practices will minimize the problem.

Some people are reluctant to use pesticides in their homes because of the potential danger to children and pets. If you care for your plants well, you may never have to resort to commercial pesticides. Begin with the least toxic method available. If it works, great. If not, you can either step up the attack, or get rid of the plant and start fresh.

Integrated Pest Management

The idea of using the least toxic method possible is one of the key principles of integrated pest management (IPM). This pest management strategy focuses on long-term prevention or suppression of pest problems through a combination of cultural, physical, chemical, and biological tools, in order to minimize health and environmental risks.

Begin by making five steps common practice:

1. Never buy a plant that isn't 100 percent clean and healthy. This doesn't mean you can't buy a plant that has a broken branch or a spent bloom stalk. Sometimes it's possible to negotiate a good deal for a less than perfect specimen. But if you see an insect on the plant, just say no.

2. Whenever you buy a new plant, isolate it for a week or two and watch carefully. Do not integrate it into your collection until you're sure it's free of pests.

3. Keep your growing areas neat and clean. Debris is a breeding ground for insects, so remove dead leaves and flowers as they fall. If you discover an infestation, clean the entire area thoroughly, including window sills, window panes, containers, and anything else in contact with the affected plants.

4. Pay attention to the cultural needs of your plants: temperature, light, food, and water. Plants are better able to survive an infestation when they're well grown and properly watered and fed, just as we are better able to fight off a cold when we're strong and well nourished.

5. Really look at every plant in your collection at least once a week. It's essential to know what your plants look like when they're healthy, so you can spot a problem as soon as it occurs. Early detection is the key; you can get rid of almost any pest if you catch it early enough.

You may monitor pests by visual inspection, or you may use sticky cards to trap insects in your growing area. Sticky cards are not insecticides, but rather a useful indicator of insect population density. Familiarize yourself not only with the appearances of the most common houseplant pests, but also with the type of damage each pest can do.

Nonchemical practices are used whenever possible to keep insect populations at a minimum. Improved sanitation will slow the spread of pests, by depriving them of places to feed and reproduce. Many insects can be eliminated with consistent care and regular application of otherwise harmless household items.

Products such as dishwashing liquid, mineral oil, and rubbing alcohol are extremely useful against certain pests. And it's always a good idea to have a few bottles of beer on hand. The brew isn't meant to slake your thirst as you scout for spider mites. Instead, it's an effective lure and solvent for slugs, the persistent mollusk capable of chewing large holes in your plants' foliage.

There are times when slightly stronger methods are required, and when wisely chosen and administered, they are harmless to humans and effective against pests. Pyrethrum-based sprays are derived from plant chemicals (from *Chrysanthemum cinerariifolium*) and are not toxic to humans. Horticultural oils are also an excellent choice. Both types of spray kill on contact, and neither spray should be used when temperatures are above 75˚F (24˚C) to 80˚F (27˚C), as foliage may be damaged. Ced-o-flora, a kerosene-based pesticide, is the number one horticultural oil in my arsenal.

In addition to horticultural oils and pyrethrum-based sprays, I use Azadirachtin. This is an especially interesting and effective pesticide derived from the oil found in the seed of the Neem tree (*Azadirachta indica*). It works against insects in several ways: as an antifeedant (impeding the ability to swallow), by interrupting the reproductive cycle, and by interfering with the molting necessary between developmental stages. Azadirachtin is effective against mites as well as insects, which makes it particularly useful to have on hand. And since it is less toxic than many pesticides (it can be used on food crops), this is an excellent choice if you need something stronger than soap and water.

If there's a smoker in your household, cigarette butts can be useful in fighting many insect pests. Cigarette filters absorb nicotine, which is an effective insecticide. Peel the paper off the used filters and poke the filters into the potting mix. The nicotine in the filter will be absorbed by the soil, then by the plants' roots, acting as a systemic poison. Systemic poisons take a while to be effective, which is why it's a good idea to use them in conjunction with a topical pesticide. Commercial systemic poisons are available in liquid or granular form.

Some plants have adverse reactions to insecticides, so whenever you spray, make sure the insecticide you've chosen is safe for the plant you're spraying. This applies to homemade remedies as well as to commercial chemicals. Test the solution on a small part of the plant before spraying all over.

For example, if you mix a soap and water solution and inadvertently use too much soap, the leaves of the sprayed plant may turn brown and look burned. Damage may be irreparable, as when I sprayed a *Crassula argentea* with a fairly benign horticultural oil. Within 48 hours the entire plant wilted and crumbled. I now know that *C. argentea* is especially sensitive to insecticides, but it's a lesson I learned the hard way.

Integrated pest management also incorporates the use of biologicals, that is, predator insects, to reduce the populations of harmful pests. Although some people may be reluctant to introduce insects into their homes, biological controls are certainly appropriate for greenhouse use. Every plant pest has a predator that can be used to control it. For example, mealybugs are eaten by *Cryptolaemus montrouzieri*, aka "the mealybug destroyer." Predator mites (*Neoseiulus fallcis*) feed on spider mites, and stingless parasitoid miniwasps (*Aphidius* species) lay their eggs inside aphids. The larvae hatch and eat the aphids from within. How cool is that? Remember, pesticides kill beneficials as well as plant pests, so stop using them several days before releasing a beneficial insect.

Using biological controls offers a fascinating opportunity to watch nature balance itself. It's also an excellent alternative to using chemicals, which is really what IPM is all about. If your plants start out healthy and you care for them well, you should never have to use anything stronger than soap and oil to keep them in peak form.

If you're interested in using biological controls to reduce a population of pests, you'll need to choose the predator insect specifically recommended for the problem you have. There are many variables to consider (area to be covered, temperature, humidity), so consult a specialist before placing an order for predators.

At some point in your growing career, a plant pest will inevitably sneak into your home. If you pay close attention to your plants, you'll be able to identify the problem quickly and eliminate it, using the least toxic methods available.

Slugs

Slugs aren't usually household pests, but they can easily ride into your home on a tropical plant from a greenhouse or nursery. Or, if you summer your plants out-

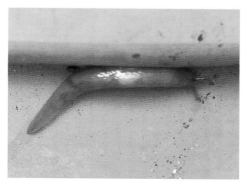

A small slug

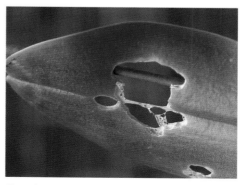

Slug damage on a *Phalaenopsis* leaf

doors, you may inadvertently bring a slug indoors in the fall. Watch for the silvery trails that both snails and slugs leave behind on plant leaves. Slugs like a warm, moist environment, and your home is a safe haven without predators such as birds or toads. Slugs are nocturnal creatures, so you won't always catch them in the act, but a few well-positioned saucers of beer work wonders. Place several among the houseplants that show signs of damage and wait. Slugs will find the beer, climb into the saucers to drink, and be dissolved by the liquid. Check your beer traps every morning and replenish them as needed. After a few weeks, you should be able to stop putting out bait.

Spider Mites

Spider mites are another noninsect plant pest. This is not merely a technicality. Spider mites are arachnids (having eight legs as opposed to six legs for insects) and in general they are susceptible to different chemicals than insects. However, the cultural practices useful when combating insect infestations are effective against spider mites, too.

Spider mites are particularly insidious because they are tiny and very hard to see. Frequently, you'll notice the damage to the plant before you detect the mites themselves. If a leaf looks yellow, dull, or mottled, or you see webbing in the leaf axils or on the underside of leaves, this may be a sign of infestation. An easy way to check for mites is by spraying water onto the leaves. Mite webbing will catch water droplets which are easier to see than the mites themselves.

Red spider mite and its characteristic webbing, magnified

Also, check the underside of a leaf with a magnifying glass. If you see red or white creatures smaller than the head of a pin moving around, you've got spider mites. If you don't have a magnifying glass but you can see little dots with your naked eye, touch one. If it moves away, it's a spider mite. Or, tap the top of the leaf while holding it over a piece of paper. If small dots fall onto the paper, they are probably spider mites.

Spider mites are sucking pests. They suck the chlorophyll out of leaves, leaving behind dead, mottled leaf tissue. A speckled, pale leaf surface is often your first clue that mites are dining on your plant. Spider mites are also highly mobile. They may travel among plants under their own steam, or you may inadvertently transport them by brushing up against an infested leaf, then touching a clean plant. If you find spider mites on one plant, check its neighbors to see if the mites have spread.

If you have mites, there are several things to do. First, remove all damaged foliage and dispose of the infested leaves. Then, accurately assess the extent of the damage. Because spider mites are difficult to detect, they often establish a strong foothold before they are noticed. A large population can be tough to eliminate. It may be preferable to dispose of the entire plant.

It is possible to kill spider mites with a solution of soap and cold water sprayed onto foliage with a mister. Or, rub dishwashing liquid up and down both sides of your plant's foliage, covering all surfaces, and let it sit. After 15 to 20 minutes, rinse off the soap. Repeat this at three-day intervals until you see no more sign of infestation.

If the population of spider mites is large, and you've decided to duke it out, you may need to use something stronger than soap and water. A combination of systemic granule and liquid spray can be effective. Once you've gotten mites under control, consider preventive measures: a rinse with soapy, cold water once every two or three weeks should keep spider mites from taking over. Small plants can be submerged in a wash basin filled with soapy water, while large specimens can be sprayed or washed by hand.

Don't confuse spider mites with spiders. Spider webs look different from spider mite webs; they are looser and more geometric in design. I welcome spiders among my plants (as long as they're not too scary) because they prey on other insects.

Scale

Scale is another insect pest that can be difficult to discover. While they are visible to the naked eye, mature insects look like little brown dots and can be mistaken for bumps on bark, especially on ficus, citrus, and other woody stemmed plants. If you scrape a dot with your fingernail and it pops off, you have scale. The hard shell is a protective covering, under which lives a sucking insect. Most sprays are ineffective against scale because they cannot penetrate the shell.

Scale on a leaf   Mealybugs on a palm, magnified

If you've caught the problem early and the scale is not widespread, remove each insect with a cotton swab dipped in alcohol. If the infestation is widespread, this can be tedious. Immature scale is difficult to see with the naked eye. The insects start out as crawlers, at which point they are shell-less, mobile, and tiny. As they mature, they grow, secrete their protective cover, and attach themselves to stems and leaves. The proboscis of the scale insect pierces the plant tissue and sucks chlorophyll out. When you remove the scale from the plant, the proboscis is left behind, so you kill the insect as you dislodge it. If you drop an insect during the removal process don't worry, it cannot reattach itself and continue to feed.

Because young insects are difficult to spot, you may not be able to remove them all with a swab. However, since they have not yet secreted their shell, they are vulnerable to spraying. After swabbing visible scale, spray the entire plant with a mixture of one part mineral oil, one part soap, and eight parts water. Test the solution on a single leaf first to make sure it does not burn the foliage. Some plants are more sensitive than others. If the leaf shows damage within 48 hours, reduce the concentration of the solution and try another test.

Mealybugs

Mealybugs are a kind of soft scale. Instead of a hard, brown shell, they are protected by a waxy, white covering. There are several different kinds of mealybugs, but all are sucking insects and feed similarly to hard scale. Like scale, immature mealybugs are mobile and difficult to see, so plan a two-fold attack. You need to eliminate all stages of mealybugs, or the reproductive cycle will continue. Remove the visible insects with a cotton swab and alcohol. You'll see the alcohol dissolve the white, cottony covering, exposing the pinkish insect body beneath. Spray the foliage with the same soap-mineral oil-water solution recommended for scale.

Aphids

Aphids are a common insect pest, and they are remarkable for the speed with which they reproduce. Aphids can both lay eggs and bear live young. and an aphid infestation can reach epic proportions very quickly. Fortunately, aphids are fairly easy to kill; they have no protective covering. If temperatures outside are warm, bring the affected plant outdoors and spray it with a strong blast of water from the hose. This will knock off most of the insects. If it's too cold to work outside, spray or wash the plant with a solution of one part dishwashing liquid, one part mineral oil, and eight parts water. Keep the plant separate from the rest of your plants for several weeks and continue treating the insects with soap and water. As with the other insect (and arachnid) pests we've discussed here, the immature stages are small and difficult to see, so it will take several sessions before you've gotten rid of them all.

Aphids on a hoya

Hoya with aphids soaking in a solution of soap, mineral oil, and water

Ants

You may see ants on your plants, and while they don't attack plants, they can indicate a problem. Ants frequently act as shepherds to mealybugs, aphids, and scale. If you see a line of ants climbing up and down the stem of a plant, follow the trail; it may lead you to a colony of sucking insects. Also, look for a sticky liquid on the plants' leaves. This is called *honeydew*, and it's a sugar-rich substance excreted by sucking insects. Ants collect the honeydew and eat it. Sooty mold is a powdery black substance that grows on the surface of honeydew. It's easier to spot than the honeydew itself and can indicate the presence of an insect problem.

Whiteflies

Whiteflies are pests that are easy to spot. Both adults and nymphs feed on the underside of tender leaves; when the foliage of a plant with whiteflies is touched, a cloud of insects flies up into the air. In addition to feeding on your houseplants, whiteflies can carry diseases from plant to plant. Certain plants are prone to whiteflies, such as lantanas, abutilons, and brugmansias. If you grow something that is known to attract whiteflies, be vigilant. The adult stage is highly mobile and can spread through a plant collection quickly. Whiteflies can be controlled with the same solution of soap and water recommended for aphids.

Fungus Gnats

Indoor growers often complain of fruit flies around their houseplants. These are in fact fungus gnats. Their larvae feed on organic matter in the potting mix and may occasionally damage root tissue. Established plants are not greatly affected by this, but seedlings may lose vigor. Fungus gnats prefer a moist, organic potting mix. Their population can be reduced by keeping the mix as dry as each individual plant will tolerate. This will kill the larvae and interrupt the reproductive cycle.

8

Plant Diseases

Diseases are more difficult to diagnose than pest infestations, but they are also more rare. Fortunately, many of the same good cultural habits that help keep your plants pest free will also reduce their chances of acquiring a disease. The best preventive measure you can take when dealing with diseases is to be constantly vigilant.

1. Check the health of each part of a plant before buying it. Make sure the leaves and stems are turgid and have healthy color. Pseudobulbs should be plump and firm. Feel and smell the potting mix. If it doesn't smell fresh, if it smells at all of mushrooms, and if the mix is wet, knock the plant out of its pot to examine the roots to make sure there is no root rot. Rotten roots are brown and slimy; healthy roots are white and plump.
2. Quarantining a new plant is as important for preventing the spread of disease as it is for monitoring insect pests. Fungal and bacterial diseases can be spread by physical contact, so keep new acquisitions isolated for a week or two while you watch for signs of disease.
3. Keep your growing areas clean. Fungal spores can remain dormant on leaves until conditions are optimal for growth. Remove plant debris that might harbor spores or bacteria.
4. Viral diseases are less common than fungal and bacterial diseases, and they can be communicated from plant to plant via a cutting blade. If you suspect a plant has a virus, do not use the same pruning shears on it that you then use

to cut another plant. Viruses can only be confirmed by laboratory analysis. While useful for commercial growers, these tests are prohibitively expensive for home growers.

5. At the risk of repeating myself, pay attention to the cultural needs of your plants: temperature, light, food, and water. Plants fight disease better when they're healthy and strong.

6. Watch your plants carefully and respond to the first signs of distress. If you are careless with maintenance, you may miss early indications of disease. As with insect pests, early detection is the key to controlling plant disease. Be aware. Be very aware.

Diseases are caused by living agents called *pathogens*. Pathogens include fungi, bacteria, phytoplasmas, viruses, and nematodes. For a disease to infect a plant, the pathogen must find a host plant susceptible to the pathogen, and the environmental conditions must be appropriate. In order to thwart a disease, remove one leg of the pathogen-host-environment triangle.

Fungal Diseases

Most plant diseases are caused by fungi, which reproduce by small spores. A spore lands on a leaf; it may be airborne, splashed on with water, or deposited by direct physical contact. If water is present on the leaf, the spore will produce a hypha (a small thread of fungus), which penetrates plant tissue.

Hyphae can penetrate directly by piercing soft, young leaves. They can also enter through leaf stomata, lenticels (stem stomata), hyathodes, or through wounds or cracks in plant tissue. Wound entry can be controlled to a certain degree by keeping the plant healthy and whole. By maintaining a clean growing area, we can also limit the chances of spores penetrating through plant openings. Beyond this there's not much a gardener can do other than provide optimal care and conditions.

Most fungi work unseen as they live off the plant tissue. A few, like powdery mildew, live on the leaf surface. The white fuzzy manifestation of powdery mildew is actually the fungal mycelium, a large web of hyphae. Pathogenic fungi kill plant cells and absorb the nutrients they need from those cells. Fungi don't have their own chlorophyll and therefore cannot photosynthesize.

There are many symptoms of fungal diseases, but the most common is leaf spot. The spots can be black, brown, or gray. If you suspect a plant has a fungal disease, there's an easy way to find out. Cut off a piece of leaf with a spot and seal it in a zip-lock bag. Put the bag someplace warm, like on top of the refrigerator, and let it sit. After a week, take the leaf out of the bag and look at it with a magnifying glass. Do you see tiny fungus stalks originating from the leaf spot? If so, your plant has a fungal disease.

Most fungi thrive in cool, wet conditions, so don't allow water to stand on plant foliage or flowers. If you water early in the day, any splashes of water should have time to dry before cooler evening temperatures provide the perfect breeding ground for fungus.

One of the most common and easily identifiable fungal diseases in a greenhouse or humid growing area is botrytis, also known as gray mold. It can penetrate al-

Fungal damage on *Phalaenopsis* flower

most any soft part of a plant and cause bulb, stem, flower, leaf, or root rot. Botrytis produces copious spores. They are fuzzy, gray, and immediately recognizable; they cover a flower or leaf like a thick carpet. They land on leaf surfaces and in humid conditions will produce hyphae. Infected cells quickly collapse, and the infected parts of the plants turn rotten and mushy. Remove any plant parts with visible botrytis spores, and amend the conditions in your growing area, specifically improving air circulation and eliminating standing water. Also, don't work with plants when the foliage is wet, to avoid unwittingly spreading spores. If the botrytis has reached the crown of the plant, the plant can probably not be saved.

A diseased plant is a breeding ground and may infect neighboring plants. If only a few leaves have been damaged, cut them off with a sterilized blade or scissors. Then, spray or dust the cut with a plant fungicide. If you need a fungicide fast and don't have one on hand, sprinkle the leaves of your plant with cinnamon. It may look funny, but cinnamon is an effective fungicide, and it smells good, too.

Bacterial Diseases

Some plant diseases are bacterial in nature. Bacteria are unicellular, much smaller than fungi, and cannot be detected with the naked eye. Like fungi, they also require a moist environment, and, like fungi, they also enter plant tissue through stomata, wounds, and hyathodes.

Symptoms of bacterial diseases can appear similar to those of fungal diseases, most commonly, discolored spots on plant foliage and flowers. If you've ruled out the possibility of a fungal disease, treat for bacteria. First, decide if your plant is worth saving. If so, cut off any damaged parts and spray with Physan or another antibacterial spray. Treat outside when possible, but if it's January in northern latitudes, bring your plant to the garage or cellar, or lay a plastic tarp down on the floor before spraying.

Phytoplasmas

Phytoplasmas are smaller than bacteria and are carried from plant to plant by insects, grafting, or dodder (a parasitic plant). They are tiny and can't live outside of plants, but they are able to reproduce independently. Phytoplasma diseases are sometimes called *yellows diseases,* because they cause foliage to yellow. Scientists suspect they work by upsetting the hormone balance of plants. Among tropicals, palms can be the victims of *palm yellows,* which are usually fatal.

Viruses

Viruses are even smaller than phytoplasmas and can only be seen with an electron microscope. Like a phytoplasma, a virus cannot function outside of a cell. It is a piece of DNA surrounded by protein; consider it a cell-hijacker. Once in the cell the virus manipulates the host plant's internal cell structures to produce more viruses. The cell then breaks open, sheds the viruses, and the cycle continues. Viruses are transmitted through sap, and by tools, insects, or fingers. They cannot reproduce independently.

Viral diseases are relatively rare, which is fortunate since they are difficult to diagnose. Symptoms to look for include stunted growth, a chlorotic mottling of the leaves, yellowing veins, or a pattern of yellow or greenish concentric rings or lines. Some plant viruses, such as impatiens necrotic spot virus, are named after a single host but may afflict numerous plants. Symptoms can be different in each plant, which makes diagnosis especially tough.

A plant can look perfectly healthy and still be infected. There is no cure for plant viruses, and they can only be confirmed by laboratory testing. Most reputable growers test for viruses periodically, and as a result, viral diseases are not widespread among tropicals. Buy your plants from growers you can trust or who give you a guarantee. If you have an infected plant, get rid of it and the potting medium it was planted in. The pot itself may be reused after soaking it for at least an hour in a solution of 1 cup bleach in 1 gallon of water.

Nematodes

Nematodes are microscopic worms which are sometimes pathogenic. Some are innocuous and feed on decaying organic matter. Some are beneficial and can be used to kill Japanese beetle grubs. Others can cause plant disease. Foliar nematodes on saintpaulias cause chlorotic mottling and may also affect begonias and other plants. Root-knot nematodes cause tumors in roots, thus preventing them from efficiently transporting water and nutrients. These tumors are easily detectable with the naked eye; affected roots are swollen and knotty. Any plant infested with nematodes should be thrown away.

The symptoms of many diseases are not immediately visible and are difficult to recognize. In general, diseases do not appear in regular patterns. So if all the leaves of a plant exhibit the same symptoms, for example, a regular pattern of small black spots, it's more likely that there's a cultural problem than there is a disease present.

To muddy the diagnostic waters even further, certain cultural problems produce symptoms that look like disease symptoms. Cold damage on a phalaenopsis leaf may produce round black spots with yellow halos. Sounds like a bacterial disease, but it isn't always. Cold water splashed onto the tender leaves of a tropical plant may produce a smattering of small black spots. Unlike black spot diseases, these spots do not enlarge or destroy the entire leaf and the tissue damage is not fatal.

Pathogens enter plants through wounds, and washing the blade of your knife or scissors won't get rid of all microscopic organisms. Therefore, be careful when

Cold damage on leaves

pruning, and sterilize the blade before moving from plant to plant. This can be done by rinsing your blade in alcohol or holding your scissors over a flame.

It can take some time for the symptoms of a disease to manifest themselves after a pathogen has invaded a host plant. Not only is it sometimes impossible to identify a plant disease until damage has already been done, but once you detect the symptoms, it can be equally difficult to pinpoint the problem. Because plant diseases are fairly rare in individual collections, this shouldn't worry you. Remain watchful and give your plants the excellent care that will keep them strong and disease-resistant.

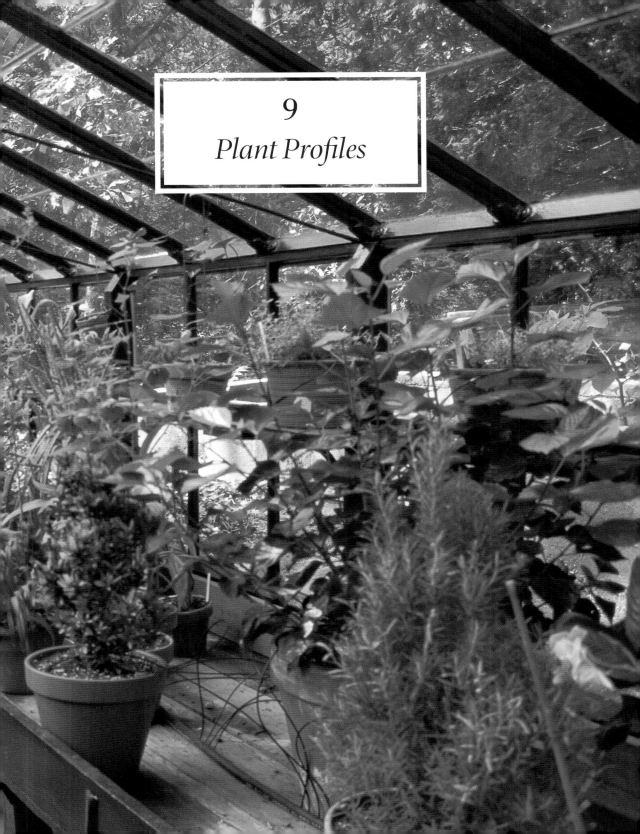

9
Plant Profiles

Abutilon megapotamicum
Abutilon ×hybridum

FLOWERING MAPLE

Malvaceae

Abutilon megapotamicum is native to Brazil; it is a colorful plant with a trailing growth habit. Upright *Abutilon ×hybridum* has been bred from various South American species. *Abutilon megapotamicum* and *A. ×hybridum* grow best in part shade, in moist, well-drained soils. Leaves are palmate with either three or five lobes and resemble those of the maple tree. Foliage can be solid green or variegated (white leaf margins or yellow speckles). Flower color and shape are highly varied, ranging from white to red to salmon to bicolor, and from open flowers to graceful bell shapes to pendent tubular blooms. Older specimens can get large and woody, so if you're not looking for a specimen plant, take cuttings to maintain juvenility. Abutilons are prone to whiteflies, so keep an eye out.

LIGHT Indoors, abutilons grow well in full sun. When grown outdoors as annuals, they should be protected from direct afternoon sun. In low light, foliage will continue to grow, but flowering will decrease or stop.

WATER Allow to dry out slightly between waterings, until the top half-inch of potting mix is dry to the touch.

TEMPERATURE Abutilons can tolerate temperatures of 45° to 50°F (7°C to 10°C), which makes them an excellent choice for a cool, bright windowsill.

SOIL Either a soilless or soil-based mix is fine for both abutilons.

FERTILIZATION Feed with a flowering plant food every other week during the growing season.

PROPAGATION Abutilons grow easily from stem cuttings. They bloom on new wood, so regular pruning not only provides material for propagation but also encourages continued flowering.

WINNING ATTRIBUTES Both *Abutilon megapotamicum* and *A. ×hybridum* offer a wide range of foliage patterns and flower colors and shapes. They quickly reach specimen size and will bloom year-round given enough sunlight.

Abutilon megapotamicum

Abutilon ×hybridum

Acalypha hispida
CHENILLE PLANT

Acalypha wilkesiana
JOSEPH'S COAT

Euphorbiaceae

Acalypha wilkesiana is native to Fiji where it grows as a shrub, reaching 15 feet in height. It is valued for its truly outrageous foliage color and patterns and grows best in full sun. Leaves are elliptical, toothed, and 3 to 6 inches long. Flowers are insignificant. *Acalypha hispida* is native to the South Pacific Islands, where it grows to be 10 feet tall. There it flowers best when grown in part sun/part shade. This plant is grown for its long, fuzzy, pendent red flowers, which can be up to 8 inches long. Leaves are medium green and ovate. Both acalyphas thrive in moist soils and high humidity. *Acalypha hispida* is dioecious; that is, male and female flowers are borne on separate plants. Female plants produce the showy red flowers. In containers, both acalyphas can grow to be sizeable shrubs, limited only by the root space available to them. To keep them small, prune hard annually, removing half to two-thirds of the top growth. Both are susceptible to spider mites and mealybugs, so keep your plants clean.

LIGHT Indoors, both *Acalypha hispida* and *A. wilkesiana* require high light; a western or southern window is best. In low light, *A. wilkesiana* will lose its variegation; *A. hispida* will not flower.

WATER Acalyphas can dry out slightly between waterings. When the potting mix is dry a half-inch below the surface, it's time to water. They also require high humidity so grow them on large drywells or in a greenhouse.

TEMPERATURE These plants like it hot; keep them out of drafts. Temperatures below 60°F (16°C) can cause leaf drop.

SOIL Use either a quick-draining, soil-based potting mix or a soilless mix.

FERTILIZATION Feed once every two weeks during the growing season. Use a balanced fertilizer for *Acalypha wilkesiana*; a bloom-booster for *A. hispida*.

PROPAGATION Acalyphas are easily propagated from stem cuttings. They are rapid growers and require annual pruning to maintain an attractive shape. Use stem tips pruned from old, leggy plants to start new plants when parent stock has outgrown its location or is no longer attractive.

Acalypha hispida

Acalypha wilkesiana

WINNING ATTRIBUTES The variegation of *Acalypha wilkesiana* is outstanding, combining copper, orange, green and purple, depending on the cultivar. The flower tassels of *A. hispida* are unique and tactile. These are exotic, showy plants.

Adenium obesum

DESERT ROSE

Apocynaceae

Adenium obesum is native to the Arabian peninsula and eastern Africa where it grows as a shrub and occasionally as a small tree reaching 15 feet. As its common name suggests, it grows in arid conditions, and its succulent trunk stores water for the dry season. This plant forms a caudex, a swollen section where the trunk joins the roots, and these caudices often become gnarled and twisted with age. It is a striking plant, whose smooth gray bark and unusual swollen trunk make it an excellent specimen plant. In nature it's deciduous and often leafless when in flower, making for a spectacular show. In containers, it rarely grows taller than 3 feet. *Adenium obesum* flowers more profusely if kept potbound. Flowers are funnelform and approximately 2 inches in diameter. They are usually shades of pink but can also be white or red. Leaves are dark green with a prominent white midrib, obovate, and 2 to 3 inches long. Sparse foliage is concentrated at the tips of branches. Mealybugs and scale are occasional problems.

LIGHT Grow *Adenium obesum* in bright light. An eastern or western window is acceptable, but southern light will produce more blooms.

WATER Water when the top inch of potting mix is dry to the touch. The stem may become slightly soft from lack of water; water well, and the tissue should become firm again. *Adenium obesum* is prone to rot, so do not overwater, especially when temperatures are cold. If a branch or stem becomes squishy, cut off the damaged tissue, leaving a clean margin, and watch for signs of recovery.

Adenium obesum

TEMPERATURE Can tolerate temperatures of 55°F (13°C). Decrease watering frequency in cooler temperatures to avoid rot.

SOIL Use a cactus soil or a soilless mix. This plant requires a fast-draining potting mix.

FERTILIZATION Feed at half strength once a month in spring and summer.

PROPAGATION *Adenium obesum* can be propagated from cutting or seed. Cuttings should be allowed to callus for several days before planting. Try pollinating the flowers with a small paintbrush.

WINNING ATTRIBUTES *Adenium obesum* has an exceptional form. Beginning as a miniature curiosity, it matures into a striking specimen with a branching, swollen shape. The flowers are the icing on the cake.

Adromischus cooperi

PLOVER EGGS

Crassulaceae

Adromischus cooperi is native to the semidesert areas of southern Africa. It grows to 3 to 4 inches tall and 2 to 3 inches wide. Individual leaves are about 2 inches long, plump, with slightly flattened leaf tips, and grow in a rosette from a central stem. Foliage is pale gray green, mottled with purple or dark green at the ends of the leaves. Flowers are trumpet-shaped, dusky purple or red, about a half-inch long, and held in loose clumps on bloom stalks about 10 inches above the foliage. *Adromischus cooperi* is a low maintenance plant and grows very well in containers. Its smooth, succulent leaves exert an almost magnetic attraction. You will need to touch them, and you should feel free. They are sturdy and can easily stand up to a little stroking. This charming miniature is an excellent choice for a sunny windowsill.

LIGHT Grow in full sun. In bright indirect light variegation will be less intense, and the plant may not flower.

WATER A small pot will need water once a week during warm weather. In winter, once every two weeks should be adequate.

TEMPERATURE Normal household temperatures are fine for *A. cooperi*. Do not let the temperature get below 50°F (10°C).

SOIL Grow in a soilless mix or a cactus mix.

FERTILIZATION Feed once a month at half strength during active growth.

Adromischus cooperi

PROPAGATION   *Adromischus cooperi* is easily propagated from leaf cuttings. Remove a leaf from the stem and allow it to callus for a week. Then, pot up the leaf, burying only as much as is necessary to allow the leaf to stand up.

WINNING ATTRIBUTES   This is a beautiful, low maintenance miniature with subtle variegation, a compact growth habit, and smooth, plump foliage.

Aeschynanthus marmoratus
Aeschynanthus radicans
Aeschynanthus speciosus

LIPSTICK PLANT

Gesneriaceae

These three vines are epiphytes from the islands of the South Pacific. There they grow in the crotches of trees where sunlight is dappled and plant roots are exposed to the air. *Aeschynanthus marmoratus* is a wildly variegated plant. The undersides of

Aeschynanthus marmoratus

Aeschynanthus radicans

its leaves are burgundy, and the tops are speckled with yellow and red. Its flowers are similarly variegated and therefore are not easily distinguished from the plant's foliage. In contrast, the flowers of *A. speciosus* stand out in bold relief from its foliage. They are bright orange and several times larger than the plant's leaves. *Aeschynanthus radicans* produces somewhat smaller flowers of a deep, cherry red; these are also larger than the neighboring leaves. Foliage is opposite, elliptical, with pointy tips; flowers are tubular, with a slight curve.

*Aeschynanthus
speciosa*

LIGHT Indoors, give all three *Aeschynanthus* species as much bright indirect light as possible: an east or west window is best. These plants will tolerate some direct sun but may sustain foliar damage (burning or bleaching) in hot afternoon sun.

WATER Aeschynanthus are drought-tolerant plants; their shiny leaves have a waxy cuticle. When the soil feels dry a half-inch below the surface, it's time to water. High humidity is appreciated.

TEMPERATURE Aeschynanthus can tolerate temperatures as low as 50°F (10°C) if watering is reduced during the cold period. A combination of cold temperatures and frequent waterings will lead to root rot.

SOIL As epiphytes, *Aeschynanthus* species grow best in a quick-draining potting mix. Use one part fir bark to three parts soilless medium.

FERTILIZATION These are not heavy feeders—once a month during the growing season is adequate.

PROPAGATION Easy to propagate from stem cuttings. In high humidity, simply pin a stem to the soil surface, where it will root.

WINNING ATTRIBUTES *Aeschynanthus marmoratus* offers excellent foliage variegation year-round. Leaf variegation is most pronounced in bright light, while shadier conditions result in muted, but still remarkable patterns. *Aeschynanthus radicans* and *A. speciosus* produce large, brightly colored flowers with great visual impact. These plants are easy to care for, drought-tolerant, and their full, mounding shapes make them attractive in hanging baskets. These are not unruly vines that require pruning or training as they have a naturally neat, cascading growth habit.

Agapanthus africanus

Liliaceae

Agapanthus africanus is a perennial native to South Africa. Leaves are slim, strap-shaped, and arching; the plant is approximately 1 to 2 feet tall. Flowers are borne on scapes about 3 feet tall. Individual, six-petalled, funnel-shaped blooms are held in

The blue flowers of *Agapanthus africanus* are set off by neighboring yellow foliage.

umbels of 20 to 30 and are usually shades of purple-blue, although white cultivars exist. In nature, *A. africanus* grows in full sun or light shade and is subject to dry and wet seasons. It flowers in spring or summer, during the rainy season. *Agapanthus africanus* makes an excellent houseplant, with a rare and lovely flower color. In containers it blooms best when potbound, and a mature plant can produce four or five umbels over several weeks. Cut back bloom stalks when flowers have passed.

LIGHT   Give *Agapanthus africanus* full sun for most impressive flowering. Southern or western light is best.

WATER   During active growth, water when the top half-inch of potting mix feels dry to the touch, probably once a week for average household temperatures. If you give your plant a cool winter rest, reduce watering to once every two weeks.

TEMPERATURE   *Agapanthus africanus* is not technically a tropical plant; it tolerates temperatures as low as 40°F (4°C). In cool temperatures, reduce watering frequency.

SOIL   Grow in a soilless mix; it requires a fast-draining medium.

FERTILIZATION   Grows well in poor soils. Fertilize once in early spring.

PROPAGATION   Easily propagated by division, this plant quickly forms clumps, and offsets can be separated from the parent plant and potted up on their own.

WINNING ATTRIBUTES   The flowers of *Agapanthus africanus* are a remarkable color. Very few other plants offer these shades of blue. Flowers are long lasting and stand high above the foliage, making an outstanding show. *Agapanthus africanus* is pest free and low maintenance.

Agave victoriae-reginae

CENTURY PLANT

Agavaceae

Agave victoriae-reginae is a succulent plant, native to the deserts of northern Mexico. Leaves are approximately 6 inches long, thick, and sharply pointed. Foliage is stiff and wedge-shaped, with white edging and tips. This coloration creates a delicate spiral pattern within a tight rosette of foliage. In nature, *A. victoriae-reginae* can reach 24 inches in both height and width. In containers, it rarely reaches half this size. It is a slow grower, making large specimens hard to come by.

LIGHT   Grow *Agave victoriae-reginae* in full sun. In low light, new foliage will be weak and thin.

Agave victoriae-reginae is the top center plant.

WATER Overwatering will lead to root rot. In summer, watering once a week is adequate. In winter, reduce watering to once every two weeks.

TEMPERATURE Can tolerate a light frost, but grows best under frost free conditions.

SOIL Requires a quick-draining soil. Use a soilless mix, or one part sand to one part soil-based mix.

FERTILIZATION Feed sparingly, no more than once a month during the growing season.

PROPAGATION *Agave victoriae-reginae* is grown from seed. It is a slow grower and rarely flowers indoors. In nature, it only flowers after reaching maturity, which can take 20 years. Because seed is rare and growth is slow, this isn't the best candidate for home propagation.

WINNING ATTRIBUTES *Agave victoriae-reginae* is a pest free plant of exceptional beauty and sculptural value. It is also one of the few *Agave* species with a small enough growth habit to make it suitable for pot culture.

Allamanda cathartica

GOLDEN TRUMPET

Apocynaceae

Allamanda cathartica is native to Brazil where it grows in full sun as a vine. Foliage is dark green, shiny, elliptical, and grows in whorls. Individual leaves are 3 to 5 inches long. When sold as a houseplant, *A. cathartica* is often pruned into a shrubby form, or treated with growth inhibitors, which obscures its natural vining habit. Be aware that even in a container this plant can climb 10 to 15 feet in a single season.

LIGHT Flowers most heavily in full sun and must have at least two or three hours of direct sun for consistent bloom.

WATER During the growing season, let the top half-inch of soil dry out between waterings. If you allow temperatures to drop in winter, reduce the frequency with which you water. High humidity is recommended in warm weather.

TEMPERATURE Keep warm, above 60°F (16°C). Leaf drop may occur under cooler conditions.

SOIL Grow in either a soilless or soil-based mix.

Allamanda cathartica

FERTILIZATION Feed at half strength every other week during active growth.

PROPAGATION Easily propagated from stem cuttings. Since the plant benefits from an annual spring pruning, you can prune and propagate at the same time.

WINNING ATTRIBUTES The flowers are large (3 inches in diameter) and a vibrant, saturated yellow. It is a fast grower and makes an impressive display.

Alocasia 'Black Velvet'
Alocasia 'Hilo Beauty'

ELEPHANT EAR

Aracea

The genus *Alocasia* is native to southeastern Asia and the South Pacific islands. Both *Alocasia* 'Black Velvet' and *Alocasia* 'Hilo Beauty' are garden hybrids grown for their exceptional foliar variegation. In nature, *Alocasia* species are understory plants and receive diffused light. Direct sun can cause leaf burn and pale foliage. Leaves are heart-shaped, with dramatic patterns, and flowers have a classic spathe/spadix form. Remove blooms to divert the plant's energy to foliage production. The leaves of *A.* 'Black Velvet' are extremely dark green with a velvety texture and a geometric pattern of silver/white veins. *Alocasia* 'Hilo Beauty' has smooth leaves irregularly variegated with white, cream, and several shades of green. Watch out for spider mites, which can gain a foothold in dry conditions.

LIGHT Grow in bright indirect light.

WATER Alocasias grow best when kept consistently moist and given high humidity. When the surface of the potting mix feels dry to the touch, it's time to water. Dry air may lead to brown leaf tips.

TEMPERATURE These hybrids require warm temperatures, above 65°F (18°C). Drafts can cause brown leaf margins. Cold temperatures combined with moist soils can lead to root rot.

SOIL A soil-based potting mix is best for *Alocasia* hybrids; it retains moisture longer than a soilless mix and provides more nutrition.

FERTILIZATION These are hungry plants. Feed at full strength every two weeks during the growing season.

PROPAGATION Remove offsets and pot them up individually. You can also divide the rhizome and treat the pieces as root cuttings.

Alocasia 'Black Velvet'

Alocasia 'Hilo Beauty'

WINNING ATTRIBUTES   These two *Alocasia* hybrids are smaller than many and therefore well-suited to indoor pot culture. Their foliage is strikingly beautiful, quintessentially tropical, and very bold.

Aloe variegata

PARTRIDGE-BREAST ALOE

Liliaceae

Aloe variegata is native to South Africa and Namibia. Foliage is succulent and grows in a rosette. Individual leaves are three-sided; they have white, horizontal markings and finely serrated edges which are not dangerously sharp. Plants grow to

Aloe variegata

about 12 inches high. Outdoors they produce spikes of tubular, coral pink flowers, held 12 to 18 inches above the foliage. *Aloe variegata* rarely blooms indoors but may flower in direct sun or in a greenhouse.

LIGHT Indoors, *Aloe variegata* can be grown under a wide range of light intensities, from the direct sun of a south-facing window to the lower intensity of incandescent and fluorescent grow-bulbs. Variegation remains strong even in northern light.

WATER Should be kept dry; water once every 10 days in warm temperatures, once every two to three weeks in winter.

TEMPERATURE *Aloe variegata* can withstand winter temperatures as low as 50°F (10°C).

SOIL Grow in a soilless medium, or in a combination of one part sand and three parts soil-based mix.

FERTILIZATION Grows well with very little fertilization. Feed once a month during the growing season.

PROPAGATION   Offsets can be separated from the parent plant and potted up individually. Wait until some roots have developed at the base of the offset before separating it from the parent plant.

WINNING ATTRIBUTES   The white markings and plump foliage of *Aloe variegata* are very attractive. Its unusual sculptural form is compact and unique. It requires very little maintenance.

Alpinia purpurata
RED GINGER

Alpinia zerumbet 'Variegata'
VARIEGATED SHELL GINGER
Zingiberaceae

Alpinia purpurata is native to the Pacific Islands where it grows in the dappled light of humid, tropical rain forests. In nature it grows to be 10 feet tall. Leaves are deep green with a prominent yellow midrib, oblanceolate, and quite large: about 20 inches long and 4 to 6 inches wide. Showy red flower heads are actually bracts; true flowers are small and white and emerge from between the bracts. The entire inflorescence is about 8 inches tall. In nature, *A. purpurata* reproduces in a fascinating way. Small plantlets sprout from among the flower bracts. The weight of the plantlets eventually forces the stems down to the ground, allowing the plantlets to make contact with the forest floor where they root and grow. New stems also grow from spreading underground rhizomes. In containers, *A. purpurata* rarely exceeds 6 feet in height. It is better suited to the greenhouse or conservatory than to the average home because of its size and high humidity requirements. *Alpinia zerumbet* 'Variegata' is native to India and Southeast Asia, where it reaches 6 to 8 feet. It is a clumping plant, producing tightly massed stems from underground rhizomes. Its foliage is dramatically striped with yellow. Leaves are lanceolate and up to 2 feet long. Pendent flower clusters are up to 12 inches long, and individual blooms open one by one. Buds are pale pink or white, and open flowers expose a yellow interior marked with red. It rarely blooms indoors, but grows well in containers where it reaches 4 to 6 feet high. *Alpinia zerumbet* 'Variegata' also requires high humidity. This, combined with its large size, makes it well suited to a conservatory room or greenhouse. Alpinias generally bloom on second-year growth; do not cut back one- year-old stems or you will curtail bloom. These plants can be summered out-

Alpinia purpurata

doors in humid climates. If allowed to grow outdoors, give them protection from hot afternoon sun. In nature these plants spread rapidly; in containers they need frequent watering and feeding during the growing season.

LIGHT These are understory plants in nature and should be grown in part sun to bright indirect light indoors.

WATER Alpinias do not like to dry out. Water when the surface of the potting mix feels dry.

TEMPERATURE Grow in normal household temperatures.

SOIL A soil-based mix is best.

Alpinia zerumbet 'Variegata'

FERTILIZATION   Feed every other week at full strength during the growing season.

PROPAGATION   Alpinias are easy to propagate by division. Cut through the horizontal rhizome and tug the roots apart, then repot.

WINNING ATTRIBUTES   These are showy, large plants that reward your careful ministrations with impressive foliage and inflorescences. *Alpinia purpurata* produces gorgeous, large heads of bracts and flowers, offset by large, deep green leaves. *Alpinia zerumbet* 'Variegata' is a magnificent foliage specimen. Its outstanding yellow stripes make it an immediate focal point, both indoors and out.

Ananas comosus

PINEAPPLE

Bromiliaceae

Ananas comosus is believed to be native to Brazil, although it has long been culti-vated by indigenous peoples throughout Central and South America. It is a terres-trial bromeliad that grows in full sun. Leaves are about 2 feet long, lanceolate, medium green, and very sharply toothed. In nature, rosettes of foliage will grow to 3 feet tall. The inflorescence is about 12 inches tall, borne above the foliage. *Ananas comosus* grows well in containers but requires bright light and high humid-ity in order to flower indoors. Pot-grown specimens may not flower until they are several years old. Indoors, fruit rarely reaches a size worth eating, nor does it be-come sweet enough to enjoy. Nonetheless, the fruit is quite decorative. Several var-iegated cultivars offer cream-striped leaves and reddish bracts.

LIGHT   Indoors grow in full sun.

WATER   Requires a moist potting mix. Water when the surface of the potting mix feels dry.

TEMPERATURE   Keep above 60°F (16°C) at all times.

SOIL   Grow in a mix of four parts soilless potting mix and one part sand.

Ananas comosus

FERTILIZATION Feed at half strength every other week during active growth.

PROPAGATION Propagating *Ananas comosus* is fun and easy. It's an excellent garden project to try with children. Slice off the top of a store-bought pineapple, including just enough fruit to hold the leaves together. Let this piece dry for a week or two. Then plant it about an inch deep in the sandy/soilless potting mix specified above, and water well. With constant moisture, high humidity, and bright sun, a new plant will grow from the top of the old.

WINNING ATTRIBUTES *Ananas comosus* has excellent structure with a highly ornamental inflorescence and attractive ripening fruit. Even if your plant doesn't flower, the stiff, recurved foliage is statuesque.

Anthurium 'Obake'

FLAMINGO FLOWER

Anthurium clarinervium

Araceae

Anthurium are native to tropical America where they grow as understory plants. Some are grown for their outstanding foliage, while others have been hybridized to produce exotic flowers. *Anthurium* 'Obake' is a garden hybrid bred for its vivid

Anthurium 'Obake'

Anthurium clarinervium

green and red flowers. A spadix holds the actual flowers and is the slim, center spike surrounded by a showy, shiny, bright-colored bract, which is the spathe. *Anthurium clarinervium* is native to Mexico; it is prized for its remarkably patterned foliage, which is dark green with silvery veins. The leaves of all *Anthurium* are heart-shaped. They require higher than average humidity and warm temperatures.

LIGHT Grow both in bright indirect light. *Anthurium clarinervium* will also grow well in the slightly less bright light of a northern window.

WATER High humidity is the key to growing these plants successfully. If you have a greenhouse, try them there.

TEMPERATURE Anthuriums are warm-growing plants and should be kept above 60°F (16°C) at all times. Cooler temperatures will result in damaged foliage.

SOIL Many anthuriums are epiphytic in nature, so plant them in a quick-draining, soilless mix.

FERTILIZATION Feed at half strength once every two weeks during the growing season.

PROPAGATION Propagation is best accomplished by division.

WINNING ATTRIBUTES The wildly colored flowers of *Anthurium* 'Obake' are its major selling point. They are long lasting and so exotic as to appear unnatural. The richly patterned foliage of *A. clarinervium* is elegant and attractive all year long.

Aporophyllum hybrid

RAT-TAIL CACTUS
Cactaceae

Aporophyllum cacti are intergeneric hybrids of *Aporocactus* and *Epiphyllum*, both of which are epiphytic cacti. In nature, both genera receive dappled light. As epiphytes, aporophyllums are trailing plants; they grow best in hanging baskets. Cultural requirements closely resemble those of *Aporocactus* species: give them protection from full sun and grow in a quick draining mix. Physical characteristics are somewhat different from those of *Aporocactus*. Foliage is slimmer, and the flowers of aporophyllums more closely resemble those of *Epiphyllum* hybrids. These large, showy flowers are orange, red, or magenta. Spines are small, sharp, and tenacious. Handle with care.

LIGHT Indoors, full sun produces the most bloom. A southern window is best, but western or eastern sun is acceptable. If you grow your aporophyllum outdoors in summer, give it some protection from afternoon sun.

WATER Unlike desert cacti, aporophyllums require weekly watering during warm weather. In cooler weather, increase the interval between waterings to once every 10 days. Pot this plant in clay to allow the potting mix to dry out somewhat between waterings. It's difficult to reach in among the spiny stems to feel the soil, so develop your watering schedule according to visual cues. If the foliage starts to look shriveled, it's time to water.

TEMPERATURE Regular household or greenhouse temperatures are best. After flowering, plants can be given a winter rest period at about 50°F (10°C), but this is not necessary. If you give your aporophyllum a winter rest, reduce watering to once or twice per month.

Aporophyllum hybrid

SOIL   Use a lightweight, quick-draining, soilless mix.

FERTILIZATION   Feed with a balanced fertilizer every two weeks during the growing season, then with a bloom-booster in late fall to guarantee regular winter flowering.

PROPAGATION   Propagation is easily done with stem cuttings. Allow cuttings to air dry for several days before planting several together in a 4-inch pot.

WINNING ATTRIBUTES   Large, bright-colored flowers create an outstanding show for several weeks in early winter. This plant is pest free and low maintenance.

Araucaria bidwillii

MONKEY PUZZLE

Araucariaceae

Araucaria bidwillii is native to the rainforests of Queensland, Australia, where it can surpass 100 feet. Needless to say, in your home it will not grow quite that large. While many people do not consider this a houseplant, it makes an excel-

Araucaria bidwillii

lent, low maintenance, long-lived specimen. A relative of *Araucaria heterophylla* (Norfolk Island Pine), *A. bidwillii* is less ubiquitous and more interesting. Foliage is pinnate, glossy dark green, and very sharp. The bark is exfoliating and reddish brown; it is especially attractive when the peeling pieces are backlit by the sun. In containers, *A. bidwillii* will grow to be 10 to 12 feet tall. Mature specimens should be pruned every two or three years as they approach the ceiling. This is a low maintenance and pest free plant, which is a good thing since working with it can be painful. Wear gloves to avoid bloodshed. If there are young children in your home, either grow *A. bidwillii* where they can't reach it, or wait until they know enough not to try.

LIGHT   Grow *Araucaria bidwillii* in bright light; a western or southern window is best.

WATER   This is a drought-tolerant plant. Large specimens will need water only once every two or three weeks, depending on the temperature of your home. A smaller plant should be watered when the top inch of potting mix is dry to the touch.

TEMPERATURE   Normal household temperatures are fine for *Araucaria bidwillii*. It can tolerate occasional temperatures in the 50°F (10°C) range.

SOIL   Grow in either a soilless or soil-based potting mix.

FERTILIZATION   Feed every other week during the growing season.

PROPAGATION   Easily propagated from fresh seed. It is a conifer, and seeds are borne in large cones, although usually not indoors.

WINNING ATTRIBUTES   *Araucaria bidwillii* makes an impressive, quick-growing specimen. Its stiff branches and pinnate leaves give the plant architectural interest, and both the bark and glossy dark leaf color are very attractive. This is one of the few conifers appropriate for indoor growing, and its unusual appearance makes it a collector's item.

Ardisia crenata

CORAL BERRY

Myrsinaceae

Ardisia crenata is native to Eastern Asia as far north as Japan. In nature, it grows to be 5 to 6 feet tall and is an understory shrub, growing in part shade and in moist, quick-draining soil. *Ardisia crenata* can be invasive in subtropical climates. In pot culture it grows to about 3 to 5 feet tall. Small, white-pink flowers open in spring, and persistent berries ripen to a bright red in late fall. Foliage is shiny, dark green, elliptic-lanceolate, with crenate margins. Individual leaves are approximately 3 to 4 inches long.

LIGHT   Bright indirect light to part sun is best.

WATER   Allow to dry out somewhat between waterings. If potting mix is kept constantly moist, foliage will yellow and drop. If household temperatures are above 75°F (24°C), grow *Ardisia crenata* on a drywell.

TEMPERATURE   Native to temperate and tropical zones, it can tolerate colder temperatures than many houseplants can; in fact, high temperatures cause the berries to drop prematurely.

Ardisia crenata

SOIL   Both soilless and soil-based potting mixes are fine.

FERTILIZATION   Feed at half strength with a balanced fertilizer every other week during the growing season.

PROPAGATION   Can be propagated from stem cuttings or from seeds. Remove the seed from inside the berry, and plant, barely covered, in a lightweight mix.

WINNING ATTRIBUTES   The bright red berries are gorgeous in contrast with the shiny, dark green foliage. Berries last for up to two years, which can give you a spectacular specimen plant. *Ardisia crenata* is not prone to any insect pests or diseases and is relatively trouble free. Staking may be necessary as the plant gets taller.

Asparagus setaceus

ASPARAGUS FERN
Liliaceae

Asparagus setaceus is native to South Africa and is not a true fern. It gets its common name from its delicate, fernlike foliage. What look like leaves are actually modified, needle-like branches, called *phylloclads*. As a young plant, *A. setaceus* is compact, but as it matures, it sends out climbing stems that can reach 3 to 4 feet in length. Indoors, you may prune the taller branches to keep the plant an appropriate size.

LIGHT   Grows best in bright indirect light or part shade. It will tolerate some sun, but leaves may become pale. Foliage should be protected from hot afternoon sun.

WATER   Despite its delicate appearance, *Asparagus setaceus* is somewhat drought-tolerant. Its root system includes water-storing nodules. Water when the top half-inch of soil feels dry, or if you notice individual needles dropping from the leaves.

TEMPERATURE   Tolerates temperatures to 50°F (10°C), although growth slows under cool conditions. If temperatures get higher than 75°F (24°C), humidity must be raised to prevent leaf drop.

SOIL   Use a soil-based mix.

FERTILIZATION   Feed at half strength every other week during the growing season.

PROPAGATION   Divide overgrown plants into smaller specimens. The root balls of all *Asparagus* species can get quite dense and usually need to be divided with a small saw or very sharp knife.

*Asparagus
setaceus*

WINNING ATTRIBUTES The foliage of this plant is so ethereal that it looks as if it's floating on air. It's a delicate plant with a graceful habit, perfect for a north- or east-facing window.

Aspidistra elatior

CAST IRON PLANT

Liliaceae

Aspidistra elatior is native from the Himalayan mountains to Japan and is technically not a tropical plant. It is capable of withstanding cool temperatures and will even tolerate the occasional light frost, although foliage may be damaged. It was a favorite of the Victorians, who named it "cast iron plant" because it did not succumb to gas fumes or cold, dark drawing rooms. Leaves are elliptical, approximately 12 to 18 inches long, with an arching growth habit. Petioles are 6 to 8 inches long. *Aspidistra elatior* rarely flowers indoors, but under greenhouse conditions watch for purple-brown flowers growing at soil level. They resemble partially open clamshells. This plant grows slowly and until recently was hard to find commercially. Now several varieties are available in the trade: the solid green species, *A. elatior* 'Variegata' (striped irregularly with cream and white); and *A.*

elatior 'Milky Way' (with yellow speckles on the leaves). Watch for spider mites and scale.

LIGHT   *Aspidistra elatior* is famous for surviving in dark corners. However, variegated varieties require higher light, and all aspidistras will grow best in bright indirect light.

WATER   Can be allowed to dry out between waterings. Water when the top inch of soil feels dry. *Aspidistra elatior* will tolerate moist soils, but not indefinitely.

Aspidistra elatior
'Variegata'

TEMPERATURE Grows well in average household temperatures. It also tolerates temperatures as low as 40°F (4°C), and can survive the occasional dip into the 30s. It should be kept on the dry side if grown under cold conditions.

SOIL Use a soil-based mix.

FERTILIZATION *Aspidistra elatior* is not a heavy feeder. Feed at half strength once a month during the growing season.

PROPAGATION Grows from a rhizomatous root system, the top of which is visible creeping along the soil surface. When the pot appears full (perhaps so full that it cracks under pressure from the root system), divide the rhizomes and roots into sections of at least two leaves to make more plants.

WINNING ATTRIBUTES This is one tough plant. That doesn't mean you can't kill it if you really try, but it's perfect for a difficult spot—dim, cold, neglected. Remember that it will survive under adverse conditions, but it will flourish with a little TLC. And while growers stress the hardiness of this plant, it is also graceful in form and variegation.

Asplenium antiquum 'Victoria'

JAPANESE BIRD'S NEST FERN
Polypodiaceae

Asplenium antiquum is an epiphyte native to China and southern Japan. The cultivar 'Victoria' has a more open vase shape than the species, and its leaf margins are slightly ruffled. This is not a frilly fern, nonetheless it is quite graceful. Fronds are a light, apple green, about 3 feet long, with pointed tips. New fronds emerge from the central crown with a classic fiddlehead shape. This fern is moderately difficult to grow. It is not as tolerant of dry air as *Davallia fejeensis* or *Platycerium bifurcatum*, nor does it require humidity as high as *Adiantum capillus-veneris*. If surrounding air is too dry, leaf margins will turn brown, marring their beauty. *Asplenium antiquum* is susceptible to scale under dry conditions. This is a large fern that may not fit into every interior landscape. If you like the unusual color but need a small, terrarium-sized plant, try *Asplenium nidus*. It has a slightly different shape, but similar cultural requirements.

LIGHT Grow these in bright indirect light; an eastern or bright northern window is best. If you grow them in a conservatory room or greenhouse, place them in the shade of taller plants.

WATER   Allow the top half-inch of potting mix to dry out between waterings. *Asplenium antiquum* does not require constantly moist soil, but it does need elevated humidity. Grow it in a greenhouse, conservatory, on a drywell, or among other plants.

TEMPERATURE   Grows well in average household temperatures.

SOIL   As an epiphyte, *Asplenium antiquum* requires a quick-draining potting mix. Make yourself a special epiphyte mix with three parts soilless mix and one part fine-grained fir bark.

FERTILIZATION   Feed at half strength once a month during the growing season.

Asplenium antiquum
'Victoria'

PROPAGATION   *Asplenium antiquum* is a true fern and is propagated from spores. However, its spores are tinier than most, and propagation is therefore difficult.

WINNING ATTRIBUTES   This is a lovely plant, graceful but not dainty. Its large size and vaselike shape make it an impressive specimen. Its fresh, apple green color is outstanding.

Tuberous *Begonia* hybrid
Begonia 'Frosty'
ANGEL-WING BEGONIA
Begonia 'Escargot'
REX BEGONIA
Begoniaceae

The genus *Begonia* is extensive and varied. Plants range from giant specimens, taller than a human being with leaves more than a foot in diameter, to miniatures with foliage the size of a dime. Several categories of *Begonia* make excellent houseplants. Tuberous *Begonia* hybrids are derived from *Begonia boliviensis,* which is native to the Andes. The flowers of these hybrids are magnificent: saturated, brightly colored, about 3 inches long, and pendent. Stems are thick and succulent. Foliage is rich, medium green, with a sharply lobed, maple leaf shape. Leaves are 3 to 4 inches long. Tuberous *Begonia* hybrids flower primarily in spring and summer and go completely dormant in winter. In autumn, allow the foliage to yellow and die, remove the tubers from their pots, cut or rub off the stems, and allow the tuber surfaces to dry. Keep in a cool, frost free closet in peat moss or sand until spring, at which time you may replant the tuber, with the hollow facing up. This is quite easy to do, and the extra effort will result in an extraordinarily beautiful hanging plant.

Angel-wing begonias are another category of begonia. They have fibrous root systems and cane-like stems. Many grow to be 4 feet tall and in containers may require staking. *Begonia* 'Frosty' has a compact growth habit that makes it a perfect houseplant. Foliage is green, frosted with silver variegation. Leaves are shaped like wings, with jagged, undulate margins. Flowers are a light coral-pink; individual blooms are an inch in diameter and held in terminal clusters. This angel-wing has both seriously lovely foliage and year-round flowers. Angel-wings respond well to pruning and can be encouraged to branch by regularly pinching out the growing tips.

Tuberous *Begonia* hybrid

Plants in the *Begonia* ×*rex-cultorum* group are rhizomatous begonias grown for their outstanding foliage. A thick rhizome grows partly exposed above the soil, sending up stems from its nodes. *Begonia rex*, native to India, is seldom grown today. Its numerous modern hybrids are grouped as *B.* ×*rex-cultorum* and are all dramatically variegated. *Begonia* 'Escargot' not only has glorious silver, purple, and green coloration, but also an unusual, spiral-edged pattern and leaf-shape. *Begonia* ×*rex-cultorum* requires higher humidity than many other begonias. Don't try to compensate for dry air by overwatering. A consistently damp soil will lead to root rot. In dry air, leaf margins may crack and brown. These plants are best grown in a greenhouse or conservatory room, or at the very least on a large drywell. A well-grown *B.* ×*rex-cultorum* is spectacular year-round.

LIGHT Tuberous *Begonia* hybrids should be given part sun during active growth. Once the top growth has died back and the plant enters dormancy, light levels are unimportant. Indoors, *B.* 'Frosty' does best in part sun. *Begonia* 'Escargot' grows best in bright indirect light; an eastern or unobstructed northern window is best. Direct sun will bleach the foliage, and insufficient light results in spindly stems and small leaves.

WATER Tuberous *Begonia* hybrids have succulent stems that store water; they are fairly drought-tolerant. Allow the top inch of potting mix to dry out between waterings. Once foliage starts to yellow, stop watering until leaves and stems die back. Water *B.* 'Frosty' when the top inch of potting mix is dry. Do not allow it to remain constantly wet, or lower foliage will drop. *Begonia* 'Escargot' requires elevated humidity. Do not, however, allow the potting mix to remain constantly moist. Allow the top half-inch of potting mix to dry out between waterings.

TEMPERATURE During active growth, tuberous *Begonia* hybrids do well in average household temperatures; during dormancy, keep them at about 50°F (10°C). Keep *B.* 'Frosty' and *B.* 'Escargot' at normal household temperatures.

SOIL Tuberous *Begonia* hybrids grow well in either a soilless or soil-based potting mix. Pot *B.* 'Frosty' and *B.* 'Escargot' in a soilless mix.

FERTILIZATION Feed tuberous *Begonia* hybrids with a bloom-booster fertilizer every other week during active growth. Feed *B.* 'Frosty' and *B.* 'Escargot' with a balanced fertilizer at half strength every other week during active growth.

PROPAGATION To propagate tuberous *Begonia* hybrids, remove a large tuber from its pot in spring before growth has started. Cut it into several sections, including

Begonia 'Frosty' is an angel-wing begonia.

Begonia 'Escargot' is a rhizomatous begonia in the *Begonia* ×*rex-cultorum* group.

a growing point in each section. The growing point will look like the eye of a potato. Dust the cut edge with sulfur powder and pot each tuber piece with the hollow facing up. *Begonia* 'Frosty' may be propagated from seed or stem cuttings. Propagating *B.* ×*rex-cultorum* is a fascinating experience; new plants will grow from leaves pinned to potting mix. If you'd like to experiment, follow the instructions in chapter 6.

WINNING ATTRIBUTES The flowers of tuberous *Begonia* hybrids are large, vibrant, and numerous. This is a showy plant. Try growing it for its outstanding blooms and to experiment with plant dormancy. *Begonia* 'Frosty' is a compact, low maintenance houseplant. It has a free-flowering habit, and its glossy, speck-led foliage is fresh and lovely. Nothing beats the foliage of *B. ×rex-cultorum*. Its coloration and patterns are visually arresting, and a well-grown specimen tells the world you've got mad skills.

Bougainvillea hybrids

PAPER FLOWER

Nyctaginaceae

Bougainvilleas are native to tropical and subtropical regions of South America and grow in full sun and dry soil. Normally evergreen, they will drop their leaves under cool conditions or extreme drought. Bougainvilleas are shrubs, producing long, thorny stems. Leaves are simple and medium green, although there are variegated cultivars. The true flowers are actually small and white. They are surrounded by large, colorful bracts, which can be white, orange, magenta, or vermillion. In na-ture, bougainvilleas flower during the dry season when many also drop their leaves. The leafless stems, covered with colorful bracts, are very showy. Keep pot-bound to encourage bloom. Bougainvilleas can be pruned heavily to keep them a manageable size. They flower on new wood, so prune annually after flowering. *Bougainvillea glabra* is native to Brazil and is commonly grown as a garden plant worldwide; it is also progenitor of many *Bougainvillea* hybrids.

LIGHT Sun! Sun! Sun! This plant requires very high light to produce worth-while bloom. Bougainvilleas will produce foliage in lower light, but need six to eight hours of direct sun per day in order to bloom indoors.

WATER *Bougainvillea* hybrids are drought-tolerant. In fact, they flower more prolifically when the top several inches of soil dry out between waterings. Under wet conditions, bougainvilleas will produce foliage, but fewer flowers.

TEMPERATURE Hot is good. Keep above 50°F (10°C).

SOIL Grow in a soilless mix. Soil that stays moist is not appropriate for this plant.

FERTILIZATION Bougainvilleas flourish in poor soils. Fertilizers high in nitro-gen will encourage foliage but discourage flower production. Feed once a month during the growing season with a low nitrogen fertilizer.

Bougainvillea
hybrid

PROPAGATION   Stem cuttings don't root easily, but rooting hormone and bottom heat improve your chances. You may also remove suckers from the parent plant and pot them up.

WINNING ATTRIBUTES   The bracts of *Bougainvillea* hybrids are vibrant and plentiful; it is a spectacular plant. It's not easy to grow well indoors, but worth trying for the exuberance of bloom.

Boweia volubulis

Boweia volubilis

CLIMBING ONION

Liliaceae

Boweia volubilis is native to southern Africa. In nature, green basal bulbs, covered with papery sheaths, grow partially under the soil. In containers, they are usually grown on top of the soil. This looks more interesting and reduces the chances of rot. The bulbs can reach 8 inches in diameter. Top growth is composed of flexible, flat stems which branch frequently, creating an intricate tangle of vine. Outdoors, *B. volubilis* grows in part shade and goes dormant during the dry season, when the twining stems yellow and fall off. In the average home, some go dormant but many do not. If your plant enters dormancy, reduce watering to almost nothing. If the bulbs start to shrivel, water them, but no more than once a month. When the bulbs begin to produce new top growth, resume your regular watering schedule. Indoors, *B. volubilis* will flower in full sun, although it is primarily grown for its foliage. Flowers are small and greenish-yellow.

LIGHT *Boweia volubilis* will grow in almost any exposure indoors. The bright indirect light of a northern or eastern window is fine, although the plant will not flower without the direct sun of a western or southern exposure.

WATER Watering once a week is sufficient. During dormancy, reduce this to about once a month, depending on the appearance of the bulbs.

TEMPERATURE Average household temperatures are fine. Do not let it get below 50°F (10°C).

SOIL Pot *Boweia volubilis* in a soilless medium or a cactus potting mix.

FERTILIZATION Do not feed during its dormancy. When the plant is actively growing, feed once a month.

PROPAGATION Bulbs produce offsets, which can be separated from the parent stock and potted up on their own.

WINNING ATTRIBUTES *Bowea volubilis* is a unique-looking plant. The substantial bulbs are in sharp contrast with the very delicate top growth, which can either be trained around an upright form or allowed to trail. It tolerates a variety of light levels and is extremely low maintenance.

Brugmansia hybrids

ANGEL'S TRUMPET

Solanaceae

In tropical America, *Brugmansia* hybrids are large shrubs or small trees, reaching 15 to 20 feet high. In nature they grow where nighttime temperatures are cool but frost free, and the air is humid. Leaves are approximately 8 inches long, and the spectacular, pendent, trumpet-shaped flowers are 8 to 10 inches long. There are double and single blooms, and many are enticingly fragrant. Many commercially

Brugmansia hybrid

available varieties are garden hybrids of *B. versicolor* and *B. suaveolens*. In containers, plants rarely grow taller than 10 feet. They bloom on new growth, and flower most heavily in early fall. You may prune brugmansias heavily once flowering has finished. If you choose to overwinter this plant in a dormant state (in a frost free location), cut back hard, leaving only a few inches of stem above ground. If you have a sunroom or conservatory, the plant can be allowed to grow actively throughout the year. This plant is narcotic; if you have a child or pet who chews or nibbles, it may not be the right plant for you. Watch for spider mites and whiteflies indoors or in dry climates.

LIGHT Indoors, brugmansias require full sun to bloom. A south-facing window is best. They are excellent plants for the greenhouse, where they'll get the sunlight they require and can be allowed to grow to specimen size.

WATER During the growing season, keep brugmansias consistently moist and give them high humidity. Water when the soil surface feels dry to the touch. If you allow your brugmansia to go dormant, water once a month throughout dormancy.

TEMPERATURE Grows best in warm to hot temperatures. Temperatures in the 40°F (4°C) range will not kill the plant, but may initiate dormancy or cause foliage to drop.

SOIL Brugmansias should be potted in a quick-draining, soil-based mix. A soilless mix is acceptable but will require more frequent fertilization.

FERTILIZATION During the growing season, feed once a week with a balanced fertilizer. No feeding is necessary during the winter months, whether the plant is dormant or not.

PROPAGATION *Brugmansia* hybrids are easily grown from seed and can also be propagated from stem cuttings. A seed-grown plant will take two to three years to bloom, while a plant grown from cuttings will bloom the first year.

WINNING ATTRIBUTES This is an impressive specimen plant that creates a tropical atmosphere wherever it grows. The huge, often fragrant, flowers are seductive and compelling.

Brunfelsia uniflora

YESTERDAY-TODAY-TOMORROW

Solanaceae

Brunfelsia uniflora is native to northern South America where it grows in full to part sun and in quick-draining soils. It is an evergreen shrub with elliptical leaves, 5 to 7 inches long. Leaf margins are undulate. Flowers bloom at the ends of branches and are fragrant. They are five-petalled, trumpet-shaped, about 2 inches wide, and initially bluish-purple. As flowers age, they turn lavender, then almost white over a period of several days. There are several other brunfelsias with similar growth habits and appearances. *Brunfelsia pauciflora* bears single, scentless flowers, and *B. grandiflora* has slightly larger flowers borne in heavier clusters. All three of these make excellent conservatory plants. They adapt well to containers, where they grow to 2 or 3 feet tall. *Brunfelsia uniflora* blooms in winter, providing a tropical feel when we need it most. It grows best in the elevated humidity of a greenhouse or conservatory and should be pruned heavily in early spring and may be pinched at any time of year to encourage bushy growth.

Brunfelsia uniflora

LIGHT Indoors, give *Brunfelsia unifora* at least four hours of direct sun.

WATER Allow the top half-inch of potting mix to dry out. If you give *Brunfelsia uniflora* a winter rest, allow the top inch to dry out between waterings. Provide elevated humidity during active growth.

TEMPERATURE Tolerates temperatures as low as 50°F (10°C). You may give it a cool winter rest, but this is not required.

SOIL Grow in a quick-draining soil-based mix.

FERTILIZATION Feed every other week during active growth.

PROPAGATION *Brunfelsia uniflora* is not easy to propagate. Tip cuttings should be treated with rooting hormone and given bottom heat. The rooting process is difficult and slow.

WINNING ATTRIBUTES The flowers are superb: large, clustered, and multi-hued. Their nighttime fragrance is an added bonus. Since this plant flowers on new growth, it can be kept compact without sacrificing bloom.

Caladium bicolor

ELEPHANT EAR

Araceae

Caladium species are native to South America and the West Indies, where they grow as understory plants, protected from direct sun. Most caladiums available to the consumer are varieties and cultivars of *Caladium bicolor*. Their heart-shaped leaves are papery thin and can reach 15 inches in length. Variegation may be red, pink, and/or white, with some leaves showing hardly any green. The flowers are the spathe/spadix type typical of many members of the Arum family. Since these plants are grown for their outstanding foliage, remove flowers that may divert energy away from foliage production. Caladiums are tender plants with a natural dormancy period. Foliage will start to yellow and wilt in the fall, at which time watering should be decreased; this mimics the dry season of the native habitat. You may move pots of dormant caladiums out of your display area (or under the greenhouse bench) until you notice new leaves starting two to four months later. During dormancy, water just enough to keep the tubers from completely drying out, once every two to four weeks. Temperatures should be maintained above 55°F (13°C).

*Caladium
bicolor*

LIGHT Indoors, caladiums will tolerate some sun, but they grow best in bright, indirect light. If you grow them outdoors in summer, place them in light shade. They can be acclimated to tolerate some direct sunlight, but will require more frequent watering.

WATER Caladiums require high humidity to produce beautiful, unblemished foliage; they should be grown on a pebble tray or in a greenhouse. Soil should not be allowed to dry out during active growth; water when the surface of the potting mix feels dry to the touch.

TEMPERATURE Caladiums require warmth to root and grow. Plant tubers when temperatures are approximately 75°F (24°C), or provide bottom heat to speed the rooting process. Throughout the growing period, regular household temperatures are fine; cold drafts can ruin foliage. During dormancy, maintain temperatures above 55°F (13°C).

SOIL Grow in a soil-based potting mix.

FERTILIZATION Feed with a balanced fertilizer every other week during the growing season. Do not feed during dormancy.

PROPAGATION Caladiums produce offsets from the parent tubers. These can be separated from the original tuber and potted up on their own when the plant goes dormant in autumn or in spring before active growth starts.

WINNING ATTRIBUTES The large, papery leaves of this plant are striking not only for their bright colors and intricate patterns, but also for their size and shape. A few pots clumped together make an outstanding display, or individual plants can be used to add spots of color throughout your greenhouse or home. If the idea of dealing with a dormancy period intimidates you, experiment with caladiums, which are easy to handle.

Calathea lancifolia

PEACOCK PLANT

Marantaceae

Calathea species are native to tropical South America where they grow on the jungle floor, often along streams. They vary greatly in leaf size and pattern of variegation, but all have remarkably beautiful foliage with markings of red, purple, silver, and several shades of green. As denizens of the forest floor, they grow best in diffuse light and high humidity. *Calathea lancifolia* has upright, lance-shaped leaves with undulate margins. Leaves are approximately 18 inches long and 2 to 3 inches wide. It has a more upright growth habit than many other *Calathea* species. The underside of its foliage is purplish red, and the top is a lovely pattern of alternating dark and light green. In dry conditions calatheas are prone to spider mites, so elevate humidity as much as possible and watch for signs of infestation. Webbing is easiest to see against the brightly colored undersides of the leaves.

LIGHT Bright indirect light is ideal. Direct sun will bleach leaf variegation, and since this plant is cultivated for the remarkable colors and patterns of its foliage, allowing the colors to fade would be counterproductive.

Calathea lancifolia

WATER During active growth, water when the soil surface feels dry. In winter, allow the potting mix to dry out a half-inch below its surface. Humidity should be kept as high as possible; grow on a drywell, in a greenhouse, or in a terrarium. Dry air can cause brown patches on the leaves, which mar the plant's beauty.

TEMPERATURE *Calathea lancifolia* is a true tropical and should be kept at temperatures above 60°F (16°C). It can survive temperatures in the 50°F (10°C) range, but watering must be reduced, and there may be foliage damage.

SOIL Grow in a soil-based mix. A specimen potted in a soilless mix dries out more quickly and requires more frequent watering and feeding.

FERTILIZATION Feed with a balanced fertilizer once every two weeks during the growing season.

PROPAGATION Propagation by division is most efficient; this plant grows quickly and can be divided every two or three years.

WINNING ATTRIBUTES The foliage variegation of *Calathea lancifolia* is both striking and subtle. The juxtaposition of light and dark green on the tops of the leaves creates an intricate pattern, and when glimpsed through the leaves, the contrasting red-purple underside spices up the color scheme.

Ceropegia haygarthii
Ceropegia linearis
ROSARY VINE
Ceropegia sandersonii
PARACHUTE PLANT
Asclepiadaceae

Ceropegia species are primarily drought-tolerant vines native to southern Africa, Madagascar, and the Canary Islands. They form tubers along their stems, as well as within their root systems. Flowers are similar in shape, all being tubular with five lobes at the top and resembling parachutes or lanterns. *Ceropegia* species are native to hot, sunny, dry climates and as such they are well adapted to the low humidity of the average home. *Ceropegia haygarthii* has flowers approximately 1 to 2 inches in height with prominent pink stamens. Succulent, gray-green stems are attractive and grow well when trained along an upright form. *Ceropegia linearis* (aka *C. woodii*) is the most commonly available *Ceropegia*. Its foliage is small and heart-

*Ceropegia
haygarthii*

shaped with a mottled pattern of white or lavender on top and pink undersides. Flowers are lavender and held upright along thin, vining stems. It is most attractive when grown in a hanging basket; vines can easily reach 6 to 8 feet in length. Both leaves and flowers are approximately three-quarters of an inch long. *Ceropegia sandersonii* has medium green, shiny leaves, approximately 1 inch in length and vaguely heart-shaped. The stems are thick and fleshy and may grow without foliage for months at a time. It is best grown trained along a trellis. Flowers are large, up to 3 inches tall, and resemble a complex parachute.

LIGHT *Ceropegia haygarthii*, *C. linearis*, and *C. sandersonii* will bloom in indirect or direct sun. *Ceropegia linearis* tolerates somewhat lower light intensities than the other species.

WATER None of the above-mentioned ceropegias require water more than once a week. Overwatering can be fatal. Do not elevate humidity; these are dry climate plants.

TEMPERATURE Average household temperatures are fine.

SOIL Use a soilless mix. These can also be grown in a cactus mix.

FERTILIZATION Do not require frequent feeding. Once a month during the growing season is adequate.

PROPAGATION All *Ceropegia* can be propagated by division. Also, *C. linearis* can be propagated by planting the individual tubers that grow along the vining stems.

Ceropegia linearis

Ceropegia sandersonii

Start *C. sandersonii* and *C. haygarthii* from stem cuttings; remember to maintain polarity.

WINNING ATTRIBUTES These are unusual, low maintenance plants with wildly odd flowers. While they are not beautiful in a romantic, flowery sense, they are so interesting that anyone who values the unusual will want to grow several. *Ceropegia* species are fairly pest free.

Cestrum aurantiacum

Cestrum aurantiacum

CESTRUM

Solanaceae

Cestrum aurantiacum is native to Central America where it grows as an evergreen shrub and can reach about 10 feet in height. It rarely gets that large in containers, topping off at 5 or 6 feet. *Cestrum aurantiacum* grows upright without support, making it useful as a container specimen. Flowers are orange or yellow. Individual blooms are small and tubular, borne in large clusters. Leaves are dark green, lance-olate, and 3 to 6 inches long. *Cestrum aurantiacum* blooms spring through early fall, both indoors and out.

LIGHT Give it full sun for optimal flowering. As light intensity decreases, so does bloom.

WATER   During the flowering season, water when the top half-inch of soil feels dry. When the plant is not in active growth, let the top inch dry out.

TEMPERATURE   Regular household temperatures are fine for *Cestrum aurantiacum*. It can survive temperatures in the 50s, but may drop some leaves.

SOIL   Grow in a soilless potting mix—it requires a quick-draining medium.

FERTILIZATION   Feed every other week with a flowering plant food during the growing season.

PROPAGATION   Propagate by stem tip cuttings. Prune after flowering to keep a neat shape and obtain propagation material.

WINNING ATTRIBUTES   This is an excellent flowering specimen for a sunroom or greenhouse. With regular pruning it can be kept as a compact tree, and in direct sun the flowers are showy and prolific.

Chlorophytum amaniense 'Fire Flash'

FIRE FLASH

Liliaceae

Chlorophytum amaniense is native to East Africa, where it grows in arid conditions. Like the more common *C. comosum*, this drought-tolerant plant has swollen, water-storing nodules as part of its root system. The foliage of *C. amaniense* grows in open rosettes. Individual leaves are lanceolate, approximately 10 to 12 inches long and 2 to 4 inches wide. Petioles and leaf midribs are a soft orange, in sharp contrast with the medium green leaves. Flowers originate from the crown of the plant and are small and white. This plant reaches a maximum of about 18 inches tall in containers.

LIGHT   Indoors, bright sun promotes intense variegation. In lower light, the orange will become muted. If you summer this plant outdoors, give it some protection from direct sun or leaves will scorch.

WATER   Water once a week during the growing season, and once every 10 to 14 days in winter. In dry air, leaf tips may turn brown, so try growing on a drywell. In addition, all chlorophytum are sensitive to fluoride in the water. If your water is fluoridated, use distilled water to avoid browning foliage.

TEMPERATURE   Regular household temperatures are fine for *Chlorophytum amaniense*. Do not allow it to get below 50°F (10°C).

SOIL   Grow in a soilless mix.

Chlorophytum amaniense 'Fire Flash'

Chlorophytum amaniense 'Fire Flash'

FERTILIZATION Feed every other week during the growing season.

PROPAGATION Propagation is best accomplished by division. Unlike *Chlorophytum comosum*, *C. amaniense* does not send out runners that put out young plantlets. Division must be from the crown.

WINNING ATTRIBUTES How many plants do you know with a large orange stripe the length of the leaf? This plant has outstanding variegation and a neat growth habit. It is low maintenance and not susceptible to insect pests. It makes a bold visual statement either alone as a specimen plant or as punctuation in a large collection of tropicals.

Cissus discolor
REX BEGONIA VINE
Cissus rotundifolia
ARABIAN WAX CISSUS
Cissus striata
MINIATURE GRAPE IVY
Vitaceae

Cissus discolor is a delicate vine native to Indonesia. Think tropical rain forest, dappled light, high humidity, seasonal rains. Leaves are heart-shaped and approximately 4 to 6 inches long. The undersides are reddish purple, while the tops are green, marked with silver. Stems are reddish, as are the tendrils that help this vine climb. It grows well in containers and looks best when trained to climb rather than allowed to trail. This plant requires elevated humidity and can be difficult to grow in the home. If you must try it without a greenhouse (and it's hard to resist) place it on a large drywell. *Cissus rotundifolia* is a succulent climber native to East Africa. It has toothed, circular leaves of varying sizes (1 to 3 inches) on thick vining stems; both stems and leaves are a bright medium green. Like *C. discolor*, *C. rotundifolia* climbs via tendrils. It is easy to grow indoors and can be trained to cover an upright form or grown in a hanging basket and allowed to hang down. This is an attractive plant but unfortunately difficult to find. If you see one, buy it and consider yourself lucky. *Cissus striata* is a charming, small-leaved vine native to Chile. It climbs via aerial roots, and its stems are slim and jointed. Leaves are 1 to 2 inches in diameter, have five lobes, and are glossy, deep green. *Cissus striata* can be trained over an upright form, grown as a ground cover, or allowed to trail over the edge of a pot. This pretty plant is exceptionally easy to grow.

LIGHT Bright indirect light is best for *Cissus discolor*; direct sun will bleach its leaves. *Cissus rotundifolia* grows well in full to part sun. *Cissus striata* tolerates a

Cissus discolor

Cissus rotundifolia

Cissus striata

wide range of light conditions, from indirect light to part sun. It will grow well in a northern, eastern, or western window.

WATER Finding the right balance here is tricky. *Cissus discolor* should be allowed to dry out somewhat between waterings. Water when the top inch of potting soil feels dry. Overwatering can cause foliage to drop. It also requires elevated humidity or the leaf edges will turn brown and crumble. *Cissus rotundifolia* is succulent and should be watered when the top inch of soil is dry. Elevated humidity is not required. *Cissus striata* is somewhat drought-tolerant; allow the top half-inch of potting mix to dry out between waterings. Elevated humidity is not necessary.

TEMPERATURE Keep above 60°F (16°C) and out of drafts.

SOIL Grow all three plants in a soilless mix.

FERTILIZATION Feed every other week with a balanced fertilizer during the growing season.

PROPAGATION These are easily started from stem cuttings. Since older specimens of *Cissus discolor* may lose their lower leaves, start new plants periodically to maintain an attractive specimen.

WINNING ATTRIBUTES *Cissus discolor* is a challenge to grow but well worth trying for its exquisite foliage. It is an excellent plant for a greenhouse and can easily be summered outdoors if you live in an area with high humidity. *Cissus rotundifolia* is an easy plant to grow, and its succulent round leaves are bright and attractive. *Cissus striata* has a versatile growth habit and tolerates a wide range of light intensities. It is an appealing, easy to grow foliage plant.

Clerodendrum speciosissimum

JAVA GLORY-BOWER

Clerodendrum ugandense

BUTTERFLY CLERODENDRUM

Verbenaceae

Clerodendrum speciosissimum is a fast-growing shrub with extremely showy panicles of flowers. It is native to Indonesia where it grows in full sun and reaches about 6 feet tall. In nature it is an aggressive grower, producing suckers. In containers, *C. speciosissimum* will grow 3 to 4 feet tall. It is not a long-lived plant, but it will last for several years and is worth growing for its huge inflorescences. Flowers are held in large panicles, about 12 inches tall. Individual flowers are orange-red, five-petalled, with protruding stamens. Leaves are heart-shaped, 6 to 10 inches wide, and covered with soft hairs. If you summer this plant outdoors, *C. speciosissimum* will attract butterflies and hummingbirds. *Clerodendrum ugandense* is native to tropical Africa where it is a shrub in full sun. It grows 6 to 8 feet tall in nature. Flowers have a delicate shape resembling that of a small butterfly. Each bloom is composed of four pale blue petals (butterfly wings) surrounding a single dark blue petal (butterfly body) and long, reflexed stamens (butterfly antennae). Flowers are held in loose panicles. The foliage of *C. ugandense* is medium green, shiny, elliptical, and about 3 to 5 inches long with a prominent, sunken midrib. Indoors, the plant will be shrubby until it reaches 3 to 4 feet in height. Then, it will start to vine,

Clerodendrum speciosissimum

at which point you may either prune it to maintain a compact growth habit or twine it around a trellis or form. Outdoors, *C. ugandense* attracts hummingbirds. Both may get spider mites in dry air.

LIGHT   Grow *C. ugandense* in bright indirect light; *C. speciosissimum* grows best in full sun.

WATER   Water both when the soil surface feels dry to the touch.

TEMPERATURE   *Clerodendrum ugandense* will tolerate occasional temperatures in the 50°F (10°C) range, but should be grown at normal household temperatures. *Clerodendrum speciosissimum* should be kept above 60°F (16°C).

SOIL   Grow both species in either a soil-based or soilless mix.

FERTILIZATION   Feed every other week during the growing season.

PROPAGATION   Both species are easily propagated from stem cuttings with bottom heat.

Clerodendrum ugandense

WINNING ATTRIBUTES The flowers of *C. ugandense* are dainty and beautifully colored. This plant grows quickly and in a single season can be a specimen plant 3 to 4 feet tall. It is easily shaped by pruning. *Clerodendrum speciosissimum* is brilliantly showy and an excellent specimen plant for a greenhouse or conservatory room. Its flowers are both delicate and enormous, nicely set off by large, lobed foliage.

Clivia miniata

BUSH LILY

Amaryllidaceae

Clivia miniata is native to the coastal forest of South Africa. It grows in quick-draining, sandy soil and is accustomed to a cool, dry rest period in fall and winter before blooming in late winter, early spring. In the home, *C. miniata* flowers best when pot-bound. Repot only when absolutely necessary; *C. miniata* may refuse to bloom for a

Clivia miniata

year or two after transplanting. Blooms are tubular and orange, with yellow at the throat. Each flower is approximately an inch wide; flowers are held in umbels of about 20 on scapes about 18 to 20 inches tall, making a showy cluster. Leaves are about 2 inches wide, 20 inches long, straplike, and dark green. They grow in pairs, arching away from each other. As the plant ages, lower leaves will yellow and should be removed. Rare cultivars with yellow flowers are available for large sums of money.

LIGHT Although it is traditionally recommended to grow *C. miniata* in bright indirect light, my plant lives in a northern window, alongside a few sansevierias and a zygocactus. It flowers brilliantly every year. Nonetheless, an eastern window is usually best. Direct afternoon sun can scorch leaves.

WATER Water *C. miniata* once a week during the growing season, then once every two weeks starting in fall until you see the bloom spike begin to poke through the center foliage. When the flower spike appears, resume weekly watering.

TEMPERATURE Grow at regular household temperatures during spring and summer. However, to ensure flowering, give it a temperature drop in autumn. *Clivia miniata* is a subtropical plant. It will grow and bloom best when given several months rest at between 45°F (7°C) and 50°F (10°C). If your clivia flowers, but the bloom is compressed between the leaves of the plant, you are not letting it get cold enough during its rest period.

SOIL Use a soilless or quick-draining soil-based mix.

FERTILIZATION Feed once a month during the growing season and not at all during its cool rest period. When the bloom spike appears, start feeding again.

PROPAGATION *Clivia miniata* is a slow grower, so while it can be propagated by division, it will take some time to grow large enough for this to be worthwhile. Try pollinating the flowers of *C. miniata* with a paintbrush. Flowers can be self-pollinated and will produce large fruits about the size of a fat cherry. When fruits ripen to a bright red color, they are ready to be harvested, and the seeds inside can be planted. It is possible that when the plant diverts energy to ripening seed, it may not produce flowers that year. However, sometimes a plant will ripen seed and still flower soon after.

WINNING ATTRIBUTES The flowers of this plant are outstanding: large and beautifully colored. They are also gently fragrant, but you have to get very close to appreciate the scent. Foliage is attractive, if subtle, the rest of the year, but grow this plant for the saturated orange flowers it produces in late winter, when the world is short on color.

Coccoloba uvifera

SEA GRAPE

Polygonaceae

Coccoloba uvifera is native to the coasts of tropical and subtropical America, where humidity is high and the sandy soils are quick-draining. It is highly tolerant of salt. In nature the tree can reach 30 feet tall. Leaves are 6 to 8 inches wide, circular, glossy, with prominent white or pink veining. New foliage has a bronze tint. The leaves are quite beautiful, and in autumn *C. uvifera* produces clusters of purple/brown, edible fruit. In containers, *C. uvifera* rarely grows taller than 8 to 10 feet tall. It is a high light plant and must have several hours of direct sun in order to flower and fruit.

LIGHT Indoors, *Coccoloba uvifera* will take as much light as you can give it. With four to six hours of direct sun, you may get flowers. The tree will grow well in bright, indirect light, but will not flower.

WATER Water when the top half-inch of potting mix feels dry. High humidity must be maintained to keep the foliage glossy and whole. In dry air, leaf margins may brown or curl.

TEMPERATURE Average household temperatures are fine.

SOIL Grow in a soilless mix. It must have fast drainage and can also be grown in a cactus mix.

FERTILIZATION Feed every two weeks during the growing season.

PROPAGATION *Coccoloba uvifera* is easily propagated from both seed and stem cuttings. Cuttings require bottom heat to root. Seeds are large and easy to handle; they require a constantly moist potting mix and high humidity to germinate.

WINNING ATTRIBUTES This is a superbly attractive small tree. The size, shape, texture, and coloration of the foliage make it an excellent specimen plant or focal point in a plant room.

Coccoloba uniflora

Cocos nucifera

COCONUT PALM

Arecaceae

Cocos nucifera is native to the Pacific Islands where it grows to 100 feet tall and is an enormously valuable plant, providing one of the world's chief sources of vegetable fat. It grows directly on the beach, in full sun and sandy soil. In the home, fortunately, *C. nucifera* will not reach such gargantuan heights. Grown in soil, it is an attractive tree, easily maintained at 4 to 8 feet tall. Grown as a novelty, in a dish of water, it will be shorter-lived and smaller, but a real conversation piece. Leaves are feathery and green to yellow-green with yellow petioles.

LIGHT   *Cocos nucifera* grows best in full sun; a south-facing window is best, but east or west is acceptable. In low light, growth will be weak, and the plant will not survive.

Cocos nucifera

WATER If you're growing *Cocos nucifera* in potting mix, water when the top half-inch of mix feels dry. *Cocos nucifera* requires high humidity and should be grown on a drywell if traditionally potted. For something completely different, place the coconut in a large dish and fill it with enough water to cover the bottom 2 inches of the nut.

TEMPERATURE Household temperatures are fine; keep it above 65°F (18°C).

SOIL Grow *Cocos nucifera* in a soilless mix or cactus mix. Plant it shallowly, leaving the top just above soil level. Or, grow it without soil, in a dish of water.

FERTILIZATION Feed once every two weeks if you are growing it in potting medium. If you are growing it in solution, alternate plain water with a weak fertilizer solution (one-quarter strength) every other week.

PROPAGATION This is one plant you will not be able to divide and share. The tree does not bloom indoors and therefore will not produce nuts. You may find sprouted nuts for sale, or you may sprout your own. To do so, place the nut on top of sand or moist, soilless mix and provide bottom heat. It may take up to six months for roots to appear; don't plant the nut until roots are visible.

WINNING ATTRIBUTES Planted in soil, *Cocos nucifera* is a graceful palm. But why not try something unusual? Growing this plant in water is an interesting experiment and a great way to watch how roots grow and work.

Codiaeum variegatum

CROTON

Euphorbiaceae

Codiaeum variegatum is native to southeast Asia, including the Pacific islands. It grows in moist soils, full sun, and high humidity. In nature, the plant has green leaves and is a small tree, reaching about 8 feet in height. The domesticated plant has been highly cultivated, and there are a large number of cultivars available with varying leaf shapes and colors. Leaves are shiny and leathery and can be lobed, elliptical, lanceolate, or linear. Commercially available plants are highly variegated, with flamboyant markings of red, yellow, orange, and purple. Patterns include stripes, blotches, and dots. In containers, *C. variegatum* rarely grows taller than 2 to 3 feet. Repot with care; the root ball is sensitive, and the plant may drop leaves after a rough transplant. As a member of the euphorbia family, *C. variegatum* ex-

*Codiaeum
variegatum*

udes a white latex when any part of the plant is broken. Some people are sensitive to this when it touches the skin; handle with care. Spider mites can be a problem in dry conditions, so elevate humidity and stay vigilant.

LIGHT Indoors, grow in direct sun. Lower light will reduce variegation.

WATER *Codiaeum variegatum* is a moisture-loving plant. Water when the soil surface is dry to the touch. The plant will drop leaves if it gets too dry. *Codiaeum variegatum* also requires high humidity; grow it in a greenhouse or on a drywell. In dry air, leaves may drop or turn brown.

TEMPERATURE Keep warm, over 60˚F (16˚C). Cold drafts can cause leaf drop.

SOIL Grow in a soil-based mix.

FERTILIZATION Feed every other week during the growing season with a balanced fertilizer.

PROPAGATION Propagate from stem cuttings to preserve leaf shape and variegation. Maintain bottom heat and high humidity while rooting the cuttings.

WINNING ATTRIBUTES The variegation of this species is exceptional. Its colors are hot and flashy, and the patterns verge on the psychedelic. This plant is so showy that less is truly more. Use a few small plants to punctuate an interior landscape or a single, large specimen as the focus of an installation.

Codonanthe carnosa

Gesneriaceae

Codonanthe carnosa is an epiphyte native to Brazil, where it grows as a dense, creeping vine with pairs of opposite, small (less than 1 inch in length), elliptical leaves. Foliage is dark, muted, forest green, slightly succulent, and lightly felted. Flowers are trumpet-shaped and white with a pinkish throat. They are about a half-inch long and often followed by a light orange, small, round fruit, about a quarter-inch in diameter. I am enchanted by *C. carnosa* and cannot understand

Codonanthe carnosa

why it isn't widely available. Its foliage is attractive and soft to the touch. It is a compact vine rather than a wild climber and perfectly suited to container-growing indoors. It flowers year-round, and its blooms are delicate and plentiful. *Codonanthe carnosa* requires little maintenance and is pest free.

LIGHT Grows best in bright indirect light to part sun.

WATER Allow the top inch of potting mix to dry out between waterings. Remember that gesneriads are especially sensitive to cold water. To avoid having foliage marred by ring spot, use tepid water.

TEMPERATURE Grow in normal household temperatures.

SOIL This plant requires a fast-draining potting medium. Grow it in a mix of three parts soilless mix with one part fine-grained fir bark.

FERTILIZATION Feed at half strength every other week during active growth.

PROPAGATION *Codonanthe carnosa* is easily propagated by stem cuttings. This plant is not widely sold. If you know someone who has one, ask for a few small pieces. You'll soon have a lovely plant of your own.

WINNING ATTRIBUTES This is a charming epiphyte with petite foliage and a neat, appealing growth habit. It blooms almost constantly and often sports fruit and flowers simultaneously. *Codonanthe carnosa* is a real winner; buy it, grow it, love it.

Coffea arabica

COFFEE

Rubiaceae

Coffea arabica is native to Ethiopia and is the shrub from which we harvest most of our coffee beans. In nature it can reach 15 feet in height and grows in the light shade of taller trees. Grown indoors it rarely exceeds 6 feet tall. The leaves of *C. arabica* are singularly attractive: glossy, dark green, with undulating leaf margins and prominent venation. Bark is exfoliating and attractive. Plants bloom when they're three to four years old. Their flowers are fragrant, white, and star-shaped, and when pollinated they produce red berries, each of which holds two seeds. These seeds, when roasted, are our coffee beans. Watch for scale and mealybug.

LIGHT *Coffea arabica* grows in bright indirect light, but flowers with direct sun. Indoors it will take as much sun as you can give it, but if you summer this plant outdoors, give it some protection from direct rays.

Coffea arabica

WATER During the growing season, water when the top half-inch of potting mix is dry. In winter, water when the top inch of potting mix feels dry. *Coffea arabica* requires the elevated humidity of a drywell or greenhouse. In dry conditions, leaf margins may turn brown or black.

TEMPERATURE Keep *Coffea arabica* above 55°F (13°C). Colder temperatures can cause leaf drop.

SOIL Grow in a soil-based mix.

FERTILIZATION Feed every two weeks with a balanced fertilizer during the growing season.

PROPAGATION Cuttings are difficult to root, although not impossible. Give them bottom heat and high humidity. *Coffea arabica* is easy to start from seed; fresh seeds germinate quickly. Remove the seeds from inside the berries before planting.

WINNING ATTRIBUTES *Coffea arabica* is a lovely tree—the combination of attractive bark and leaves, in addition to fragrant flowers, make it an excellent ornamental houseplant. You may even be able to brew your own cup of custom blend java.

Colocasia esculenta 'Black Magic'

BLACK ELEPHANT'S EAR

Araceae

Colocasia esculenta is native to Fiji and Hawaii. Leaves are large, heart-shaped, and primarily green. *Colocasia esculenta* 'Black Magic' is a cultivar with outstanding black leaves and red veins and stems. There are numerous similarly named cultivars with equally intense variegation: 'Black Knight', 'Jet Black Wonder', and 'Jet Black Bead' are several. Leaf stems may be 3 to 4 feet tall and rise directly from tubers to form thick clumps. The leaves themselves are 16 to 18 inches long and 12 inches wide. This is a plant that requires high humidity; in dry conditions, *C. esculenta* is prone to spider mites.

Colocasia esculenta
'Black Magic'

LIGHT   Indoors this is a full sun plant, requiring six to eight hours of sun for optimal variegation and strong growth. If you summer it outdoors, give it full or part sun.

WATER   *Colocasia esculenta* loves moisture; keep the potting mix constantly moist. Or, submerge the pot in an indoor water garden, providing both the high humidity and moist soil it requires.

TEMPERATURE   Grow in normal household temperatures. The tuber will go dormant in autumn; leaves will yellow and eventually wither. Cut back the foliage and store the pot in a dark, frost free place until new growth starts in spring.

SOIL   Grow in a heavy, soil-based mix.

FERTILIZATION   *Colocasia esculenta* is a heavy feeder. Fertilize every week during the growing season.

PROPAGATION   Tubers produce offsets during the growing season. These can be separated and potted up on their own in spring.

WINNING ATTRIBUTES   The foliage of *Colocasia esculenta* is wondrous. Large size and extraordinary color make this an unbeatable specimen for a greenhouse or conservatory. This plant is spectacular as part of a water garden, where its reflection doubles the impact.

Columnea 'Fujiyama'

GOLDFISH PLANT

Gesneriaceae

Columneas are gesneriads native to tropical America. Many are epiphytic and make excellent houseplants. They have fleshy leaves, a generally cascading growth habit, and tubular flowers with an unusual hooded shape that resembles that of a cobra ready to strike. Don't let the image deter you. The flowers are large, vibrant and numerous; with their semi-upright habit they really stand out. *Columnea* 'Fujiyama' has bright vermillion flowers, about 2 inches tall. It blooms year-round, but most profusely in winter and early spring. Dark green leaves are neatly arranged in opposite pairs, closely spaced along the stems. This plant appreciates elevated humidity but should not be misted; sunlight on wet leaves will burn the foliage. Initially, growth will be upright; as stems lengthen they will arch and trail. If older specimens get leggy, take cuttings to propagate new plants. Regular pinching encourages branching.

LIGHT   Grow in bright indirect light to part sun. Full sun may cause foliage to scorch.

WATER   Water when the top half-inch of potting mix is dry. Do not use cold water, or ring spot may disfigure the foliage. Elevate humidity.

TEMPERATURE   Grow in average household temperatures. Giving your plant a winter rest at about 55°F (13°C) may increase subsequent flowering.

SOIL   *Columnea* 'Fujiyama' grows best in a quick draining epiphytic mix of three parts soilless mix and two parts fine-grained fir bark.

FERTILIZATION   Feed with a half-strength fertilizer when buds become visible. Continue through the growing season.

PROPAGATION   *Columnea* 'Fujiyama' is easily propagated from stem cuttings. As soon as they have rooted, pinch to encourage branching.

WINNING ATTRIBUTES   The flowers are truly outstanding: large, colorful, and unusually shaped. Their brilliant color stands out against dark green foliage. This plant blooms from an early age. It can be grown as a standing specimen when small; when its stems begin to trail it makes an excellent hanging basket.

Columnea 'Fujiyama'

Cordyline terminalis

TI PLANT

Dracenaceae

Cordyline terminalis is native to Papua, New Guinea, and has spread throughout Australasia and Indonesia. In nature it grows to 10 feet tall. These are usually single-stemmed plants that do not branch. Young plants are shrubby but lose their lower leaves as they age, developing a tree-like shape with a crown of lanceolate foliage. Leaves are 12 to 24 inches long and 2 to 4 inches wide. They are sessile and grow in whorls around the stem. New foliage is a rich red color and ages to reddish-green. Immature specimens are easy to find, but a mature, flowering plant is a rarity indoors. Flowers are large branching sprays of small white blooms, which are usually fragrant. This plant does well in containers, where it grows to be 3 to 6 feet tall. While *C. terminalis* blooms infrequently indoors, you can successfully flower this plant given appropriate light and water. It is wonderfully rewarding to watch large panicles (8 inches across) of tiny flowers mature, a process that takes several weeks. Cultivars provide a range of variegation and leaf size; shading is always reddish-purple. *Cordyline terminalis* is prone to spider mites indoors.

LIGHT Bright indirect light is best. Direct sun may scorch leaves.

WATER Water when the top half-inch of potting mix is dry. This plant benefits from elevated humidity.

TEMPERATURE Grow in average household temperatures. Keep it warm and away from all drafts.

SOIL Grow in a soil-based mix.

FERTILIZATION Feed at half strength every other week during the growing season.

PROPAGATION A woody *Cordyline terminalis* can be rejuvenated by air layering. Tip cuttings can be rooted with rooting hormone, bottom heat, and high humidity as long as they are not woody. Also, 2-inch sections of leafless stem may produce new growth if you make sure each section contains at least one bud—look and feel for a swelling under the bark. Maintain polarity when potting your stem sections, or, press them horizontally into moist potting mix. Use rooting hormone to dust the buried portion of the stem, maintain high humidity, and give your cuttings bottom heat. It's thrilling to see a new plant grow from a small piece of bare stem.

*Cordyline
terminalis*

WINNING ATTRIBUTES Most people grow *Cordyline terminalis* for its deeply variegated foliage, which is rich and lovely. Dainty, fragrant flowers are the true accom-
plishment. As a small tree, it fits nicely into the back of your interior garden, and as a
compact, young plant it can be placed anywhere that receives adequate light.

Costus malortieanus

SPIRAL GINGER

Zingiberaceae

Costus malortieanus is native to Central America where it grows up to 6 feet tall in dappled sunlight and humid conditions. Leaves are obovate, about 12 inches long and 4 to 8 inches wide. They are arranged in a spiral pattern around the stem. Foliage is lovely: medium green with subtle, darker green stripes. Undersides are covered with silky hairs. Flowers are 2 to 3 inches long and tubular. They are white outside, with yellow and rust colored interiors. Bracts are held in a tight, green cone formation; flowers open from between the bracts, a few at a time. In containers, *C. malortieanus* grows to about 4 feet. It requires elevated humidity, and this, combined with its large size, makes it best suited to a greenhouse or conservatory. In dry conditions, *C. malortieanus* is prone to spider mites.

LIGHT Indoors, grow in bright indirect light to part sun.

WATER Grows best in moist potting mix; water when the soil surface feels dry. This plant also requires elevated humidity.

TEMPERATURE Grow in average household temperatures.

SOIL Use a soil-based mix.

FERTILIZATION Feed every other week during the growing season.

PROPAGATION Propagate by dividing clumps in spring.

WINNING ATTRIBUTES The foliage of *Costus malortieanus* is subtly variegated and richly hued. The leaf arrangement is also attractive and unusual. This is a lovely plant, even when it's not in bloom; the flowers are an outstanding bonus.

Costus malortieanus

Cotyledon ladismithiensis

BEAR'S PAW

Crassulaceae

Cotyledon ladismithiensis is native to South Africa where it may grow to be about 8 inches tall. Foliage is thick, gray-green, and fuzzy. The leaf tips have several blunt points which give the leaf its paw-like appearance. Flowers are rich orange, pendent, and bell shaped. They are held in groups of two or three on stalks several inches above the foliage and look like they have been generously sprinkled among the leaves. In containers, *C. ladismithiensis* makes an excellent groundcover, filling in around the base of a single large succulent, or in a specialized planting like a cactus garden. It can also be grown on its own as a miniature succulent with a pleasing shape and an unusually colored flower.

LIGHT Grow in full sun. Inadequate light results in weak, leggy growth and no flowers.

WATER Water when the top inch of potting mix is dry.

TEMPERATURE Keep in average household temperatures.

SOIL *Cotyledon ladismithiensis* does best in a quick-draining cactus mix.

FERTILIZATION Feed with a balanced fertilizer at half strength once every two weeks during active growth.

Cotyledon ladismithiensis

PROPAGATION Propagate from leaf cuttings. Allow them to callus for a week before planting.

WINNING ATTRIBUTES The plump leaves of this miniature succulent are very attractive; you'll want to touch them. *Cotyledon ladismithiensis* flowers freely; its rich orange flowers are unusual and add a bright splash to your indoor landscape.

Crassula 'Morgan's Pink'

PROPELLER PLANT

Crassulaceae

Crassula 'Morgan's Pink' is native to southern Africa. It thrives under hot, dry, sunny conditions. This is a prostrate succulent with plump, blue-gray foliage; in nature it creeps along the ground. Its trailing growth habit is especially attractive in containers. Leaves are opposite and closely spaced, clasping the stem; stems resemble the form of a Hawaiian lei. Salmon pink flowers are borne in terminal clusters. This plant will flower indoors with a few hours of direct sun. Overwatering can cause stem rot.

Crassula 'Morgan's Pink'

LIGHT   Give *Crassula* 'Morgan's Pink' as much light as possible indoors. It will flower in a sunny eastern, western, or southern window. In bright, indirect light, the plant will grow but may not flower.

WATER   Water once every two weeks. If you notice the foliage looks shriveled or soft, decrease the interval between waterings by a day or so, until foliage once again looks turgid and healthy.

TEMPERATURE   Keep temperatures above 55°F (13°C).

SOIL   Grow in a soilless mix or in a special cactus mix.

FERTILIZATION   Feed once a month during the growing season.

PROPAGATION   *Crassula* 'Morgan's Pink' is easy to propagate by leaf cuttings. Remove leaves from the parent stock and allow them to callus for several days. Then, plant the calloused tip of the leaf in a sandy or soilless potting mix. Water once every 10 days until new top growth appears, then treat as a mature plant. *Crassula* 'Morgan's Pink' also produces basal offsets that can be cut from the parent plant, callused, and potted up on their own.

WINNING ATTRIBUTES   The color and texture of this foliage are outstanding and unusual. Trailing stems, thickly clothed in succulent foliage, make *Crassula* 'Morgan's Pink' a tactile, irresistible plant.

Crossandra infundibuliformis

FIRECRACKER PLANT

Acanthaceae

Crossandra infundibuliformis, native to India and Sri Lanka, is a small, evergreen shrub from 1 to 3 feet tall. It grows in full to part sun. Foliage is glossy, medium green, lanceolate, and undulate, with prominent venation. Leaves are approximately 3 inches long. Flowers are a rich, cantaloupe orange, and there is also a yellow-flowered cultivar. Blooms are five-lobed, flat, and arranged in a fan shape. They are held in groups of two and three on spikes approximately 3 to 4 inches above the foliage. The effect is quite wonderful as the soft, rich color of the flowers contrasts with the shiny leaves. This plant blooms year-round. Indoors, *C. infundibuliformis* averages 12 to 18 inches tall. Pruning and pinching encourage branching and keep the growth habit compact; the resulting cuttings can be used

*Crossandra
infundibuliformis*

for propagation. Remove spent flowers for continued bloom. In dry air, spider mites can be a problem, so elevate humidity as much as possible.

LIGHT Bright light is best. An eastern window is fine in summer, but in winter a western or southern window is better and will result in more bloom.

WATER Water when the soil surface is dry to the touch. It benefits from elevated humidity and should be grown on a drywell or in a greenhouse.

TEMPERATURE Keep above 65˚F (18˚C).

SOIL Grow in a soil-based potting mix.

FERTILIZATION Feed every other week at half strength during the growing season.

PROPAGATION Propagate from tip cuttings. Give it bottom heat and elevated humidity while rooting.

WINNING ATTRIBUTES This plant blooms year-round. Its growing habit is mounded and compact, and the contrast between the glossy green foliage and the warm orange flowers is stunning. There's something about the reflective, shiny leaves and the soft plentiful flowers that is both perplexing and satisfying. How can something be soft and hard at the same time? Grow *Crossandra infundibuliformis* and you'll find out.

Cryptanthus bivittatus

EARTH STAR

Bromeliadaceae

Cryptanthus bivittatus is a terrestrial bromeliad native to Brazil, where it grows as a ground cover. Its foliage is star-shaped. Leaves are striped pink and green or white and green; leaf margins are undulate. In containers, individual leaves grow to be 4 to 6 inches long. Flowers are held in the leaf axils and are relatively insignificant, compared to the showy foliage. Indoors, *C. bivittatus* almost never blooms. The stiff, sculptural shape of its foliage is what makes growing this plant worthwhile. Leaf margins are sharply toothed, so handle with care. It is sometimes sold as *C. bromelioides* var. *tricolor*.

Cryptanthus bivittattus

LIGHT   *Cryptanthus bivittatus* should have bright indirect light to maintain variegation. A few hours of morning sun will intensify coloring, but protect foliage from hot afternoon sun.

WATER   Water when the top half-inch of potting mix feels dry. The leaf tips may brown in dry air. Grow it on a drywell or in a terrarium.

TEMPERATURE   *Cryptanthus bivittatus* grows well in regular household temperatures.

SOIL   Use a soilless mix.

FERTILIZATION   Feed with a balanced fertilizer every other week during the growing season.

PROPAGATION   This is a slow grower, but offsets can eventually be separated from the parent plant and potted up once they've developed roots.

WINNING ATTRIBUTES   This is a beautiful plant, useful in many ways to the indoor gardener. It can be grown alone in pots or planted en masse at the base of a small tree as a ground cover. It is lovely in terrariums and on epiphyte trees. *Cryptanthus bivittatus* is low maintenance and relatively pest free.

Cycas revoluta

SAGO PALM

Cycadaceae

Cycas revoluta, native to southern Japan, grows in full to part sun where it can reach 10 feet tall. In nature, trees are long-lived (50 to 100 years), and older specimens expose thick trunks as lower foliage falls away. Pinnate leaves are glossy dark green and stiff, growing in a rosette pattern from the center of the plant. Leaves arch outward and are 2 to 3 feet long. The midribs are pale yellow and spiky. This is a slow-growing plant, sometimes producing only one new leaf per year. The crown is a fuzzy, light-brown mound. While the leaves may resemble those of a palm, the plants are not related. (Cycads are ancient gymnosperms; they coexisted with dinosaurs. Palms are more recently evolved monocot angiosperms.) *Cycas revoluta* makes a superb houseplant but is often poorly grown. In containers, it usually grows to about 2 to 3 feet tall. It is frequently sold as bonsai, but as such is restricted to just a few leaves. The plant is much less attractive when grown this way. *Cycas revoluta* may occasionally get mealybugs.

Cycas revoluta

LIGHT Give *C. revoluta* bright sun to keep the rosette bushy and compact. In inadequate light, new leaves will be longer and more loosely formed than the original foliage. If a new leaf starts to form in a lower light situation, remove the leaf and move the plant to a sunnier spot.

WATER Water when the top inch of potting mix is dry.

TEMPERATURE You may give *Cycas revoluta* a winter rest period at about 50°F (10°C), in which case reduce watering frequency. *Cycas revoluta* can also grow in average household temperatures year-round.

SOIL Grow in a quick-draining soil-based mix.

FERTILIZATION Feed once in spring before active growth starts and again in midsummer.

PROPAGATION *Cycas revoluta* occasionally produces offsets, which can be removed and potted up. It can also be propagated by seed but does not usually produce viable seed indoors.

WINNING ATTRIBUTES The decorative value is outstanding. A well-grown, mature specimen is lush and expansive and makes an excellent centerpiece for an indoor garden. The high gloss of its foliage is very appealing.

Cyperus alternifolius

PAPYRUS

Cyperaceae

Cyperus alternifolius is native to Madagascar. There it grows in wet or boggy soils, in full or part sun, and reaches 3 to 6 feet tall. Its stems are three-cornered and hollow and are topped by a whorl of bracts that look like blades of grass; these bracts are 6 to 10 inches long. Small whitish-green flowers are borne in whorls inside the bracts. Indoors, *C. alternifolius* can be grown in a water garden or simply by sitting its pot in a container of water to keep the soil wet. *Cyperus alternifolius* grows quickly and may need annual repotting or division. It is a large plant, but not massive; its stems are slim, and the overall effect is delicate. It is a useful plant for creating a layered effect, since you can see through the stems to what is planted behind it. The form is unusual and exotic, and its yellow-green color makes a nice accent. This is not a flashy plant: it has a sophisticated and sleek appearance. In dry air, watch for spider mites.

LIGHT   Give full to part sun. If very few new stems are produced, this indicates light levels are too low.

WATER   *Cyperus alternifolius* should be grown in wet soil. Sit its container in a saucer or bucket of water, keeping the roots wet at all times. High humidity is also required. If bract tips become brown, this is a sign that the humidity is too low. However, if you grow it sitting in water, the humidity should be adequate.

TEMPERATURE   Grow in normal household temperatures. You may give it a cool rest period in winter at 50˚F (10˚C) to 55˚F (13˚C).

SOIL   Grow in a rich, heavy, soil-based mix. Incorporating water-retaining polymer into the soil mix is a good idea.

FERTILIZATION   Feed every other week during the growing season with a high nitrogen fertilizer.

PROPAGATION   *Cyperus alternifolius* can be propagated by division or from cuttings. Cut off the whorl of bracts and pin it upside down to moist potting mix. Roots and a new stem should form within three to four weeks. Or float the cutting upside down in water and watch roots form, then plant the rooted cutting.

WINNING ATTRIBUTES   *Cyperus alternifolius* is graceful, impressively tall, and will sway in the slightest breeze, adding movement to your interior landscape. This plant will quickly reach specimen size. The pale yellow-green color is a useful highlight in a massed planting, and its exotic form is understated and elegant.

Cyperus alternifolius

Cyrtomium falcatum

HOLLY FERN

Polypodiaceae

Cyrtomium falcatum is native to Asia. Furry rhizomes produce fronds about 2 to 3 feet long. Fronds are pinnate, and individual pinnae are shiny and dark glossy green. They are toothed, approximately 2 to 3 inches long, and elliptical with a sickle-shaped tip (rather like a holly leaf). Pinnae are thicker and more substantial than those of many other true ferns, and as a result, more tolerant of low household humidity. It is not a tropical plant but is well-adapted to indoor culture. *Cyrtomium falcatum* grows well in containers and is an excellent choice for a bright, but not directly sunny, location. Its arching shape is graceful, and its dark color is rich and attractive. This is an excellent choice for someone who likes ferns but cannot provide the elevated humidity usually required.

LIGHT   Bright indirect light is best; try an unobstructed northern or eastern window.

WATER   Water when the top half-inch of potting mix feels dry. If you give your plant a cool winter rest, allow the top inch of potting mix to dry out between waterings.

TEMPERATURE   *Cyrtomium falcatum* is not a tropical plant and can withstand cool temperatures. It can even tolerate light frost. It also grows well in normal household temperatures. Above 70°F (21°C), be sure to grow on a drywell.

Cyrtomium falcatum

SOIL Grow in a soil-based mix.

FERTILIZATION Feed at half strength every other week during the growing season.

PROPAGATION *Cyrtomium falcatum* can be propagated by division or from spores. When dividing the rhizome, be sure to leave three or four fronds per division.

WINNING ATTRIBUTES This plant has an interesting shape and glossy dark green leaves. It is elegant and graceful. It can be showcased as a specimen plant or used to provide a rich backdrop in a larger installation. *Cyrtomium falcatum* is usually pest free.

Cyrtostachys renda

SEALING WAX PALM

Aracaceae

Cyrtostachys renda is native to Malaysia, New Guinea, and Indonesia, generally growing in swampy coastal areas. In nature it reaches 20 to 30 feet tall. Fronds are pinnate with arching midribs. One look at this tree will tell you why it is so highly prized. Brilliant scarlet petioles and pseudostems contrast sharply with the medium green fronds. This is not a plant for everyone; however, it is worth trying if you have a large, warm growing space. It is slow-growing and does well in containers, where it gets to be about 10 to 12 feet tall. *Cyrtostachys renda* requires the elevated humidity of a greenhouse and constant warmth in order for the bright red stems to fully develop. It is a true tropical plant and does not adapt well to nontropical conditions. If you are successful, the reward is spectacular. *Cyrtostachys renda* is gorgeous and vivid and is an immediate focal point in any interior landscape.

LIGHT This plant needs full sun.

WATER Keep moist at all times.

TEMPERATURE Keep above 60°F (16°C) at all times.

SOIL Grow in a soil-based mix.

FERTILIZATION Feed every other week at half strength during active growth.

PROPAGATION *Cyrtostachys renda* is propagated from fresh seed, which will not be produced indoors. If you order seed, soak it in water overnight and plant immediately. Give it bottom heat and high humidity. Germination can take one to three months.

Cyrtostachys renda

WINNING ATTRIBUTES If you have an appropriate spot (large, sunny, humid, warm), *C. renda* is a must-try. This is a true connoisseur's plant: rare, spectacular, and heart-stoppingly beautiful.

Datura metel

DEVIL'S TRUMPET

Solanaceae

Datura metel is native to southern China. It grows in full sun and can reach 5 feet in height. All parts of the plant are poisonous when ingested. Do not grow this plant if you have pets or family members who graze indiscriminately. Flowers are held erect and are trumpet-shaped with fluted edges. They may be double or single and are 8 to 10 inches long. Blooms are white, yellow, or purple and usually fragrant. Foliage is ovate, medium green, 6 to 8 inches long, and basically unremarkable. The plant is prized for its large and lovely flowers. The spiny seed pods that follow flowers are also attractive. Indoors, *D. metel* requires a pot at least 12 inches in diameter in order to reach specimen size. It usually grows to about 3 feet in containers. *Datura metel* is prone to spider mites in dry conditions.

LIGHT This is a full sun plant. Do not bother to grow it if you cannot give it southern light. If you plan to use your plant outdoors in summer you can overwin-

Datura metel

ter it in an eastern or western window, but growth may be sparse, and it will not flower well. Cut back leggy growth before moving *D. metel* outdoors in late spring.

WATER Water when the top inch of potting mix feels dry.

TEMPERATURE Grow at normal household temperatures. It can be given a dormant period in winter, in which case it should be cut back to 6 inches above soil level and kept in a cool (but frost free), dark place.

SOIL Grow in a soil-based mix.

FERTILIZATION Feed every other week during the growing season.

PROPAGATION *Datura metel* is easily propagated from seed and will grow to 3 feet in a single growing season. Bottom heat speeds germination. It can also be propagated from stem cuttings.

WINNING ATTRIBUTES The flowers are extravagant, and a large plant covered with bloom is a show-stopper. Their fragrance is strongest at night, so you'll enjoy their perfume when you're home in the evenings. *Datura metel* quickly reaches specimen size and is easy to grow from seed.

Davallia fejeensis

SQUIRREL'S FOOT FERN

Davalliaceae

Davallia fejeensis is native to Fiji, where it grows as an epiphyte. Woody rhizomes, covered with silvery brown hairs, creep along tree trunks or the forest floor, sending out roots from below and foliage from above. As a plant of the forest floor, *D. fejeensis* receives indirect, dappled light. Individual fronds are triangular, finely cut, and 12 to 18 inches in length. The growth habit of this fern is unusual: instead of originating at a common growing point, fronds are produced at intervals along the rhizome. *Davallia fejeensis* has a bushy, upright form. This is an excellent fern for growing indoors and does well in average household humidity. Remove the occasional brown frond. Its feathery foliage is soft and quintessentially fern-like, yet this plant requires less maintenance than many other ferns. In a hanging basket, the rhizomes will eventually encircle the pot, giving you an unusual specimen with fronds extending from every direction. *Davallia fejeensis* can also be bark-mounted as a hanging plant.

LIGHT Best suited to indirect light; a northern window is recommended. In direct sun the foliage will bleach and become less attractive.

Davallia fejeensis

WATER Water when the top half-inch of potting mix is dry. As the rhizomes cover the surface of the pot, it will become more difficult to poke your finger through to the potting mix, so get to know your plant's needs. Depending on the light and temperature, *Davallia fejeensis* will need water once every 7 to 10 days. Bark-mounted specimens should be submerged and their root balls soaked for 5 or 10 minutes.

TEMPERATURE Average household temperatures are fine; *Davallia fejeensis* will tolerate winter temperatures as low as 55°F (13°C), but this may damage some fronds. Water less frequently in cooler temperatures.

SOIL As an epiphyte, *Davallia fejeensis* requires a fast-draining mix; grow it in a soilless medium. It can also be mounted on a bark slab, where the rhizomes will attach themselves after a few months.

FERTILIZATION Feed at half strength every other week during the growing season.

PROPAGATION *Davallia fejeensis* is easily propagated by division. You may divide the plant as you would any other, or you can cut off a piece of rhizome with several nodes and pin it to the surface of the potting mix. Water it well, give it heat and high humidity, and you'll get both root growth and foliage from the rhizome. This is a great project to do with kids.

WINNING ATTRIBUTES *Davallia fejeensis* has many things to recommend it. It is a low maintenance, pest free fern. The delicate looking foliage is actually quite sturdy, and its rhizomes are furry, tactile, and attractive. This is an excellent plant for introducing children to the wonderful world of horticulture.

Dioscorea elephantipes

ELEPHANT'S FOOT

Dioscoreaceae

Dioscorea elephantipes is native to southern Africa, where its tuber was once a subsistence food for hunter gatherers. Today it is valued for its wildly unusual form. A large tuber grows partially above ground and in nature may reach 3 feet in diameter. Its surface is covered with a thick, woody, plated bark and resembles a tortoise shell. Vines emerge from the top of these tubers and produce medium green,

Dioscorea elephantipes

heart-shaped leaves, about 2 inches long. This plant grows very well in containers, where vines may either be allowed to trail or trained over an upright form. It is a slow growing plant: in containers, tubers rarely exceed 1 foot in diameter. Vines grow to about 6 feet long. *Dioscorea elephantipes* may or may not go dormant. If foliage yellows, remove it and withhold water until a new vine starts from the top of the tuber. Dormancy may last several months.

LIGHT Indoors, *Dioscorea elephantipes* grows best in full to part sun.

WATER Allow the top inch of potting mix to dry between waterings. If your plant goes dormant, withhold water entirely until new growth begins to emerge.

TEMPERATURE *Dioscorea elephantipes* grows well in normal household temperatures.

SOIL Grow in a soilless mix or cactus potting mix.

FERTILIZATION Feed at half strength every other week during active growth.

PROPAGATION You can propagate *Dioscorea elephantipes* from seed. It grows slowly and will take several years to form its distinctive caudex.

WINNING ATTRIBUTES This is a rare, exotic plant; if you appreciate unusual forms, *Dioscorea elephantipes* belongs in your collection. It is a low maintenance, pest free plant, and a true conversation piece.

Dischidia ovata

WATERMELON LEAF

Dischidia pectinoides

RAVIOLI PLANT

Asclepiadaceae

Dischidia ovata is native to the South Pacific. It is also an epiphyte and grows in high humidity and dappled light. Its leaves are ovate and about an inch long. Foliage is dark green and veins are white; the contrasting pattern is very attractive. *Dischidia ovata* has a compact, trailing growth habit and looks best in a hanging basket. Flowers are small, green with purple stripes, and like all *Dischidia* flowers, they have a tight bell shape. It is a charming miniature and adds a subtle splash of variegation to a plant collection. *Dischidia pectinoides* is native to the Philippines. It is also an epiphyte and grows in the dappled light and high humidity of the tropical rain forest. This plant is prized for its dual leaf shapes. Leaves are gray-green. One type is small and elliptical, about an inch in length. The other form is large, circular, and inflated, about 2 inches in diameter; there are roots inside each leaf pouch. In

Dischidia ovata

nature these leaves provide shelter for colonies of ants, which benefit the plant in several ways. Ant feces are absorbed by the interior roots as a source of nitrogen for the plant. Ants also protect the plant from predators. While the extra nitrogen is useful to epiphytes in nature, indoors *D. pectinoides* grows well in a soilless mix with a balanced plant food. The plant does *not* attract ants indoors. Flowers are cherry red and quite small; even when fully open, they don't appear to be. *Dischidia pectinoides* is frequently sold stuffed inside large, ornamental snail shells. It will not survive in these shells for long, so repot it promptly. It looks best when trained along an upright form.

LIGHT Both *Dischidia* species grow best in the bright indirect light of an eastern window. In lower light they will not flower, and in higher light the leaves become pale and washed out.

Dischidia pectinoides

WATER Do not overwater. These plants cannot tolerate constantly moist soils. Allow the top inch of potting mix to dry out between waterings. High humidity is helpful.

TEMPERATURE Grow both in regular household temperatures.

SOIL Dischidias are epiphytes and therefore require a quick draining potting mix. Use a soilless mix, or a combination of three parts soilless mix and one part fine-grained fir bark.

FERTILIZATION Feed at half strength once a month during the growing season.

PROPAGATION Dischidias are easily started from stem cuttings; they produce aerial roots along the length of their stems. You may either root cuttings in a soilless mix with rooting hormone or wrapped in a moist paper towel inside a plastic bag.

WINNING ATTRIBUTES *Dischidia pectinoides* is a curiosity with its two very different leaf shapes. Year-round, cherry red flowers add to its appeal, but because individual flowers are small, the effect is subtle. *Dischidia pectinoides* can be trained along an upright form, giving you vertical interest. *Dischidia ovata* has a graceful, trailing growth habit and is an excellent small plant for the grower with limited space. Its outstanding leaf pattern is lovely.

Duranta erecta

SKY FLOWER, GOLDEN DEWDROP

Verbenaceae

Duranta erecta, native to Mexico and South America, is an evergreen shrub that reaches 10 to 15 feet tall. Leaves are ovate, 2 to 3 inches long, with serrated margins. Spines up to 1 inch long are held in the leaf axils, although some plants are spineless. Flowers are sky blue with whitish throats and dark purple streaks on the lower petals. They are borne in pendent terminal clusters. Individual blooms are trumpet-shaped and about a half-inch wide; inflorescences are about 6 inches long. Flowers are followed by clusters of yellow-orange berries which hang like bunches of miniature, golden grapes. They are poisonous, however, so don't grow

Duranta erecta

this plant around kids or pets who might nibble. *Duranta erecta* does well in containers, growing up to 6 feet tall. It is a fast grower and blooms on new growth, so prune regularly to keep the shrub compact and floriferous. It may be pruned to grow in a tree shape or as a shrub. This plant grows best in elevated humidity. If you'd like to try it but are short on space, grow it outside in summer and overwinter it in a dormant state. Cut it back to 6 inches tall and store it in a dark, cool, but frost free place.

LIGHT Indoors *Duranta erecta* requires full sun to bloom.

WATER Water when the top inch of potting mix is dry. If you allow your plant to go dormant, water only when the top 2 or 3 inches of mix are dry; this will be once every four to six weeks.

TEMPERATURE Grow in average household temperatures. A dormant plant can tolerate temperatures as low as 50°F (10°C).

SOIL Grow in a soil-based potting mix.

FERTILIZATIO Feed at half strength every other week during the growing season.

PROPAGATION Propagate from stem cuttings or from seed.

WINNING ATTRIBUTES The flowers are numerous and lovely. The straight species is a delicate, pale blue, and various cultivars with showy markings are also available. The tiny, golden fruit are abundant and attractive.

Epiphyllum ackermannii
ORCHID CACTUS
Epiphyllum oxypetalum
QUEEN OF THE NIGHT
Cactaceae

The genus *Epiphyllum* is native to the tropical rain forests of Central and South America, where most grow as epiphytic cacti. *Epiphyllum ackermannii* has a pendent growth habit, and is sometimes sold as *Nopalxochia ackermannii*. Stems are flat, 1 to 2 inches wide, with wavy margins; spines are short or nonexistent. On this plant, the stems are the photosynthetic organs. Its stiff, freely branching stems give the plant sculptural value at all times, but when *E. ackermannii* blooms, everything else is incidental. Flowers are huge, 8 inches across with many petals and numerous, prominent white stamens. They are unscented, but who cares? Buds ripen over a period of weeks, prolonging the anticipation. Flowers last for a few days. This is a very low maintenance, exotic plant. *Epiphyllum oxypetalum* has an upright growth habit and in nature may be 6 feet tall. It grows just as tall in containers, but needs to be staked or it will topple under its own weight. Stems are flat, 2 to 4 inches wide, and spineless. Flowers are large (6 to 8 inches across), scented, and pure white. They have numerous petals and stamens. Flowers open after dark and last only one night; make sure you stay up to see the show. This is one of several cacti that share the common name "queen of the night." It is a low maintenance plant that puts on a brief but spectacular show.

LIGHT Both epiphyllums grow well in part sun. Indoors, an eastern or western window is best. If you summer these plants outdoors, give them some protection from full sun.

Epiphyllum ackermannii

Epiphyllum oxypetalum

WATER These are true cactus and therefore fairly drought-tolerant plants. However, they are rain forest cacti and need more frequent watering than desert cacti do. Allow the top inch of soil to dry out between waterings. High humidity is appreciated but not required.

TEMPERATURE Grow both in normal household temperatures. Winter temperatures near 50°F (10°C) may increase bloom for *E. oxypetalum*.

SOIL Grow both epiphyllums in a combination of three parts soilless mix and one part fine-grained fir bark.

FERTILIZATION Feed at half strength every other week during the growing season.

PROPAGATION Propagate from cuttings. Take a tip cutting about 6 inches long and allow it to callus for about a week. Plant the cut end deep enough to keep it upright. You may need to stake the cutting while roots are established.

WINNING ATTRIBUTES *Epiphyllum ackermannii* has unusual architectural value even when it's not in flower. In bloom, it is beyond compare. *Epiphyllum oxypetalum* is slightly awkward most of the year: large, with an interesting shape. It is worth growing because of its large, fragrant, night-blooming flowers. Both are easy, low maintenance plants that are exceptionally rewarding.

Episcia cupreata

FLAME VIOLET

Gesneraceae

Episcia cupreata, a native of northern South America, grows as a groundcover in light shade. Leaves are hairy, oval, and 2 to 4 inches long. There is great variety within the species: some plants have leaves with an embossed appearance and others are smooth. Some are marked with silvery pink and others have more coppery tones. All are vividly variegated foliage plants with a creeping growth habit. Flowers grow from the leaf axils and are tubular in shape. They are about 1-inch long and slightly fringed. Most are vermillion or red with yellow throats, although some cultivars have pink or white flowers. *Episcia cupreata* produces stolons with plantlets at the ends. In a hanging basket, these plantlets hang down for dramatic effect. However, since this plant requires more humidity than other gesneriads, a hanging basket is only appropriate for a greenhouse or conservatory. Foliage will curl under and turn brown if surrounding air is too dry. You can also grow *E. cupreata* as a groundcover in a terrarium or potted traditionally and placed on a drywell.

Episcia cupreata

LIGHT   Grows best in bright indirect light; direct sun will burn the leaves. It also grows well under fluorescent lights.

WATER   Allow the top half-inch of potting soil to dry out between waterings. *Episcia cupreata* requires elevated humidity. Grow it on a drywell, in a greenhouse or conservatory, or in a terrarium.

TEMPERATURE   Keep temperatures above 60°F (16°C).

SOIL   Grow in a soil-based mix.

FERTILIZATION   Feed with a flowering plant food at half strength every other week during the growing season.

PROPAGATION   *Episcia cupreata* is very easy to propagate. It produces stolons with plantlets at the end, much like those of the garden strawberry. You may pin these plantlets to the surface of some potting mix while they are still attached to the parent plant, allowing roots to form, then sever the connecting stolon. Or you can cut the stolon first and pot the plantlet on its own. If you choose the latter, be sure to give *E. cupreata* extremely elevated humidity while roots are forming.

WINNING ATTRIBUTES   The leaves of this plant are beautiful; they shimmer as either a ground cover or hanging basket. Bright red flowers are wonderfully offset by the silver leaf variegation.

Eranthemum nigrum

Acanthaceae

Eranthemum nigrum is native to the Solomon Islands where it grows as a shrub up to 5 feet tall with spectacular foliage. Leaves are dark purple, almost black. They are elliptical and 3 to 5 inches long. Flowers are 1 inch in diameter, five-petalled, and trumpet-shaped. They are white with magenta spots at the throat. Numerous blooms are held in terminal clusters. The extreme contrast between the dark foliage and bright white flowers is outstanding. This plant grows to about 3 feet tall in containers but can also be maintained as a smaller specimen by restricting root size. Pinch to encourage branching.

LIGHT Indoors grow in full to part sun.

WATER Allow the top half-inch inch of potting mix to dry out between waterings.

TEMPERATURE Grow in average household temperatures.

SOIL Grow in a soil-based mix.

FERTILIZATION Feed every other week at half strength during active growth.

PROPAGATION Propagate from cuttings.

WINNING ATTRIBUTES The foliage is a show-stopper. Its rich, deep color adds depth to the indoor landscape and contrasts highly with its bright, delicate flowers.

Eranthemum nigrum

Euphorbia fulgens
SCARLET PLUME EUPHORBIA

Euphorbia milii
CROWN OF THORNS

Euphorbia obesa
BASEBALL PLANT

Euphorbia tirucalli
PENCIL CACTUS

Euphorbiaceae

The genus *Euphorbia* is large and extremely varied. (The most famous member of the family is *Euphorbia pulcherrima*, the poinsettia.) Flowers of all euphorbias are similar in that most are composed of showy bracts surrounding small, yellow flowers. Also, all euphorbias exude a milky latex when cut or broken. This may irritate sensitive skin, so handle with care. Most euphorbias have small root balls in proportion to their top growth, so they may look top-heavy. Do not be fooled into repotting; these plants grow well when tightly potted.

Euphorbia fulgens, a native of Mexico, is a deciduous shrub that grows to about 5 feet tall. Lanceolate leaves are borne on slim, arching branches. Foliage is 2 to 3 inches long and may be green or almost purple in intense light. Bracts are an electric vermillion with tiny yellow flowers at the center; the color contrast between leaves and inflorescences is sharp and striking. *Euphorbia fulgens* grows well in containers, but usually does not exceed 18 inches in height. It is a graceful, vivid plant.

Euphorbia milii is native to Madagascar, where it grows to be 4 feet tall. It does very well in containers, reaching 2 to 3 feet. It has an extremely thorny, woody stem; handle with care. Leaves are sparse, medium green, oblanceolate, and 2 to 3 inches long. They cluster at the ends of stems; older plants may have extended stretches of stem with no leaves. Heavy pruning of bare stems will usually stimulate branching and new growth. Small yellow flowers are surrounded by rich, cherry red bracts. Inflorescences are borne in pairs on bloom stalks 1 to 2 inches long. There are numerous hybrids of *E. milii*; flowers may be yellow, white, pink, or red, 0.5 to 1.5 inches in diameter. This plant is somewhat drought-tolerant but should not be treated like a cactus. It is sensitive to repotting and should only be transplanted when absolutely necessary.

Euphorbia fulgens

This *Euphorbia milii* cultivar has extra large flowers.

Euphorbia obesa

Euphorbia tirucalli

Euphorbia obesa is a succulent, native to South Africa. It is almost completely round when young and gradually elongates. In nature it may be 8 inches tall and 6 inches wide. In containers it rarely outgrows a 4-inch pot. *Euphorbia obesa* has no spines. The inflated stem is a lovely bluish-green and has eight almost flat sides with fine reddish vertical lines.

Euphorbia tirucalli is a succulent, native to eastern and southern Africa and the Arabian peninsula where it may be 20 feet tall. In containers it does not usually grow taller than 6 feet. The smooth, thin stems of *E. tirucalli* are photosynthetic. They bear small leaves (about a half-inch long) that quickly fall off the plant. The multibranching habit of this plant gives it a wonderful structure. It is delicate, sculptural, and very low maintenance.

LIGHT *Euphorbia milii, E. fulgens, and E. obesa* grow best in full to part sun. *Euphorbia tirucalli* tolerates a wide range of light conditions, from bright indirect light to full sun. Give *E. fulgens* short daylight hours in autumn to stimulate bloom.

WATER Water *Euphorbia fulgens* when the top half-inch of potting mix is dry. *Euphorbia milii, E. obesa*, and *E. tirucalli* are more drought-tolerant; allow the top inch of potting mix to dry between waterings.

TEMPERATURE Keep these euphorbias at normal household temperatures. Dramatic temperature changes (in either direction) can cause dramatic leaf drop.

SOIL Grow in a soilless mix.

FERTILIZATION Feed every two weeks at half strength during active growth.

PROPAGATION *Euphorbia fulgens, E. milii*, and *E. tirucalli* are easily propagated from cuttings; allow then to callus for three to five days before planting them. *Euphorbia obesa* is propagated from seed, but rarely flowers indoors.

WINNING ATTRIBUTES These very different euphorbias are all winners. Grow *Euphorbia fulgens* for its outrageously vivid foliage and flowers. *Euphorbia milii* offers numerous, bright blooms and a treelike structure. *Euphorbia obesa* is a compact succulent with beautiful, subtle coloring. *Euphorbia tirucalli* is a large specimen with an imposing yet delicate structure. Grow them all—I do.

Ficus deltoidea
MISTLETOE FIG

Ficus rubiginosa 'Variegata'
RUSTY FIG

Moraceae

Ficus deltoidea is native to Malaysia where it may grow to 6 feet tall. It is well suited to growing indoors and in containers grows to a maximum of 3 feet tall. This is the only indoor fig that produces fruit on a regular basis. Figs are small and inedible, but ornamental. They are yellowish, pea-size, and grow singly from short stems originating in the leaf axils. Leaves are shaped like the Greek letter delta. They are 1 to 3 inches long, medium green, with a matte finish and a pattern of small spots or pits. It is smaller than most figs (which tend to be trees) making it convenient for indoor growing. This plant is occasionally sold as *F. diversifolia. Ficus rubiginosa* 'Variegata' is a beautiful small tree native to eastern Australia where it grows to be 30 feet tall; in containers it rarely exceeds 8 to 10 feet. This tree has strong horizontal branches and a full shape. Foliage is lovely; leaves are 3 to 6 inches long,

Ficus deltoidea

Ficus rubiginosa 'Variegata'

ovate, and shiny. Undersides are rusty red, and the tops are marbled green and creamy yellow. Watch for scale, which can occasionally be a problem.

LIGHT *Ficus deltoidea* grows best in bright indirect light to part sun. *Ficus rubiginosa* 'Variegata' grows best in part to full sun.

WATER Water both figs when the top inch of potting mix is dry. Overwatering causes lower leaves to drop.

TEMPERATURE Both of these grow well in average household temperatures.

SOIL Pot in a soil-based potting mix. These plants grow best when rootbound, so do not overpot. Wait until roots emerge from the drainage hole or are visible on the surface of the potting mix.

FERTILIZATION Feed with a half-strength fertilizer every other week during the growing season.

PROPAGATION *Ficus deltoidea* may be propagated from stem cuttings. Use root hormone and bottom heat to facilitate the process. *Ficus rubiginosa* 'Variegata' is best propagated by air-layering, which takes four to eight weeks. Air layering may sound difficult, but it is actually quite straightforward. For instructions, see chapter 6. You will feel wonderfully accomplished when you succeed.

WINNING ATTRIBUTES The foliage of both ficuses is outstanding. That of *Ficus deltoidea* has a matte finish, an unusual shape, and an interesting pattern of spots. It also bears fruit year-round. The leaves of *F. rubiginosa* 'Variegata' are outstandingly variegated and highly glossy. A specimen tree adds a large splash of shiny color to your interior landscape.

Fittonia verschaffeltii

MOSAIC PLANT, NERVE PLANT

Acanthaceae

Fittonia verschaffeltii is a ground cover native to the tropical rainforests of South America, mostly Peru. In nature it grows in light shade and high humidity. *Fittonia verschaffeltii* var. *argyroneura* has silver veins, while *F. verschaffeltii* has deep pink veins. Both plants are creepers in nature, with opposite, ovate leaves approximately 2 inches long. Stems root as they grow along the forest floor. In containers, the creeping form of *F. verschaffeltii* makes it appropriate for a hanging basket or ground cover. Direct sun will damage leaves.

Fittonia verschaffeltii

LIGHT Grows best in indirect light; either a northern or eastern window is recommended.

WATER *Fittonia verschaffeltii* should not be allowed to dry out between waterings; it will swoon dramatically, its foliage going limp and flat. If you catch this within 24 hours and water well, the plant will perk up again. Don't let this happen often, however, as it stresses the plant. Conversely, keeping the potting mix too wet will cause rot and foliage drop. Water when the soil surface feels dry to the touch and give it elevated humidity. Grow on a drywell, in a terrarium, or among other plants.

TEMPERATURE Average household temperatures are fine. Don't place it in drafts of below 55°F (13°C), which may damage foliage.

SOIL Grow *Fittonia verschaffeltii* in a soil-based potting mix. Fittonias are generally shallow-rooted, so try growing them in a short container like an azalea pot.

FERTILIZATION Feed at half strength every other week during the growing season.

PROPAGATION *Fittonia verschaffeltii* is easily propagated from stem cuttings or layering.

WINNING ATTRIBUTES The venation of this plant is truly lovely, as if it were finely etched onto the leaf. The rich, dark, rose color of the veins is beautifully complemented by the medium green leaf. It grows well in low light situations and is suitable for terrariums and as a groundcover for larger trees, as well as for individual planting. *Fittonia verschaffeltii* is relatively pest free, but may get leggy as it grows older. Start new plants from cuttings to maintain attractive specimens.

Fortunella margarita

OVAL KUMQUAT

Rutaceae

Fortunella margarita is native to southern China where it grows in full sun and can reach approximately 15 feet in height. The genus *Fortunella* is closely related to the genus *Citrus*, and the resemblance between them is strong, with *Fortunella* being smaller in stature. *Fortunella margarita* is a highly decorative and productive plant. Its leaves are approximately 3 to 4 inches long, lanceolate, and a glossy, medium green. White, five-part flowers are less intensely scented than many citrus flowers, although still fragrant. The fruit of *F. margarita* is oval in shape and a brighter orange than other species. The tree itself has fewer thorns than other fortunellas. It grows very well in containers, to about 5 feet tall. Watch for scale and spider mites.

LIGHT This is a sun-loving plant. While it will grow in eastern or western light, give it a southern exposure for maximum flowering.

WATER In winter, allow the top inch of potting mix to dry out between waterings. In summer, water when the top half-inch feels dry.

TEMPERATURE Although *Fortunella margarita* can tolerate cool temperatures (to 50°F [10°C]), it grows best in warmer, household temperatures. Exposure to cold will cause foliage to drop, and plants will cease active growth. A winter rest at 60°F (16°C) is fine.

SOIL Grow in a quick-draining, soil-based potting mix. Mature plants should be top-dressed annually in early spring.

FERTILIZATION Fortunellas are heavy feeders. Feed once a week during the growing season with a balanced fertilizer. When buds appear, switch to a high potash fertilizer for two months, then return to a balanced plant food. Do not feed during winter.

PROPAGATION *Fortunella margarita* is easily propagated from seed, although it may take three to four weeks to germinate. This is a fun project to try with children.

Fortunella margarita

Eat the fruit, plant the seed, and watch it grow. Bottom heat will speed the process. *Fortunella margarita* can also be started from cuttings, which requires bottom heat, high humidity, and rooting hormone.

WINNING ATTRIBUTES *Fortunella margarita* not only makes an attractive specimen tree, but it is one of the most reliable citrus type plants for blooming and fruiting indoors. The fruit are both attractive and tasty and should be eaten whole, including the skin.

Gardenia jasminoides

CAPE JASMINE

Rubiaceae

Gardenia jasminoides is native to southern China and Japan where it can grow to be 6 feet tall. Leaves are a dark, glossy green, lanceolate, and 2 to 3 inches long. Flowers are double in form, and 2 to 3 inches in diameter. They are headily fragrant and age from white to cream-colored. In containers, the plant is a bushy, small shrub, growing to 2 to 3 feet tall. *Gardenia jasminoides* is not the easiest plant to grow, but it is well worth a try. It has a reputation for bud blast, which is usually the result of

Gardenia jasminoides

inadequate light and humidity. Make sure your plant gets enough of both, as well as nighttime temperatures of approximately 70°F (21°C), and you should get flowers. Watch for spider mites and scale.

LIGHT   *Gardenia jasminoides* grows well in part sun. An eastern or western window is best for encouraging bloom. If you move your plant outdoors in summer, give it dappled light.

WATER   Water when the top half-inch of potting mix feels dry. In winter, allow the top inch of potting mix to dry out. *Gardenia jasminoides* requires high humidity year-round. Leaf margins will curl and turn brown in dry air. Grow in a greenhouse or on a drywell. In summer, bring *G. jasminoides* outdoors if you live in a humid climate, but protect it from direct sun.

TEMPERATURE   This is tricky. When the plant is in bud, keep temperatures between 60°F (16°C) and 65°F (18°C) to avoid bud drop. At other times of year, keep temperatures between 60°F (16°C) and 75°F (24°C). Higher temperatures may prevent bud formation, and lower temperatures will cause foliage to yellow and drop.

SOIL   Use a soil-based potting mix that includes peat. This plant will not tolerate alkaline soils.

FERTILIZATION   Feed with an acid plant fertilizer every other week during the growing season.

PROPAGATION   *Gardenia jasminoides* can be propagated from stem cuttings, using bottom heat and rooting hormone. Give cuttings high humidity and use a peat-based potting mix, which will have an acidic pH.

WINNING ATTRIBUTES   Nothing beats the fragrance of a fresh gardenia flower. It's a complex scent and a beautiful flower with heavy, silky, creamy petals. This is a lush, sensuous plant when in bloom, and even without flowers the highly glossy foliage is very attractive. Don't be put off by its reputation. It's not a plant for beginners, but neither is it as difficult to grow as lore would have it.

Gasteria verrucosa
FOX TONGUE
Liliaceae

Gasteria verrucosa is native to South Africa. It is a succulent plant and quite drought-tolerant. It usually grows in the shade of other plants and is best suited to indirect light. Foliage is covered with small warty bumps the size of the head of a pin. Leaves are plump, stiff, and 8 to 10 inches long. Each leaf ends in a point that is needle sharp. Leaves are arranged in parallel rows, emerging from a central crown. Flowers are small, tubular, red or orange and held 12 or 18 inches above the foliage in loose spikes of numerous blooms. This is a pest free plant well suited to growing in containers indoors. It tolerates low humidity, and in winter can occupy a drafty window where temperatures in the 50°F (10°C) range encourage it to flower more profusely in spring. Gasterias interbreed freely, so it is sometimes difficult to know which one you have. Most require similar care, and all make excellent houseplants.

LIGHT Grow in bright indirect light. It will live in northern light, but probably will not flower. For a better chance at bloom, keep it in an eastern window. Direct sun will result in browned foliage.

WATER Water when the top inch of soil feels dry, about once a week in summer. If you keep your plant cool in winter, once every two weeks may be adequate.

TEMPERATURE Normal household temperatures are fine. If you give *Gasteria verrucosa* a cool winter rest, adjust watering accordingly.

SOIL Grow in a soilless mix or a cactus mix.

FERTILIZATION Feed at half strength once a month during the growing season. If your plant is reluctant to bloom, try a bloom-booster at half strength every other week starting in spring.

PROPAGATION *Gasteria verrucosa* will flower and produce seed indoors, but it is a slow-growing plant. A plant started from seed will take several years to reach blooming size. You can also propagate by division or from leaf cutting. An offset with roots

Gasteria verrucosa

can be potted on its own. An offset without roots or a leaf cutting should be allowed to callus for several days before being planted.

WINNING ATTRIBUTES The plump, stiff structure and bumpy texture of this plant make it visually interesting. It is small enough to fit on almost any windowsill and tolerates a wide range of light intensities.

Gelsemium sempervirens

CAROLINA JESSAMINE

Gelsemiaceae

Gelsemium sempervirens is native to the southwestern United States, Mexico, and Guatemala where it grows as a climbing vine and as a groundcover. As an understory plant, it receives dappled sunlight. Stems are slim and flexible, leaves are

Gelsemium sempervirens

slim, lanceolate, 2 to 3 inches long, and tinged with red, especially in high light. Flowers are fragrant, profuse, funnel-shaped, and a vibrant yellow. Individual blooms are an inch in diameter and 1.5 inches long. *Gelsemium sempervirens* is a rapid climber and grows to about 10 feet long. Indoors it is best grown trained on a form for vertical interest. This plant flowers in the depths of winter and brings the beauty of vivid bloom into the dark days of the season. All parts of the plant are poisonous, so keep it out of reach of nibbling children and animals.

LIGHT Grow in the bright light of an eastern or western window.

WATER Water when the top half-inch of soil is dry to the touch.

TEMPERATURE *Gelsemium semper-*

virens is not a tropical plant and can withstand outdoor temperatures in mild temperate climates. Indoors it adapts to household temperatures and is a good choice for a bright cool room or entryway.

SOIL   Grow in a quick-draining, soil-based mix.

FERTILIZATION   Feed with an acid plant food at half strength every other week during the growing season.

PROPAGATION   Propagate from stem cuttings.

WINNING ATTRIBUTES   *Gelsemium sempervirens* offers saturated yellow blooms in winter when any bright flower is especially treasured. Its profuse flowers are gently fragrant, and its leaves are subtly variegated. Rapid growth means this plant will quickly cover a trellis form or topiary.

Geogenanthus undatus

SEERSUCKER PLANT

Commelinaceae

Geogenanthus undatus is native to Peru, where it grows as a ground cover in humid habitats. It is a rapid grower and quickly covers a large area. Indoors, *G. undatus* is grown for its remarkable foliage, which is exceptionally textured and variegated. The leaf surface is puckered, hence its common name. Leaves are oval, 3 to 5 inches long and 2 to 4 inches wide. The undersides are maroon, and the tops are green striped with silver. The flowers of *G. undatus* are also attractive: pale purple, fringed, and about a half-inch wide. Each flower lasts for only a day.

LIGHT   Grows best in bright filtered light. An eastern or unobstructed northern window is best.

WATER   Water when the top half-inch of potting mix feels dry. *Geogenanthus undatus* requires elevated humidity. Grow it on a drywell, in a terrarium, or in a greenhouse.

TEMPERATURE   Household temperatures of at least 65°F (18°C) are best.

SOIL   Use a soil-based potting mix.

FERTILIZATION   Feed with a balanced fertilizer at half strength every two weeks during the growing season.

PROPAGATION   *Geogenanthus undatus* can be propagated by stem cuttings or by layering.

Geogenanthus undatus. Photo by Ty Strode, Agristarts

WINNING ATTRIBUTES   This is an outstanding foliage plant, combining prominent leaf variegation with an unusual puckered texture. It is relatively pest free and fast-growing, although it does require high humidity. Use *Geogenanthus undatus* to underplant specimen trees or as a ground cover in a terrarium.

Hatiora rosea

EASTER CACTUS

Cactaceae

Hatiora rosea is an epiphytic cactus native to Brazil. It is a segmented, trailing cactus, with stems and flowers reminiscent of those of the Christmas cactus. However, *H. rosea* has a more refined beauty. Stems are edged in red, providing interesting variegation year-round. They may be either flat or angled (with three to five sides), and are slimmer than those of the more common Christmas cacti. Plentiful flowers are about 1 to 2 inches in diameter, star-shaped, and produced either singly or in pairs at the ends of stems. Petals are gently reflexed, and the pistils and stamens are distinct and attractive. For years this plant was sold as *Rhipsalidopsis rosea,* and you may still find it labeled as such. It blooms at the onset of spring and is a welcome signal that the growing season has begun.

Hatiora rosea

LIGHT   Grow in bright indirect light to part sun.

WATER   Water when the top inch of potting mix is dry. Remember, this is a tropical rainforest cactus, not a desert cactus. It will tolerate the high humidity of a greenhouse or the lower humidity of the average home.

TEMPERATURE   Grow in average household temperatures. Unlike many holiday cacti, this plant does not require a temperature drop in autumn to initiate bloom.

SOIL   Pot in soilless mix or a combination of three parts soilless mix and one part fine-grained bark mix.

FERTILIZATION   Once buds have appeared in early spring, feed every two weeks with a half-strength fertilizer solution. Continue until active growth stops in mid to late fall.

PROPAGATION   *Hatiora rosea* is easily propagated from stem cuttings. Allow them to callus for several days before planting them.

WINNING ATTRIBUTES   *Hatiora rosea* bursts into flower just as the daffodils bloom, letting you know that spring has truly arrived; it is now officially the growing season. Flowers are numerous, delicate, and lovely. Their color is echoed by the reddish margins of the stem segments. This plant has an attractive, cascading growth habit and makes an excellent hanging specimen.

Haworthia truncata

CLIPPED WINDOW PLANT

Liliaceae

Haworthia truncata is a small succulent plant native to South Africa. The tops of its leaves are transluscent. In nature its leaves are frequently partially buried in sand, which protects foliage from the burning rays of the sun but also blocks light. The translucent windows at the tips of the leaves let light into the plant tissue so photosynthesis can take place. This is a unique plant, easy to grow indoors, but not always easy to find. Like other haworthias, the leaves of *H. truncata* grow in stemless rosettes. Often the rosette is modified to appear linear, like the leaves of gasterias. *Haworthia truncata* produces smooth, absolutely flat-topped foliage of a plain, dark green. Leaves rarely grow more than 2 inches tall; this is an excellent miniature for a gardener with limited space.

LIGHT Unlike many succulents, haworthias do not like direct sun. Bright indirect light is best.

WATER Water once a week during the growing season and once every two weeks the rest of the year. This plant will not tolerate overwatering.

TEMPERATURE *Haworthia truncata* can tolerate occasional temperatures into the 40°F (4°C) range, but grows best in average household temperatures. A drop in winter temperature to about 60°F (16°C) is appreciated but not necessary.

SOIL Grow in a soilless mix or a cactus mix.

FERTILIZATION Do not feed. If your plant looks weak or its growth has slowed significantly, repot it in fresh soil.

PROPAGATION Offsets form readily at the base of the parent plant. They can be removed and potted up on their own. If the

Haworthia truncata

offset has roots, pot it immediately. If the offset is unrooted, allow it to air-dry for three days before planting.

WINNING ATTRIBUTES This is a slow-growing, sculptural plant with a modern, minimalist appearance. Its leaves are succulent and uniquely shaped. It is pest free and easy to grow, but unfortunately not always easy to locate. If you see one, buy it.

Hedera helix 'Patty's baby'

ENGLISH IVY

Araliaceae

Hedera helix is native to the temperate climates of Asia, Europe, and North Africa. While the straight species is frost-hardy and grows best outdoors, many named cultivars are well suited to growing indoors. *Hedera helix* is not an unusual plant; however, there are many cultivars with spectacular variegation and deeply lobed and ruffled foliage. In fact, shortly after discovering your first unusual cultivar, you may find yourself building an entire collection. *Hedera helix* 'Patty's baby' is highly variegated; its leaves are more white than green and are intricately marbled. Indoors it tolerates a range of light intensities, although variegation decreases in a bright northern window. *Hedera helix* cultivars grow best if kept cool in winter, at approximately 50°F (10°C). They can be allowed to trail in hanging baskets, or trained onto topiary forms.

LIGHT Depending on the cultivar, *Hedera helix* tolerates shade, dappled light, or bright indirect light. In general, the more highly variegated cultivars require brighter light. A few are suited to full sun, but most are not.

WATER *Hedera helix* should dry out somewhat between waterings. Water when the top inch of potting mix feels dry. In hot, dry conditions, *H. helix* is susceptible to spider mites, so grow on a drywell in winter if temperatures are high.

TEMPERATURE This plant tolerates colder temperatures than most houseplants, as low as 40°F (4°C). This makes it an excellent candidate for an unheated guest room or entryway. In fact, it will grow best if given a cool winter rest.

SOIL Grows well in either a soil-based or soilless mix.

FERTILIZATION Feed every other week at half strength during the growing season.

PROPAGATION Cuttings can be started with rooting hormone. The plant can also be propagated by layering.

Hedera helix 'Patty's baby'

WINNING ATTRIBUTES There's a *Hedera helix* to fit every taste; choose the form and color that suits you best. *Hedera helix* 'Patty's baby' has outstanding variegation. It is an undemanding and versatile plant that can be allowed to trail or trained on a form. Because it is cold-tolerant, it can be used in a bright, drafty spot where many houseplants would fail.

Heliconia humilis

LOBSTER CLAW

Heliconiaceae

Heliconia humilis is native to northern South America where it can grow as tall as 15 feet. Its natural habitat is in moist soils at the edge of tropical rainforests, where light and humidity are high. Leaves are large (1 to 3 feet long) and paddle-shaped. True flowers are inconspicuous, small, white, and partially hidden inside huge, vivid bracts. These bracts are scarlet with green margins and grow upright in an alternate pattern from a central stem. They are triangular and pointed, and each is 2

Heliconia humilis. Photo by Dency Kane

to 3 inches long. The entire inflorescence can be 6 to 8 inches in length. This very showy plant is sometimes sold as *Heliconia bihai*. Many covet the *Heliconia*, but few can grow it. It requires constant warmth and humidity and can become quite large. In containers, *H. humilis* grows 4 to 5 feet tall. If you have a greenhouse or conservatory, grow *H. humilis* with *Cyrtostachys renda*, whose similar cultural requirements and color scheme make it a natural companion. The growth habit of *H. humilis* is sympodial, which means that it grows laterally, from one side of its pot to the other. Regular repotting will be necessary to recenter the plant as it grows. Watch for spider mites.

LIGHT   Grow in the bright sun of a southern exposure.

WATER   Water when the top half-inch of potting mix is dry.

TEMPERATURE   Requires warm temperatures of at least 65°F (18°C).

SOIL   Grow in a soil-based mix.

FERTILIZATION   Feed with a bloom-booster fertilizer (high potassium) at half strength every week during the growing season.

PROPAGATION   Propagate by division.

WINNING ATTRIBUTES   This is an extremely showy plant in both size and color. Its bloom stalks make excellent, long-lasting cut flowers. If you can give *Heliconia humilis* the warmth, light, and humidity it requires, you will be rewarded with an impressive, showy plant.

Hemigraphis alternata

PURPLE WAFFLE

Acanthaceae

Hemigraphis alternata is a creeping ground cover native to southeast Asia. Leaves are approximately 3 inches long and 2 inches wide, basically oval in shape, with toothed margins. Variegation is high; foliage is purple underneath and green and purple on top. *Hemigraphis alternata* will flower in bright light. Blooms are small and bright white, making a nice contrast with the dark foliage. Veins are sunken, creating a waffle-like texture on the leaf surface. In containers, *H. alternata* averages about 8 inches tall and will cascade over the side of a pot. It is a decorative, textured plant.

LIGHT   Grows best in bright indirect light and will tolerate some sun; an eastern or western window is best. In low light it may get leggy.

WATER Water when the soil surface feels dry. Elevate humidity by growing it on a drywell. In dry conditions, leaf edges may curl and brown.

TEMPERATURE Keep *Hemigraphis alternata* above 65°F (18°C) for optimum growth. An occasional dip in temperature won't harm the plant, but prolonged exposure will slow growth and damage foliage.

SOIL Grows well in either a soil-based or soilless mix.

Hemigraphis alternata

FERTILIZATION Feed every other week at half strength during active growth.

PROPAGATION Easily propagated from stem cuttings.

WINNING ATTRIBUTES The high coloration of *Hemigraphis alternata* is quite attractive, and its quilted texture is also appealing. This is a fast grower, useful as a groundcover or conservatory specimen. It is pest free and low maintenance.

Hoffmania refulgens

QUILTED TAFFETA PLANT

Rubiaceae

Hoffmania refulgens is native to Mexico where it grows in dappled sun and fertile, well-drained soils. In nature it reaches 6 feet tall. In containers, *H. refulgens* grows to be 3 to 4 feet tall. Foliage is elliptical to obovate and slightly hairy. Leaves are 10 to 12 inches long and 3 to 4 inches wide and iridescent: purple underneath and reddish-green on top. A prominent midrib is silver, and veins are sunken, giving the leaf an attractive quilted pattern. Flowers are small and insignificant when compared to the fabulous foliage. This plant thrives in the high humidity of a greenhouse or conservatory. *Hoffmania refulgens* can be pruned regularly to encourage branching and keep it small. Scale is occasionally a problem.

Hoffmania refulgens

LIGHT   Grow in part to full sun for optimal variegation.

WATER   Water when the top half-inch of potting mix is dry. Elevate humidity.

TEMPERATURE   *Hoffmania refulgens* does well in normal household temperatures; keep it away from drafts.

SOIL   Grow in a soil-based potting mix.

FERTILIZATION   Feed at half strength every other week during the growing season.

PROPAGATION   Use rooting hormone to propagate from stem cuttings. Provide high humidity while cuttings are rooting.

WINNING ATTRIBUTES   The foliage is shimmering and regal. Its color and texture combine with the impressive size of this plant to make it a show stopper.

Homalocladium platycladum

RIBBON BUSH

Polygonaceae

Homalocladium platycladum is native to the Solomon Islands. There it grows to about 10 feet in sun or part shade. The structure of this plant is fascinating. Green stems are segmented and flattened, about 1 inch wide. There are small leaves that drop quickly, leaving the stems to photosynthesize. Small, greenish flowers form

Homalocladium platycladum

directly on the stems and are followed by dark purple fruit. *Homalocladium platy-cladum* grows quickly both indoors and out, as much as 2 to 3 feet in a season. It can be allowed to grow as a shrub or pruned to maintain a desired shape and size. This plant is relatively new to the houseplant market and until recently was a rare curiosity. It makes an excellent specimen plant due to its quick rate of growth and unique form.

LIGHT *Homalocladium platycladum* is highly adaptable to various light conditions. It grows as well in a sunny greenhouse as it does in a bright northern window, although it may not flower in lower light.

WATER Allow the top inch of soil to dry out in winter. During active growth, water when the top half-inch of soil feels dry. Elevated humidity is not required.

TEMPERATURE Grow in average household temperatures.

SOIL Can be grown in either a soilless or soil-based potting mix.

FERTILIZATION Requires minimal fertilization. Feed once a month at half strength with a balanced fertilizer during the growing season.

PROPAGATION Can be propagated from cuttings; bottom heat will speed the rooting process.

WINNING ATTRIBUTES This plant is easy to grow and pest free, with a unique structure. It quickly reaches specimen size (within one growing season) and responds well to pruning. *Homalocladium platycladum* is relatively rare in the market but is bound to grow in popularity. It is too interesting to be ignored.

Hoya caudata
Hoya onchyoides
Hoya serpens

WAX PLANT

Asclepiadaceae

The genus *Hoya* includes approximately 200 species, most native to the South Pacific, although a few species are from as far north as the Himalayan foothills. They are generally epiphytic vines in nature; as understory plants they receive dappled light and as epiphytes they require fast drainage and minimal feeding. Their nutrition comes primarily from forest canopy debris and rainwater. In the home, hoyas should be grown in hanging containers or trained on a trellis. Flowers are borne in umbels, and many are highly fragrant. While the size and coloration of hoya flowers vary greatly from species to species, all are star-shaped. Most species rebloom from existing peduncles, so do not cut these off when flowering has finished. In general, hoyas have small root systems, so resist the urge to repot until you see roots growing through the drainage hole. They bloom best when tightly potted. *Hoya caudata* requires higher humidity and higher light than most hoyas, but rewards you with almost constant flowers and a beautiful, textured leaf. Foliage is elliptical, approxi-

Hoya caudata

Hoya onchyoides

Hoya serpens

mately 3 inches long, and subtly mottled with white and red. Flowers are white and ruby red with fringed petals. *Hoya onchyoides* produces the most visually spectacular of all hoya blooms. Individual flowers are 2 inches across, dark pink, with a highly recurved shape. Its foliage is modest by comparison: plain green, elliptical, and 3 to 4 inches long. *Hoya serpens* is native to the Himalayan foothills, where temperatures are cool but the climate is frost free. *Hoya serpens* has a reputation for being difficult to bloom, which it is. Provide a nighttime temperature drop of approximately 10°F (about 6°C) in summer for late summer bloom. Foliage is round, slightly variegated with white, and about a half-inch in diameter. Flowers are greenish with pink centers and larger than the leaves. Congratulate yourself when you get this one to bloom. Hoyas are generally pest free but sometimes beset by mealybugs.

LIGHT In general, hoyas grow best in bright indirect light, although all will tolerate some direct sun indoors. In western and southern windows the foliage may fade and become less attractive, however these plants often flower very well. Try *Hoya serpens* and *H. onchyoides* in an eastern window and *H. caudata* in western or southern light.

WATER Hoyas are quite drought-tolerant. Most have succulent leaf tissue, capable of storing water, and thick cuticles that slow the loss of water via transpiration. In the average home, water a hoya once a week or less, depending on pot size. In a greenhouse or under artificial lights, you may need to water more frequently. In every case, allow the top inch of potting mix to dry out between waterings. Most hoyas do not require elevated humidity.

TEMPERATURE Average household temperatures are fine. Many species tolerate winter temperatures as low as 50°F (10°C). In cooler temperatures, watering frequency should be reduced. *Hoya serpens* is prompted to bloom by a nighttime temperature drop, so try moving this one outdoors in summertime, or leaving it next to an open window.

SOIL Hoyas require a fast-draining mix. Use a soilless potting medium, or a combination of three parts soilless mix to one part fine-grained bark mix.

FERTILIZATION Hoyas are not heavy feeders. Feed once a month at half strength during the growing season.

PROPAGATION Can be propagated from cuttings. Woody stemmed species will require bottom heat. Trim the leaves of large-leafed species to reduce water needs during rooting. Hoyas also produce seeds; however, pollination is infrequent indoors, and seeds are viable for a very short time.

WINNING ATTRIBUTES Hoyas are the perfect houseplant. They are low maintenance, beautiful foliage plants that produce fragrant bloom on a regular basis. Over 200 species provide a wide range of leaf sizes, shapes, and colors. Flowers range from tiny to huge, from fragrant to scentless. Hoyas rule.

Impatiens niamniamensis 'Congo Cockatoo'

Balsaminaceae

Impatiens niamniamensis is native to central Africa where it grows in moist, shady forests. It has slim, straight, succulent stems and ovate leaves, 4 to 6 inches long with crenellated margins. Foliage is sparse. Numerous small, brightly colored blooms originate from the leaf axils. Flowers are about an inch long and unusually shaped. They look like inflated pouches with prominent spurs that curve under the body of the bloom. They may be combinations of pink, purple, and red, or in the case of *I. niamniamensis* 'Congo Cockatoo', bright yellow and red. In nature, this

Impatiens niamniamensis

plant grows to be 3 feet tall; in containers it may be kept more compact by heavy pruning every few months. New growth begins almost immediately, and *I. niamniamensis* will soon bloom again. In hot, dry conditions this plant is prone to spider mites. Grow it on a drywell to increase humidity.

LIGHT   Indoors, grow it in bright indirect light.

WATER   Water when the surface of the potting mix feels dry. Impatiens wilt dramatically when they get too dry. In hot weather they need frequent watering.

TEMPERATURE   Grow in average household temperatures. Cold air will cause leaf drop.

SOIL   Grow in a soil-based potting mix.

FERTILIZATION   Feed every other week during active growth.

PROPAGATION   Roots easily from tip cuttings and grows quickly. New cuttings can be blooming plants within 6 weeks.

WINNING ATTRIBUTES   The flowers of *Impatiens niamniamensis* 'Congo Cockatoo' are petite but profuse. Their vivid candy colors and unusual shape make them stand out in any garden.

Ixora coccinea

JUNGLE FLAME

Ixora hookeri

WHITE IXORA

Rubiaceae

Ixora coccinea is a tropical shrub native to southeast Asia. In nature it grows to about 4 feet tall by 5 feet wide in full sun to part shade. Dark, glossy foliage is elliptical, 2 to 3 inches long, and about an inch wide. Flowers are borne in large, showy umbels and are primarily vermillion, although there are cultivars with yellow, orange, or pink blooms. This is a slow-growing plant that does well in containers, where its rounded shape makes it a natural focal point. *Ixora coccinea* will bloom year-round if given enough light. *Ixora hookeri* is a much larger plant, native to Madagascar. It reaches 6 to 8 feet in containers and is impressive both in bloom and out. Foliage is glossy, large, elliptical, and tinged with red. Flowers are white, four-petalled, and intensely fragrant. Scale and mealybugs are occasional problems for ixoras.

Ixora coccinea

Ixora hookeri

LIGHT *Ixora coccinea* requires at least four hours of direct sun in order to bloom; in full sun it will flower nonstop. *Ixora hookeri* will grow and bloom best in the full sun of a southern exposure.

WATER During active growth, allow the top half-inch of potting mix to dry out between waterings. In winter, water when the top inch of mix feels dry. Grow ixoras on a drywell in winter.

TEMPERATURE Normal household temperatures are fine for *I. coccinea* and *I. hookeri*. *Ixora coccinea* can tolerate occasional drops into the 50°F (10°C) range, but be sure to reduce watering frequency accordingly.

SOIL Use a quick-draining, soil-based potting mix for both *Ixora coccinea* and *I. hookeri*.

FERTILIZATION Feed with a bloom-booster at half strength every other week during the growing season.

PROPAGATION Propagate from cuttings with rooting hormone and bottom heat.

WINNING ATTRIBUTES *Ixora coccinea* is a small showy shrub that will bloom year-round if given adequate light. The vermillion flowers are perfectly offset by highly glossy foliage. *Ixora hookeri* makes an impressive, fragrant specimen tree, appropriate to a greenhouse or conservatory room because of its large size.

Jasminum sambac

JASMINE

Oleaceae

Jasminum sambac is native to India, Myanmar, and Bangladesh, where it is an evergreen shrub. Leaves are dark green, glossy, ovate, and 2 to 3 inches long. This plant is treasured for its white, fragrant blooms, which are frequently used to perfume tea. Flowers are approximately 1 inch in diameter, funnel-shaped, and borne in clusters of three to five flowers. They age to a pale pink color. Remove spent flowers to promote additional bloom; with conscientious deadheading, *J. sambac* will bloom most of the year. As it grows, *J. sambac* becomes less shrubby and more vining in its growth habit. You can either train it around a trellis, or prune it to maintain a compact shape. Pinching will encourage branching. This plant is prone to spider mites in dry air and may drop leaves if its soil gets too dry. A well-grown specimen is both visually and aromatically pleasing.

LIGHT Grow in a southern or western window.

WATER Water when the top half-inch of potting mix is dry. *Jasminum sambac* grows best in elevated humidity; grow it on a dry-well.

TEMPERATURE Grow in regular household temperatures, above 60°F (16°C).

SOIL Use a soil-based mix.

FERTILIZATION Feed at half strength every other week during the growing season.

PROPAGATION Propagate from stem cuttings.

WINNING ATTRIBUTES The fragrance is intoxicating. Its flowers are more fragrant at night, which means you will probably be home

Jasminum sambac

to enjoy their perfume. Leaves are a lovely, glossy green, and the shape of this plant can be kept compact or allowed to ramble depending on your interior landscape.

Jatropha integerrima

PERIGRINA

Jatropha podagrica

BOTTLE PLANT

Euphorbiaceae

Jatropha integerrima is native to the West Indies where it grows to be 10 to 12 feet tall. It's an attractive shrub, with glossy, dark green lobed leaves about 3 to 5 inches long. In high light, foliage takes on reddish undertones. Flowers are richly saturated vermillion or magenta. Each flower is five-petalled, about an inch wide, and clusters of bloom are about 6 inches across. In containers, *J. integerrima* will grow to be 4 to 6 feet tall. It is sensitive to transplanting, so don't repot unless absolutely necessary. This is an excellent specimen plant for a greenhouse or conservatory room and will flower year-round. It requires extreme tropical conditions, however, and this, combined with its large size, may make it difficult to grow successfully in the average home. *Jatropha podagrica* is native to Central America. It also flowers year-round, and its flowers are also richly colored. A cyme (approximately 2 inches in diameter) of delicate, bright orange flowers is produced at the plant's growing point. Flowers are long lasting. *Jatropha podagrica* is considerably more appropriate for the average home than *J. integerrima*. It is smaller in stature, growing to 2 to 3 feet tall in containers. It forms a thick caudex where the stem meets the roots, creating a bottle-shaped trunk. Leaves are sparse, large (up to 8 inches in diameter), and three-lobed. This is a truly unusual plant, a collector's item. Both are relatively pest free. Like all members of the *Euphorbia* family, they exude a milky latex when cut that irritates some people's skins.

LIGHT Grow *Jatropha integerrima* in full sun. *Jatropha podagrica* will flower in eastern, western, or southern light. Bloom will be heavier with stronger light.

WATER These are drought-tolerant plants. Water when the top inch of soil feels dry.

TEMPERATURE *Jatropha integerrima* requires high heat all the time. It is better grown in a greenhouse than in a home where temperatures may fluctuate too

Jatropha integerrima

Jatropha podagrica

Jatropha podagrica

much. It will drop its leaves at below 65°F (18°C). *Jatropha podagrica* grows well in household temperatures but may drop leaves if temperatures fall below 60°F (16°C).

SOIL Grow both in a soilless mix.

FERTILIZATION Feed once a month during the growing season.

PROPAGATION Both can be started from seed; *Jatropha integerrima* grows quickly, *J. podagrica* does not.

WINNING ATTRIBUTES *Jatropha integerrima* combines large size and glossy, attractive foliage with almost continuous bloom of a deep, rich color. It makes an excellent focal point in a tropical conservatory. *Jatropha podagrica* is well suited to growing in the home. Its manageable size and interesting, swollen shape, combined with attractive foliage and brightly colored flowers make it an excellent addition to a collection of unusual tropicals.

Justicia aurea
GOLDEN CANDLES
Justicia brandegeana
SHRIMP PLANT
Acanthaceae

The genus *Justicia* has been reorganized in recent years and now includes plants that were formerly in several different genera. *Justicia aurea* (formerly known as *Pachystachys lutea*) is a shrub native to Peru where it grows to 5 feet in dappled light. It is known for its bright yellow, upright, overlapping bracts. True flowers are tubular and white and emerge from among the bracts. The entire inflorescence is 4 to 6 inches tall. Individual flowers last for a few days, but the bracts remain colorful for up to two months. Leaves are lanceolate, shiny, dark green, and about 6 inches long. They have prominent veins and a slightly puckered surface. This plant grows well in containers, where it can be 18 to 24 inches tall. Older, leggy specimens can easily be replaced by new plants started from cuttings. *Justicia brandegeana* (formerly known as *Beloperone guttata*) is a shrub native to Mexico that grows up to 4 feet tall. It is a full sun plant grown for its unique shrimp-like bracts. True flowers are small and white and emerge from between the overlapping, multi-hued, reddish-orange bracts. As with *J. aurea*, the white flowers last a few days, but bracts remain vibrant for several months. Inflorescences are 4 to 5 inches long and are produced in abundance year-round. Leaves are a fresh, medium green, oval, and 1 to 3 inches long. There are also cultivars with white foliar variegation. In containers, *J. brandegeana* grows to about 2 feet tall. It gets leggy with age, so to keep a compact shape, prune heavily in spring, cutting back the plant by as much as half. Also, pinch out growing points during the year to encourage branching. Both are susceptible to whiteflies.

LIGHT Grow *Justicia aurea* in bright, indirect light. It will not flower in inadequate light, but direct sun is too strong. *Justica brandegeana* is a full sun plant, and inadequate light will result in leggy growth and a paucity of bloom.

Justicia aurea

Justicia brandegeana

WATER   These plants are relatively drought-tolerant. Water when the top half-inch of potting mix feels dry. Elevate humidity by growing on drywells.

TEMPERATURE   Grow well in normal household temperatures.

SOIL   Grow in a soilless mix.

FERTILIZATION   Feed with a balanced fertilizer at half strength every other week during the growing season.

PROPAGATION   Both plants can be propagated easily from stem cuttings. Since older specimens can be leggy, consider starting new plants from cuttings.

WINNING ATTRIBUTES   *Justica aurea* has nicely patterned foliage as well as large, vivid, upright bracts. Inflorescences are long-lasting, and their sunshine yellow color is outstanding. The multi-hued bracts of *J. brandegeana* have an interesting curved, pendent shape and provide a rich splash of color. Both bloom prolifically year-round.

Kaempferia rotunda 'Raven'

PEACOCK GINGER

Zingiberaceae

Kaempferia rotunda is native to southeast Asia. It is an understory plant, and in nature it experiences a dry season during which it goes dormant. This ginger is well suited to pot culture; in nature and in containers, it grows to be about 12 inches tall. *Kaempferia rotunda* 'Raven' is a cultivar with exceptional foliage. While I have read that flowers precede foliage when *K. rotunda* breaks dormancy, this has not always been my experience. Foliage may be the first thing to emerge when dormancy ends in spring. Leaves are lanceolate, and with their petioles are 8 to 18 inches long. They are purple/maroon on the bottom and green with blotches of silver on top. The pattern of colors is regular but not rigidly so; it looks as if it had been applied by hand with a paint brush. Fragrant flowers are 1 to 2 inches in diameter, purple and white, and grow at ground level. *Kaempferia rotunda* 'Raven' will go dormant in late fall; leaves will yellow and die. Reduce watering and watch for new shoots in early spring. When you see the first signs of new growth, resume the old watering schedule. This ginger has highly aromatic roots and is used in cooking and in Eastern medicine.

LIGHT   Grows best in bright indirect light. This is one of the best gingers for growing in shade.

WATER During the growing season, water when the surface of the potting mix feels dry; in addition, elevate humidity by growing on a drywell or in a greenhouse. During dormancy, water when the top inch of potting mix feels dry.

TEMPERATURE Grow in average household temperatures.

SOIL Use a soil-based mix.

FERTILIZATION Feed at half strength every other week during active growth.

PROPAGATION Propagate by dividing the rhizomes. Place the rhizome so that new shoots or eyes are facing upward, then cover with about 1 inch of potting mix and firm into place. Water once, then not again until the top inch of potting mix is dry. When growth becomes visible, begin watering whenever the surface of the potting mix feels dry.

Kaempferia rotunda
'Raven'

WINNING ATTRIBUTES   While the variegation of this foliage is similar to that of some marantas and calatheas, its pattern is much more graceful. I would grow this plant for its lovely leaves alone; the fragrant flowers are a welcome bonus.

Kalanchoe thyrsiflora

PADDLE PLANT

Kalanchoe uniflora

CORAL BELLS

Crassulaceae

Kalanchoe thyrsiflora is native to South Africa where it is accustomed to a dry winter season and full sun. It is an unusual looking succulent with large, wedge-shaped leaves held on its stem in a floret-like arrangement. Leaves are silvery green and leaf margins are bright red. In nature, *K. thyrsiflora* can grow to be 2 feet tall; in containers, however, it rarely gets taller than 8 to 10 inches. *Kalanchoe thyrsiflora* grows well indoors if given enough light. *Kalanchoe uniflora* is a succulent trailer native to Madagascar. In cultivation it is grown primarily for its lovely and profuse coral-colored tubular flowers, which are quite a bit larger than its small (1 inch diameter), succulent leaves. It will grow well in bright indirect light and flower most heavily in direct sun. Older plants shed their lower leaves and look leggy, so prune regularly to keep *K. uniflora* looking neat.

LIGHT   Indoors, both kalanchoes grow best in full sun, although they will tolerate bright indirect light as well.

WATER   Kalanchoes are succulent plants and should not be overwatered. Water when the top inch of potting mix is dry to the touch. Normal household humidity is fine.

TEMPERATURE   Both grow best with winter temperatures of about 60°F (16°C). Place them close to (but not touching the glass of) a window, where temperatures are lower.

SOIL   Grow in a soilless or special cactus mix.

FERTILIZATION   Feed once a month when kalanchoes are in active growth.

PROPAGATION   Propagate *Kalanchoe uniflora* from stem cuttings. Allow cuttings to callus for two or three days before potting them up. *Kalanchoe thyrsiflora* can be started from leaf cuttings. Detach a leaf from the parent plant, allow it to callus for several days, then plant the calloused end in soilless or cactus mix.

Kalanchoe thyrsiflora

Kalanchoe uniflora

WINNING ATTRIBUTES *Kalanchoe uniflora* rewards your lack of attention with a lavish display of bloom. *Kalanchoe thyrsiflora* is large, showy, and really weird-looking in a way that makes you want to touch it. Anyone interested in succulents or unusual forms should definitely grow this plant. Both are relatively pest free.

Ledebouria socialis

WOOD HYACINTH

Liliaceae

Ledebouria socialis is native to South Africa. It is a succulent bulb, well adapted to the arid conditions of its native habitat. This is a geophyte; its bulbs are often half exposed, half buried. Bulbs are purple, shiny, and attractive. Each bulb produces two to six leaves, with an understated, mottled pattern. The underside of the foliage is a muted purple, while the top is silver flecked with green. Leaves are succulent, straplike, and 4 to 6 inches long. Small, bluish-white, tubular flowers are borne on spikes. Clumps of bulbs spread over time, but the plant never exceeds 6 to 8 inches in height. *Ledebouria socialis* grows well in containers, adding subtle variegation to a windowsill garden or collection of miniatures. It is well suited to a bright, cool (perhaps drafty) windowsill. It is not technically a tropical plant and tolerates colder temperatures. Old leaves dry up and shrivel as they are replaced by new leaves at the bulb's tip.

LIGHT   Grow in bright indirect light or part sun.

WATER   Water when the top half-inch of potting mix is dry. If you give your *Ledebouria socialis* a winter rest, reduce watering; water when the top inch of mix feels dry.

TEMPERATURE   Cool to average household temperatures are fine. Try to keep temperatures below 75°F (24°C). You may give this plant a winter rest period at about 50°F (10°C).

SOIL   Grow in a soilless mix or a cactus mix.

FERTILIZATION   Feed at half strength once a month during active growth.

PROPAGATION   Propagate by division. Separate bulblets from the parent bulb and pot them up on their own. Bury each bulb halfway in the potting mix, leaving the top half of each bulb exposed.

WINNING ATTRIBUTES   Its small stature allows *Ledebouria socialis* to fit into almost any plant collection. It requires little maintenance and tolerates cool conditions. The lovely, subtle variegation adds interest to any interior landscape without upstaging the rest of your plants.

Licuala grandis

FAN PALM

Arecaceae

Licuala grandis is native to the Republic of Vanuatu (formerly the New Hebrides) where it grows in part shade in sandy soils. In nature it grows to be about 10 feet tall. This is a spectacularly beautiful palm with huge, almost circular leaves. The leaf blade is pleated, and the outer edge of the foliage is evenly toothed. Individual leaves are about 3 feet in diameter. This is not an easy palm to grow indoors, but it is so beautiful that it's worth trying. It requires high heat and humidity at all times, in addition to a very well drained soil. *Licuala grandis* grows well in containers if the above conditions are met. Potted specimens grow to be about 6 feet tall. As with any palm, watch for scale and spider mites. If you love palms and have succeeded with some of the easier species, try *L. grandis*. It is not a beginner plant and is best suited to the greenhouse or conservatory.

Ledebouria socialis

Licuala grandis

LIGHT Indoors, grow in bright indirect light to part sun. You may summer this plant outdoors, but give it some protection from direct sun.

WATER Grows best with consistent moisture; water when the surface of the potting mix feels dry. Elevated humidity (above 50 percent) is also required.

TEMPERATURE Keep above 60°F (16°C).

SOIL *Licuala grandis* must have a quick-draining potting mix. Try a combination of four parts soilless mix with one part sand.

FERTILIZATION Feed every other week during active growth. Since you'll be growing this plant under greenhouse conditions, your growing season will be pretty much year-round.

PROPAGATION *Licuala grandis* can be propagated from seed, or you can remove suckers from the parent plant and pot them up on their own.

WINNING ATTRIBUTES The foliage is superb. The giant, pleated, fan-like leaves make it an immediate focal point in any greenhouse or conservatory.

Lithops marmorata

LIVING STONES

Aizoaceae

Lithops marmorata is native to extremely hot and dry environments in South Africa and Namibia. It is a succulent plant composed of pairs of fleshy, upright leaves fused at the base. The diameter of the combined leaves is approximately 1 to 2 inches. Foliage resembles smooth stones and may be gray, brown, green, or a combination of all three. Markings may be wavy or circular. New foliage and daisy-shaped yellow, orange, or white flowers emerge from the crevice between the paired leaves. Flowers are considerably larger than the foliage, and when *L. marmorata* has finished flowering, the existing leaves frequently wither and die. A new pair will appear soon after, sustained by the water in the plant's large tap root and its old leaves. This plant grows well in containers as long as it is not overwatered. While you might expect to give it a shallow pot, the root can be quite long, so don't. This is a slow-growing miniature, well suited to a small growing space.

LIGHT Grow in full sun.

WATER Water sparingly at all times. During the growing season, water once every two weeks. In fall and winter, water once a month.

Lithops marmorata

TEMPERATURE Grow at regular household temperatures. You can give it a winter rest at 50°F (10°C), but this is not necessary. If you do give *Lithops marmorata* a winter rest, withhold water until temperatures rise in spring. Don't be alarmed if existing foliage becomes somewhat shriveled.

SOIL Grow in a sandy, fast-draining cactus mix.

FERTILIZATION Fertilization is not necessary.

PROPAGATION Can be propagated from seed. It will take several years to reach flowering size.

WINNING ATTRIBUTES These are true curiosities and tactile plants. Because it's hard to believe they are living, photosynthetic flora rather than stone, you have to touch them to be sure. The subtle patterns and variegation of the smooth leaf surfaces vary from plant to plant. Anyone with an interest in succulents will want to have several.

Lotus berthelotti

PARROT'S BEAK

Fabaceae

Lotus berthelotti is native to the Canary Islands where it grows in full sun as a groundcover reaching 8 inches tall. Foliage is needle-shaped and feathery soft; leaves are silvery gray and 1 to 2 inches long. Flowers are sickle-shaped, red and yellow, and about an inch long. They are borne at the ends of vining stems. Pinch stem tips to encourage branching. In nature, stems may grow indefinitely; in containers, individual vines grow to be 4 to 6 feet long. *Lotus berthelotti* is not easy to cultivate. It is temperature-sensitive: cool temperatures in spring initiate bloom; high summer heat inhibits flowering; when nighttime temperatures are high, it will stop blooming. Over- or underwatering can cause foliage to drop. Nonetheless, it is worth trying for its superb combination of complementary textures and colors.

LIGHT Grow in full to part sun.

WATER Water when the top half-inch of potting mix is dry. If you keep your plant cool in winter, reduce watering frequency; then, water when the top inch of potting mix is dry.

TEMPERATURE *Lotus berthelotti* will benefit from a cool winter rest. You may overwinter it in a bright location where temperatures are about 40°F (4°C).

SOIL Pot in a soil-based mix.

FERTILIZATION Feed at half strength every other week during active growth.

PROPAGATION Propagate by stem cuttings.

WINNING ATTRIBUTES The brilliant red and yellow flowers are perfectly offset by the plant's soft, spiky, gray foliage. This plant makes an unusual, exotic hanging basket or can be grown as a groundcover.

Lotus berthelotti

Ludisia discolor

JEWEL ORCHID

Orchidaceae

Ludisia discolor is native to southeastern Asia, Indonesia, and southern China. It is a terrestrial orchid, growing in light shade, and in nature the thick stems creep along the ground, putting out roots as they grow. Leaves are an extremely dark green, almost black. They are approximately 3 inches long, elliptical, and velvety, with fine, parallel veins in pink or red. This plant is prized for its foliage, but it also blooms once a year, producing 6-inch spikes of small, pretty, white and yellow flowers. *Ludisia discolor* grows well in containers under average household conditions. The elevated humidity of a drywell is appreciated but not required. This plant spreads across the top of its pot; some stems will cascade over the pot's edge, and some will grow upright. This makes it a good choice for either a hanging basket or a standing pot. Be careful when watering. Water drops may leave permanent white marks on the foliage, which mar its beauty.

LIGHT Grows best in bright indirect light. In an unobstructed northern window,

Ludisia discolor

it will produce foliage but may require the brighter light of an eastern window in order to bloom. Direct sun will cause foliage to fade.

WATER The stems are thick and succulent, capable of storing water for times of drought. Water when the top inch of potting mix feels dry. If you grow your plant in a fine-grained orchid mix, give it a thorough soaking every other time you water. Be sure not to drip water on the plant's leaves.

TEMPERATURE Grow at normal household temperatures.

SOIL Grow in either a soilless mix or a fine-grained orchid mix.

FERTILIZATION Feed once a month at half strength during the growing season.

PROPAGATION Stem cuttings can easily be rooted in either a soilless mix or a glass of water.

WINNING ATTRIBUTES The foliage of this plant is unbeatable. Where else can you find velvety black leaves finely etched with soft red veins? *Ludisia discolor* is a beautiful plant year-round, and once a year offers the added bonus of delicate bloom. This plant is pest free and low maintenance.

Malvaviscus arboreus

Malvaviscus arboreus

PIPESTEM HIBISCUS

Malvaceae

Malvaviscus arboreus is native to tropical America where it grows in full to part sun. In nature it is a shrub growing to 10 feet tall. Leaves are medium green, ovate, hairy, about 2 inches long, with serrated margins. Its flowers are profuse and bright red with protruding stamens. Flower texture is crepepapery, like those of the more familiar tropical hibiscus plant. Unlike this related plant, the flowers of *M. arboreus* remain folded like a closed umbrella. Stamens protrude prominently. In containers, *M. arboreus* will quickly grow to be 4 to 5 feet tall. It is an excellent specimen plant for a sunny room or conservatory and will appreciate elevated humidity. Watch for spider mites and whiteflies, especially in dry air.

LIGHT   Grow in the bright sun of a southern or western window.

WATER   Water when the top half-inch of the potting mix feels dry.

TEMPERATURE   Regular household temperatures are fine.

SOIL   Grow in a soilless mix.

FERTILIZATION   Feed at half strength once a month during the growing season.

PROPAGATION   *Malvaviscus arboreus* is easily started from stem cuttings.

WINNING ATTRIBUTES   This is a floriferous plant; in bright sun it is covered with red blooms. The charm of its flowers lies in their apparently coy refusal to open. Prominent stamens extend from the bloom. *Malvaviscus arboreus* quickly reaches specimen size, and its flower color stands out in the interior landscape.

Mandevilla splendens
Mandevilla ×amabilis

MANDEVILLA

Apocynaceae

Mandevilla splendens is native to the mountain forests of Brazil. Foliage is leathery, glossy, ovate, approximately 2 to 3 inches long, and 1 to 1.5 inches wide. In high light it may acquire reddish undertones. The flowers of *M. splendens* are trumpet-

Mandevilla splendens

Mandevilla ×amabilis

shaped, about 2 to 3 inches in diameter, and may be deep rose, pale pink, or white, depending on the cultivar. The flower's throat is always a rich yellow color. This is one of the sprawling mandevillas, and while it can be trained around an upright form, it is also well displayed in a hanging basket or cascading over the edge of a planter. *Mandevilla splendens* can be pruned to maintain a compact, shrubby growth habit or allowed to grow as a vine, in which case its stems will need your assistance to twine. On the other hand, *M.* ×*amabilis* (a garden hybrid) is a very vigorous climber and can easily shoot up 8 to 10 feet in a single season. Its foliage is larger and coarser than that of *M. splendens,* and its flowers are somewhat larger: 3 to 4 inches in diameter. While often sold in hanging baskets, *M.* ×*amabilis* is best twined around a trellis or upright form. Both plants flower on new growth, so prune after blooms have passed to encourage the production of new, flowering shoots. To the casual consumer, these plants are quite similar; they are often mislabeled, one as the other. Cultural requirements are basically the same for each, but their growth habits are quite different. Foliage is your best indicator: rough leaf texture = strong climber, smooth leaf surface = sprawling vine. Both produce excellent, numerous flowers. The genus was formerly known as *Dipladenia*, and you may still find plants labeled with that name. Mealybugs occasionally pester these plants.

LIGHT   Grow both mandevillas in as much bright sun as possible. They will live in an eastern, western, or southern exposure, and will flower more heavily in more intense light. If your plant doesn't flower well, increase light levels.

WATER   Allow the top half-inch of potting mix to dry out between waterings. Grow on a drywell if possible.

TEMPERATURE   Grow both mandevillas in average household temperatures.

SOIL   These mandevillas grow best in a quick-draining potting mix, either soilless or soil-based.

FERTILIZATION   Feed at half strength every other week during active growth.

PROPAGATION   Propagate both from stem cuttings.

WINNING ATTRIBUTES   Mandevillas are profuse bloomers, producing heavy crops of large, pink (usually) flowers in bright sun. As vines, they fill several niches: *Mandevilla splendens* is an excellent hanging plant because of its cascading growth habit and smooth, shiny leaves. *Mandevilla* ×*amabilis* offers striking vertical interest when trained up a trellis or other upright form.

Medinilla myriantha

ROSE GRAPE

Melastomataceae

Medinilla myriantha is native to the Philippines, Indonesia, and southeast Asia where it can grow to 4 feet tall. It grows both as an epiphyte and as a terrestrial plant. In cultivation it is often grown in a hanging basket. Leaves are glossy, dark green, ovate, and about 12 inches long, and they grow in pairs, arching up and out from the stem. Leaf veins are prominent and create an attractive pattern. The flower clusters of *M. myriantha* are magnificent. Flower stalks are 12 to 18 inches long and bear pendent clusters of small pink flowers that resemble bunches of grapes. Berries are pinkish purple and also ornamental. This plant is not easy to grow; it requires high humidity and is best suited to a greenhouse or conservatory. In dry air, it is prone to spider mites. *Medinilla myriantha* is sometimes mislabeled as *M. magnifica*, but is actually easier to grow. *Medinilla magnifica* is distinguished by large and conspicuous bracts at the base of the inflorescence. Both are very showy plants.

LIGHT *Medinilla myriantha* grows best in bright, indirect light to part sun.

WATER Water when the top half-inch of potting mix is dry. Grow on a drywell or in a greenhouse; it requires elevated humidity.

TEMPERATURE *Medinilla myriantha* should be kept above 65°F (18°C).

SOIL Grow in a mixture of three parts soil-based potting mix and one part fir bark.

FERTILIZATION Feed at half strength every other week during the growing season.

PROPAGATION *Medinilla myriantha* is difficult to propagate from cuttings. It requires very high temperatures and humidity in order to root.

WINNING ATTRIBUTES The flowers of this plant are unusual, abundant, and long-lasting. Foliage is also large and attractive. This is an exceptional, exotic beauty.

Medinilla myriantha

Musa acuminata var. *sumatrana*

BLOODLEAF BANANA

Musaceae

Musa acuminata var. *sumatrana* is native to Australasia where it grows in full to part sun. In nature it may be 15 feet tall. It has a spreading root system that sends up suckers, forming large clumps of pseudostems, which are actually composed of leaf bases that wrap around each other. This plant does well in containers, where it grows to be about 6 or 7 feet tall. *Musa acuminata* var. *sumatrana* is grown for its foliage; it does not flower or fruit. Leaves are a bright, light green, covered with a splotched, burgundy pattern. Foliage is paddle-shaped. The petiole is 3 to 4 feet long, and the blade is 2 to 3 feet long. Lower leaves may yellow as the season progresses; remove them at the petiole base. Because of its large size, *M. acuminata* var. *sumatrana* is well suited to a greenhouse or conservatory room. If you'd like to try this plant but your growing space is limited, grow it outdoors in summer and overwinter it in a dormant state. Cut the pseudostem back to a few inches above ground level and store it in a cool, dark, but frost free place. In spring, bring the pot out into the light and resume watering. Spider mites may be a problem in dry air, so elevate humidity. *Musa acuminata* var. *sumatrana* is sometimes sold as *M. acuminata* 'Zebrina'.

Musa acuminata var. *sumatrana*

LIGHT Grows best in full to part sun.

WATER Water when the surface of its potting mix feels dry. Elevate humidity. A dormant banana does not require watering.

TEMPERATURE Grow in average household temperatures. A dormant plant may be overwintered at temperatures above 45°F (7°C).

SOIL Grow in a soil-based mix.

FERTILIZATION *Musa acuminata* var. *sumatrana* is a heavy feeder; fertilize every week at full strength during the growing season.

PROPAGATION Since *Musa acuminata* var.

sumatrana does not flower or fruit, it cannot be propagated by seed. Remove suckers from the parent plant and pot them up on their own.

WINNING ATTRIBUTES   Nothing says tropical paradise like the huge leaves of a banana tree. The intense variegation of *Musa acuminata* var. *sumatrana* makes it doubly desirable. This is a showy specimen.

Mussaenda 'Queen Sirikit'

LADY FLOWERS

Rubiaceae

Mussaenda erythrophylla is native to tropical western Africa where it grows 10 to 20 feet tall in full sun. Most pink *Mussaenda* hybrids are derived from it, including *Mussaenda* 'Queen Sirikit'. This plant grows well in containers but may get leggy with age. Regular pruning will keep it compact and branching. Potted specimens rarely exceed 5 feet in height. Flowers are small, yellow, trumpet-shaped, and surrounded by large, showy, pink sepals. These sepals look like bracts and may be 2 to 3 inches long. Inflorescences form huge clusters at the ends of branches, causing the branches to bend under their weight. Foliage is attractive, with prominent veins, and covered with silky hairs. Leaves are ovate and 4 to 6 inches long. *Mussaenda* 'Queen Sirikit' is a showy shrub, requiring high humidity and lots of space. It is best suited to a greenhouse or conservatory. In dry air it is prone to spider mites. This plant is sometimes sold as *M. philippica* 'Queen Sirikit'.

LIGHT   Indoors, grow in full sun.

WATER   Water when the top half-inch of potting mix is dry. Elevated humidity is required.

Mussaenda 'Queen Sirikit'

TEMPERATURE   *Mussaenda* 'Queen Sirikit' thrives above 60°F (16°C). Lower temperatures may prove fatal.

SOIL   Grow in a quick-draining, soil-based mix.

FERTILIZATION   Feed at half strength every other week during the growing season.

PROPAGATION   Propagate from stem cuttings. Rooting hormone and bottom heat will speed the process.

WINNING ATTRIBUTES   The flowers of *Mussaenda* 'Queen Sirikit' are outrageous. This is a flamboyant plant, and a well-grown specimen that will produce prolific bloom all year-round.

Nelumbo nucifera

SACRED LOTUS

Nelumbonaceae

Nelumbo nucifera is an aquatic species native to southern Asia and northern Australia. Its leaves stand 4 to 6 feet above water level, and the plant may be 4 feet wide. Leaves are light green, waxy, almost circular, and up to 10 inches wide. Leaf stalks emerge from an underwater rhizome and grow straight up. They attach to the center of the leaf, giving it a marked center point that is slightly concave and from which leaf veins radiate. Foliage is very attractive. Flowers may be white or pink and are fragrant. They develop into highly ornamental seed pods, which are often dried and used in arrangements. *Nelumbo nucifera* grows well in containers, but its rhizome must be handled carefully as the growing tip is easily damaged. This is an excellent plant for a large indoor water garden, perhaps at the center of a greenhouse or conservatory room. Fill a pot halfway with heavy, clay soil, add aquatic fertilizer, and place the rhizome on top. Pin it into place with several pieces of wire bent into a "U" shape, then add gravel to the surface of the potting soil around the rhizome. This will keep soil from floating away. Submerge the entire pot below the water surface. *Nelumbo* was once classified with *Nymphaea* (water lily) but unlike *Nymphaea*, *Nelumbo* holds its leaves and flowers high above the surface of the water.

LIGHT   Indoors, grow in full sun.

WATER   *Nelumbo nucifera* should be grown with the potted rhizome entirely submerged in water.

TEMPERATURE   Grow in average household temperatures. Water should also be maintained at room temperatures.

Nelumbo nucifera

SOIL Plant in a heavy, clay soil.

FERTILIZATION Plant the rhizome along with a time-release aquatic fertilizer. Replenish the fertilizer annually.

PROPAGATION Rhizomes may be divided in spring; make sure you include several nodes in each division. You can also grow *Nelumbo nucifera* from seed. Sow seed in heavy soil, place gravel on top, then submerge pots and maintain a temperature of at least 70°F (21°C) while the seed germinates.

WINNING ATTRIBUTES Both the foliage and flowers are large and lovely. Flowers are fragrant and develop into ornamental seed pods. An indoor water feature planted with *Nelumbo nucifera* is breathtaking.

Neoregelia 'Morris Henry Hobbs' × 'Elegance'
Neoregelia 'Pemiento'

Bromeliaceae

Neoregelias are semi-epiphytic bromeliads native to South America, mainly Brazil. Most grow as epiphytes, but some grow on the ground, although their roots do not penetrate the soil. Many species have outstanding red variegation in striking patterns of stripes and speckles. Flowers are borne low in the central cup; they are small, usually blue or white. After flowering, the parent plant gradually dies back, but not before producing offsets. Some leaves are barely serrated, but many have weapons grade teeth. Handle with care or you may get splinters or irritated skin. Foliage forms low rosettes which range from several inches to several feet in diameter. *Neoregelia* 'Morris Henry Hobbs' × 'Elegance' is a superbly varie-

Neoregelia 'Morris Henry Hobbs' × 'Elegance'

Neoregelia 'Pemiento'

gated hybrid. Its rosette is 12 to 15 inches in diameter, and the inner leaves are almost entirely red, with greenish-brown speckles. A ring of outer leaves is brownish-green, nicely contrasting with the inner red leaves. Leaf margins are toothed. *Neoregelia* 'Pemiento' is also highly variegated. Its rosette is 10 to 12 inches wide, and its leaves are very glossy. Leaf margins are sharply toothed and green with a bright red central stripe. Its variegation reflects its heritage. One of its parents is *N. carolinae*, the most widely grown *Neoregelia*. The foliage of *N. carolinae* has a cream-colored stripe down the center, and all *N. carolinae* hybrids exhibit similar patterns with varying degrees of variegation. In dry air, *Neoregelia* foliage may turn brown at the tips. A drywell should provide sufficient humidity to avoid this.

LIGHT   Grow in bright indirect light. Direct sun will damage foliage, and insufficient light will cause variegation to fade. Both of these grow well under fluorescent lights.

WATER   Allow the top inch of potting mix to dry out between waterings. Fill the center cup with water each time you water; be sure not to let it dry out. The extra humidity provided by a drywell will keep leaf tips from browning.

TEMPERATURE   Grow well in average household temperatures.

SOIL   Grow in a fine-grade fir bark mix or a combination of half soilless mix and half fine-grained bark mix.

FERTILIZATION   Feed at half strength once a month during active growth. Use the same half-strength fertilizer solution to fill the cup of the bromeliad.

PROPAGATION   Propagate by separating offsets from the parent plant. If roots have already formed on the offsets, treat them as mature plants. If no roots are present, treat them as cuttings (elevated humidity and warmth) until roots are established. You may also cut back the parent plant and leave the offsets in place to form a clump.

WINNING ATTRIBUTES   These rosettes of foliage are stiff and sculptural. Variegation is outstanding, and carefully placed specimens add rich, concentrated color to the indoor landscape.

Nepenthes hybrids

PITCHER PLANT

Nepenthaceae

Nepenthes species are native to tropical Asia where they grow as epiphytes in swampy areas. Leaves grow from a central rosette and are medium green. They are usually lanceolate, but their size varies greatly according to the species. Flowers are relatively inconspicuous and borne in spikes above the central leaves. In cultivation, this plant rarely flowers; it is grown for its eponymous pitchers, which are actually modified leaves that allow the plant to supplement available nutrients through the passive capture of insects. The insects are attracted to the reddish-brown pitchers and drown in the liquid held inside. (Small amphibians are sometimes trapped in larger pitchers.) Special digestive enzymes allow the plant to absorb the resulting nutrients as food. *Nepenthes* hybrids are usually sold in hanging baskets. Foliage is 10 to 12 inches long and 2 to 3 inches wide. Pitchers of these hybrids are 6 to 8 inches long. They are reddish-brown and often have complex mottled patterns of yellowish-green. These plants require very high humidity and grow best in a greenhouse or terrarium. If you can provide appropriate conditions, you will have an impressive, intriguing specimen.

LIGHT   Grow in very bright indirect light.

WATER   Water when the surface of the potting mix is dry. Elevated humidity is required.

TEMPERATURE   Keep above 65°F (18°C).

SOIL   Grow in a mix of three parts soilless mix and one part fine-grained fir bark.

FERTILIZATION   You don't have to feed insects to your *Nepenthes*; give it a commercial fertilizer at half strength once a month. While some carnivorous plants stop producing pitchers when fed supplementally, *Nepenthes* hybrids continue to produce theirs.

PROPAGATION   These can be propagated from stem cuttings, but it is a slow process. Even with intense bottom heat, cuttings may take two months to root.

WINNING ATTRIBUTES   The pitchers of *Nepenthes* hybrids are carnivorous death traps. This is one of the most exotic tropical plants available to the indoor gardener. It is a true conversation piece for the greenhouse or conservatory.

Nepenthes hybrid

Nerium oleander

ROSE BAY

Apocynaceae

Nerium oleander is native to the Mediterranean, both northern Africa and southern Europe. In nature it is a large, evergreen shrub, growing as tall as 20 feet. Leaves are lanceolate, deep green, 1 to 1.5 inch wide, 3 to 6 inches long, with a prominent midrib. There is a variegated cultivar with cream markings on the leaves. Flowers are five-petalled, flared, 1 to 2 inches in diameter, and borne in terminal clusters. Blooms may be white, pink, yellow, salmon, or cerise; they can be single or double. This plant flowers on new growth. In containers, it usually does not exceed 6 feet in height and blooms most heavily in summer. It is easily trained into a standard form or can be allowed to grow in its natural, shrubby shape. Because it blooms on new growth, heavy pruning does not curtail bloom. Watch for scale and spider mites. All parts of this plant are extremely poisonous when ingested. Do not grow it where nibblers can nibble it. Like all Apocynaceae, *N. oleander* exudes a white, milky latex when cut. This may irritate some people's skin.

LIGHT Grow in full or part sun.

WATER *Nerium oleander* is a drought-tolerant plant once established. Water when the top inch of potting mix is dry. Elevated humidity is not necessary.

Nerium oleander

TEMPERATURE *Nerium oleander* is not a tropical plant. It can tolerate cool winter temperatures and will even withstand a light frost. This is a good candidate for a cold, bright, unheated space, but it also easily adapts to normal indoor temperatures.

SOIL Grow in a soilless mix.

FERTILIZATION Feed once a month during the growing season.

PROPAGATION You can propagate from stem cuttings. Use rooting hormone and bottom heat.

WINNING ATTRIBUTES This is an excellent tree for the indoor garden, tolerating a wide range of temperatures. It can be kept compact and bushy without sacrificing flowers, since it blooms on new growth. It can also easily be trained into tree form, if that shape is appropriate for your landscape. A range of flower color allows you to tailor your choice of plant precisely.

Pachira aquatica

GUIANA CHESTNUT

Bombacaceae

Pachira aquatica is native to Mexico and northern South America where it grows over 50 feet tall in sunny estuaries. Despite its imposing stature in nature, *P. aquatica* adapts well to container growth, where it can easily be maintained at 6 to 8 feet by restricting the root zone. Once your tree has reached the desired height, do not increase pot size. Root-prune your tree every two to three years and replace it in its original container. Thick trunks are attractive with smooth gray bark. Foliage is dark green, large, and deeply lobed. Five to nine leaflets, each 5 to 10 inches long, meet at a center point to form a star shape. *Pachira aquatica* does not often flower indoors, but if yours does, you're in for a treat. Cream-colored petals curve back to reveal more than 200 purple-red and white stamens, giving the inflorescence the appearance of a large, old-fashioned shaving brush.

LIGHT Grow in full to part sun.

WATER Water when the surface of the potting mix feels dry. This plant naturally grows in estuaries where soil is constantly moist.

TEMPERATURE Grow in normal household temperatures.

SOIL Use a soil-based potting mix.

FERTILIZATION Feed every other week during active growth.

Pachira aquatica

PROPAGATION *Pachira aquatica* is propagated from seed or by tip cuttings. Give cuttings bottom heat to speed rooting.

WINNING ATTRIBUTES This is a fast-growing statuesque tree with attractive bark and a large, interesting leaf shape. *Pachira aquatica* is an excellent foliage specimen for a sunny location.

Passiflora trifasciata
Passiflora violacea

PASSIONFLOWER

Passifloraceae

Most passifloras are native to South America. All species are vigorous. Some produce delicious, edible fruit, while others are valued for their flowers. *Passiflora trifasciata* is native to Venezuela, Brazil, and Peru. It is one of the few passifloras grown primarily for its foliage. It has tri-lobed leaves marked along the center veins with purple, silver, and green. New growth has a maroon tint. Flowers are small (about an inch in diameter) and yellowish-green. They are not nearly as flashy as the flowers of most passifloras but have the same complex, layered structure and are nicely fragrant. *Passiflora trifasciata* grows well in containers where its vining stems can grow from 10 to 15 feet long. Give it something to climb: a trellis, a window frame, or another plant. *Passiflora violacea* is a garden hybrid from Brazil. This is grown for its flowers, which are huge, complex, and fragrant. The layers of detail are amazing. A lilac-pink outer layer of petals and sepals is topped by a wheel of long, thin, lavender filaments with white tips. Showy stigmas and anthers form the center of the flower. Individual blooms are 3 to 4 inches in diameter. Leaves are usually tri-lobed, about 4 inches across, and glossy medium green. *Passiflora violacea* grows well in containers and will climb quite high (20 feet) when given proper support. Passifloras climb via tendrils; stems are thin and flexible enough to be trained without difficulty. Pinch growing tips to encourage branching. Passifloras flower on new growth, so pruning will not inhibit bloom. However, do not cut all the way back into hard wood. Watch for spider mites.

LIGHT *Passiflora violacea* flowers best in full to part sun. *Passiflora trifasciata* grows well in bright indirect light and will also be fine with more sun. Since this vine is usually grown for its foliage, the direct sun required for flowering is less important.

Passiflora trifasciata

Passiflora violacea

WATER   Water when the top half-inch of potting mix feels dry. If you give your passiflora a cool winter rest, allow the top inch of mix to dry out between waterings.

TEMPERATURE   Average household temperatures are fine for both passifloras. If possible, give your plants winter temperatures of about 60°F (16°C).

SOIL   Grow both passifloras in a soilless mix.

FERTILIZATION   Feed at half strength with a bloom-booster every other week during the growing season. Overfertilizing may result in lush foliage and little bloom.

PROPAGATION   Both passifloras are easily propagated from stem cuttings.

WINNING ATTRIBUTES   These are impressive vines that quickly climb to great heights. The foliage of *Passiflora trifasciata* is lovely and can be woven among the plants of your collection or trained up a vertical support. The flowers of *P. violacea* are most visible when the plant is trained up and overhead. Blooms will hang down through the leaves where their lovely scent and complex structure are easily appreciated.

Pavonia multiflora

Malvaceae

Pavonia multiflora is native to Brazil where it is a shrub growing to 6 feet tall. Leaves are narrowly elliptical, 6 to 8 inches long, and medium green. The flowers of this plant are quite unusual looking and are actually a combination of bracts and flowers. Outer bracts are bright red and surround purple-red petals; prominent protruding stamens are bluish-purple. The entire inflorescence is almost 2 inches long. Flowers are borne singly in terminal leaf axils. Since this plant blooms on new wood, it can be allowed to grow as a tall shrub or standard or kept compact without sacrificing bloom. Watch for whitefly. While this plant is usually sold as *P. multiflora*, you may sometimes see it labeled *Pavonia* ×*gledhilli*. Cultural requirements remain the same, no matter which name is used.

LIGHT   Indoors, grow in full to part sun.

WATER   Water when the top half-inch of potting mix is dry. Elevate humidity.

TEMPERATURE   Grow in average household temperatures.

SOIL   Pot in a soil-based mix.

FERTILIZATION   Feed every other week at half strength during the growing season.

PROPAGATION   *Pavonia multiflora* is easily propagated from stem cuttings.

Pavonia multiflora

WINNING ATTRIBUTES The flowers are showy, plentiful, unusually shaped, and offer a unique color combination of red and purple. It is impressive, whether grown as a large specimen or a small plant.

Pelargonium peltatum
IVY-LEAVED GERANIUM
Pelargonium 'Vancouver Centennial'
Geraniaceae

Pelargonium peltatum is native to South Africa, and many ivy-leaved hybrids have been derived from it. It has trailing, jointed stems up to 3 feet long, and deep green, glossy, ivy-shaped leaves, 1 to 2 inches wide. Flower color varies and may be pink, red, white, salmon, or lavender; flower shape may be double or single. This plant grows well in containers; it looks especially nice in a hanging basket or a pot placed on a high shelf where the stems can be allowed to trail. *Pelargonium peltatum* tolerates cooler temperatures and higher humidity better than most other pelargoniums. If possible, give it cool nighttime temperatures as low as 50° to 55° (10°C to 13°C). It is an excellent candidate for summering outdoors or hanging by an open

*Pelargonium
peltatum*

*Pelargonium
'Vancouver
Centennial'*

window. Plants grown in low light or hot, dry conditions will not be attractive, but well-grown plants are sleek and elegant with their dark, shiny foliage and delicate, bright blooms. Pinch stems to encourage branching. *Pelargonium* 'Vancouver Centennial' is a fancy-leaved, zonal geranium. (The zone refers to the color demarcation typical of all the pelargoniums in this category.) It is a hybrid of several species native to hot, dry South Africa. Humid air may result in mildew diseases, and consistently moist soil can result in rot. *Pelargonium* 'Vancouver Centennial' has leaves with brick red centers bordered by a thin edging of light yellow-green. Leaf shape vaguely resembles that of a maple leaf. Flowers are bright red and are held in loose clusters several inches above the foliage. Some growers remove flower buds from plants, so all energy will be directed to foliage growth. *Pelargonium* 'Vancouver Centennial' has a wonderful, fresh scent although it is not classified as a scented geranium. The smell is fresh and gentle. Faded leaves should be removed from the plant. A leggy specimen can be pruned heavily to rejuvenate its shape. In general, both pelargoniums grow and bloom best when tightly potted.

LIGHT   Grow *Pelargonium peltatum* in full sun for optimal bloom. *Pelargonium* 'Vancouver Centennial' grows well in full to part sun. Variegation will be more intense in brighter light.

WATER   Water when the top half-inch of soil is dry.

TEMPERATURE   Grow both pelargoniums in normal household temperatures. *Pelargonium peltatum* may be given cool nighttime temperatures or a cool winter rest.

SOIL   Grow these in either a soilless or soil-based potting mix.

FERTILIZATION   Feed every other week at half strength during the growing season.

PROPAGATION   Both can be propagated from stem cuttings.

WINNING ATTRIBUTES   *Pelargonium peltatum* makes an excellent hanging basket. Its contrasting flowers and foliage make it a bright spot in the interior landscape. *Pelargonium* 'Vancouver Centennial' is a highly variegated foliage plant that would be worth growing even if it didn't produce bright red flowers throughout the year. It has a compact growth habit and can be kept small by frequent pruning.

Peperomia ferreyrae

PINCUSHION PEPEROMIA

Piperaceae

Peperomia ferreyrae is native to Peru, where it is an epiphyte growing to about a foot tall. Leaves are succulent, pale lime green, linear, and about 2 inches long. They are creased along the midrib and have translucent windows the length of the top of the leaf. The windows allow light to penetrate to the interior of the leaf tissue, just as they do on *Haworthia truncata*. *Peperomia ferreyrae* grows well in containers. It has a shallow root system (typical of peperomias), and so is well suited to shallow pots and planters. Foliage is arranged in whorls along lime green stems. As they lengthen, stems may bend under their own weight. You may allow them to trail, or, if you prefer to keep your plant compact and upright, prune regularly. Repeated pruning will result in a woody stem; in fact, *P. ferreyrae* can be used for bonsai if you're into plant bondage. This is a trouble-free, drought-tolerant plant.

LIGHT   Grow in part to full sun. Inadequate light will result in weak stems.

WATER   Water when the top inch of potting mix is dry. During active growth this may be once a week; in winter it may be once every two weeks. Overwatering may cause lower foliage to drop and eventually result in root rot (and plant death).

TEMPERATURE   Grow in average household temperatures.

SOIL   Pot in a soilless potting mix or a combination of two parts soilless mix to one-part cactus mix.

FERTILIZATION   Feed with a half-strength fertilizer solution every other week during active growth.

PROPAGATION   Propagate from stem cuttings. Allow them to callus for several days before planting.

WINNING ATTRIBUTES   I confess to a fondness for many peperomias, but *Peperomia ferreyrae* is especially noteworthy. Its unusual leaf shape, light colored foliage, and petite stature make it an excellent addition to a collection of miniature succulents.

*Peperomia
ferreyrae*

Pilea involucrata 'Silver Tree'

FRIENDSHIP PLANT

Urticaceae

Pilea involucrata is native to the tropical rainforests of Peru, where it grows in hot, humid conditions. In nature it gets dappled light and grows to about 12 inches tall. *Pilea involucrata* 'Silver Tree' is a cultivar with especially vibrant markings: almost black leaf margins are offset by bright silver centers. Foliage is ovate, quilted, and 1 to 2 inches long. This plant branches freely and has a mounding growth habit; in containers it may be 8 to 12 inches tall. *Pilea involucrata* 'Silver Tree' requires a tropical environment to thrive. It is an excellent terrarium plant, and in a greenhouse or conservatory may be used as a ground cover or to underplant specimen trees. Older plants may become leggy, and tall stems may bend under their own weight. Regular pruning keeps the shape compact and attractive and also provides cuttings for propagating new plants. You may find *P. involucrata* 'Silver Tree' sold as *P. spruceana* 'Silver Tree' or *P.* 'Silver Tree'.

LIGHT   Indirect light is best. Direct sun bleaches the foliage.

WATER   Water when the top inch of potting mix is dry. *Pilea involucrata* 'Silver Tree' requires elevated humidity. Grow it on a drywell, in a terrarium, or in a greenhouse.

TEMPERATURE   Keep above 65˚F (18˚C).

Pilea involucrata
'Silver Tree'

SOIL   Grow in a quick-draining, soil-based mix.

FERTILIZATION   Feed at half strength every other week during the growing season.

PROPAGATION   *Pilea involucrata* 'Silver Tree' is very easily propagated from tip cuttings. You may also pin a stem (still attached to the parent plant) to the surface of some potting mix and allow it to root this way.

WINNING ATTRIBUTES   The foliage of *Pilea involucrata* 'Silver Tree' is exceptional. Individually its colors are eye-catching; together they make a strong statement.

Pinguicula ehlserserac × *P. oblingoloba*

BUTTERWORT

Lentibulariaceae

Pinguicula ehlserserac × *P. oblingoloba* is a manmade hybrid. *Pinguicula* species are native to many parts of the world, in both temperate and tropical climates. Their native habitats are invariably poor soils that provide little nutrition, but the dearth of soil nutrients is balanced by their ability to trap and digest insects. *Pinguicula ehlserserac* × *P. oblingoloba* is a small plant, catching mostly fruit flies, fungus gnats, and other small insects on its petite (less than 1 inch long), elliptical leaves. Neat, low-growing rosettes of foliage are pale, yellowish green. Leaves are slimy to the touch due to the digestive enzymes that cover them. Inquisitive insects light on foliage and are caught in the sticky sliminess, then gradually digested. From spring through fall, bright purple-magenta flowers are held on stalks 8 inches above the foliage. Flowers are about 1.5 inches long, with two petals pointing upward, three pointing downward, and a prominent spur on the back. This plant is easier to grow in the home than many other carnivorous plants, if you keep the soil adequately moist and humidity sufficiently high. It is an excellent insect suppressant in terrariums where fungus gnats may be a problem.

LIGHT   Grow in bright indirect light or part sun.

WATER   This plant grows best when the potting mix is kept consistently wet. Since foliage quickly covers the surface of the potting mix, it may be difficult to determine manually when the mix is starting to dry out. Place your pot in a shallow bowl or saucer of water and keep the saucer constantly filled. This ensures that your potting mix will always be moist and also elevates humidity.

TEMPERATURE   Regular household temperatures are fine.

SOIL Grow in a soilless mix or in a combination of four parts peat moss and one part sand.

FERTILIZATION Like most carnivorous plants, *Pinguicula ehlserserac × P. oblingoloba* grows in poor soils. The plant supplements its nutrition by digesting the insect bodies that collect on its sticky leaves. If your plant does not catch insects, you should feed at half strength twice during the growing season.

PROPAGATION *Pinguicula ehlerserac × P. oblingoloba* is shallow-rooted and spreads quickly. As rosettes of foliage spread across the pot, they may grow over the pot's edge and fall off. Place individual rosettes on top of wet potting mix and press into the mix, making contact between the roots and potting medium. Or, remove individual leaves with a bit of stem attached, allow them to callus for a few days, then lay the leaf on top of the potting mix. Keep warm and very humid while new plantlets develop.

Pinguicula ehlerserac
× P. oblingoloba

WINNING ATTRIBUTES This is a very cool plant. Flowers are vibrant magenta, the leaves act as a natural insect suppressant, and you can never overwater it. It's a rapid grower and very easy to divide, if you'd like to share the wealth.

Piper ornatum

ORNAMENTAL PEPPER

Piperaceae

Piper ornatum is native to the Indonesian island of Sulawesi, where it grows both as a scrambling ground cover and as a climber. It grows in dappled light and high humidity. Stems may be 10 to 15 feet long. Leaves are puckered, highly glossy, heart-shaped, and 2 to 4 inches long. Variegation is exceptional: a complex, mottled pattern of green, pink, and silver. The undersides of the leaves are purplish-red. *Piper ornatum* rarely flowers indoors. This is a high-humidity plant and grows best in a greenhouse, conservatory room, or on a drywell. It is also an excellent terrarium plant. The leaf pattern is finely mottled, like a pointillist painting. Grow it as a climbing or trailing vine for vertical interest or as a groundcover.

LIGHT Grow in bright indirect light for optimal leaf variegation.

WATER Water when the top half-inch of potting mix is dry. Elevate humidity as much as possible.

Piper ornatum

TEMPERATURE This plant is a heat-lover. Keep it above 60°F (16°C).

SOIL Grow in a soil-based potting mix.

FERTILIZATION Feed at half strength every other week during the growing season.

PROPAGATION Propagate from stem cuttings or by pinning a stem to the surface of the potting mix and allowing it to root while still attached to the parent plant. Once roots have formed, you may separate the stem and pot it up on its own.

WINNING ATTRIBUTES *Piper ornatum* has an exceptionally versatile growth habit. It can be grown in a hanging basket and allowed to trail. It can also be trained as an upright or planted as a ground cover under large specimen trees. Its beautifully variegated leaves are intricately detailed and create a striking mosaic.

Platycerium bifurcatum

STAGHORN FERN

Polypodiaceae

Platycerium bifurcatum is native to Australia and several South Pacific islands where it grows as an epiphyte in tropical rain forests. It is most remarkable for its two different types of leaves. The upright, fertile fronds can be 2 to 3 feet long and are shaped like stag's antlers, deeply lobed at the ends. Fertile fronds are covered with a gray fuzz, giving them a soft, silvery color. (Do not rub off the fuzzy covering.) Spores form on the backside of the tips of these fronds. Sterile fronds at the base of the plant clasp the branch or tree trunk where *P. bifurcatum* perches. These fronds anchor the epiphytic fern in place. They emerge pliable and pale green, then age to a parchment-like, medium brown. Sterile fronds (sometimes called mulch fronds) flare outward at the top; debris falling from the forest canopy catches in the pocket and provides nutrition for the fern. *Platycerium bifurcatum* does very well indoors where it can be grown in a traditional pot, in a hanging basket, or bark-mounted. Taller fronds may lean outward as they grow, giving the plant a graceful, spreading shape. Scale and mealybugs may occasionally be pests.

LIGHT Bright indirect light is best. Direct sunlight may burn its leaves or cause foliage to become pale.

WATER Do not overwater this plant; it is more drought-tolerant than many ferns. The fuzzy gray leaf covering slows the loss of water via transpiration, and mulch leaves reduce moisture loss from the surface of the potting mix. If your

Platycerium bifurcatum

plant is bark-mounted, soak the mount (and mulch fronds) in a large bowl of water once a week for 15 minutes.

TEMPERATURE Average household temperatures are fine for *P. bifurcatum*. It will tolerate winter temperatures as low as 50°F (10°C).

SOIL Grow in a soilless mix. As an epiphyte it requires a lightweight, fast draining potting medium. *Platycerium bifurcatum* can also be bark-mounted as a hanging specimen.

FERTILIZATION You may never need to feed *Platycerium bifurcatum*. As new mulch fronds grow, the old, interior leaves decay into compost. They are incorporated into the potting mix, providing nutrients.

PROPAGATION Propagate from spores or by division.

WINNING ATTRIBUTES This plant has excellent structure; it is imposing, upright, and spreading, yet not stiff. The gray-green foliage adds color variety to the indoor garden. Its two different types of leaves are especially interesting. *Platycerium bifurcatum* may be hung or potted, according to your placement needs. This is a low maintenance fern and does not require elevated humidity.

Plumbago auriculata

CAPE LEADWORT

Plumbaginaceae

Plumbago auriculata is native to South Africa where it grows in hot, dry conditions as an evergreen, shrubby climber. As a young plant the shape is bushy; as it ages, the plant produces long climbing stems up to 12 feet long. Maximum height is about 6 feet; unstaked branches bend to the ground. Leaves are elliptical, medium green, and about 2 inches long. They have small stipules at the leaf base, and foliage has a downward curl. Flowers are borne in terminal clusters. Individual blooms are sky blue with a thin, darker blue line down the center of each petal. Flowers are five-petalled, about an inch wide, and have long (2-inch) floral tubes. There is a white-flowered variety, but it is not nearly as lovely. Pinch *P. auriculata* to encourage branching. This plant blooms on new growth, so prune according to your needs. If you want to keep your plant compact and floriferous, cut back hard after flowering has finished. If you'd rather grow your *P. auriculata* as a tall vining specimen, prune only the side branches until the desired height is reached.

LIGHT   This is a high light plant; give it full sun for lots of bloom.

*Plumbago
auriculata*

WATER Let the top half-inch of potting mix dry out between waterings. Foliage will wilt and fall off if the plant gets too dry. It may revive if caught in time, but flowering will be inhibited.

TEMPERATURE Most of the year, average household temperatures are fine. If possible, give your plant cooler winter temperatures (to about 50°F [10°C]). This is not necessary but will stimulate bloom.

SOIL Grow in a quick-draining, soil-based potting mix.

FERTILIZATION Feed with a bloom-booster once a month during the growing season.

PROPAGATION Propagate from stem cuttings. Pieces should be neither woody nor entirely young and soft. Use rooting hormone, bottom heat, and elevated humidity.

WINNING ATTRIBUTES The flowers of *Plumbago auriculata* are plentiful, delicate and a lovely pale blue. Its form is highly adaptable; it can be trained along an upright form for a vertical column of bloom, or kept small if your growing space is limited.

Plumeria rubra

FRANGIPANI

Apocynaceae

Plumeria rubra is a tree that grows to 25 feet in full sun in its native Central America. It branches freely, and its criss-crossing, mottled gray branches create a complex structure. Leaves are dark green, glossy, large, elliptical, and grow up to 16 inches long and 4 inches wide. Venation is white and nicely patterned. This plant is native to areas where there are distinct dry and rainy seasons, and *P. rubra* has adapted accordingly. During the dry season, it drops all its leaves and stores water in its thick, gray trunks and stems. It blooms as soon as the rainy season starts, usually before the tree has leafed out again. Flowers are borne in clusters at the ends of branches, and a plentiful display of large flowers on a leafless tree is a wonderful sight to see. Individual blooms are about 2 inches wide, with five flared petals. Flowers come in many colors: white, yellow, pink, or red. They are also wonderfully fragrant; the scent varies with the cultivar. *Plumeria rubra* grows well in containers. Plumerias hybridize readily, and numerous hybrids are sometimes difficult to identify. *Plumeria rubra* blooms best when given a temperature drop in winter.

LIGHT This is a full sun plant. It must have at least six to eight hours of direct sun in order to thrive and bloom.

WATER Do not overwater this plant. In summer, elevate humidity and water when the top inch of potting mix is dry. If you give it a cool winter rest, let the top 2 inches of potting mix dry out between waterings.

TEMPERATURE Most of the year, grow *Plumeria rubra* in average household temperatures. In winter, give it a rest at 50°F to 55°F (10°C to 13°C); plants won't go completely dormant but will drop some leaves. *Plumeria rubra* will survive temperatures as low as 40°F (4°C), but will drop all its leaves and take longer to resume active growth. A temperature drop in winter encourages subsequent flowering.

SOIL Grow in a quick-draining soilless or soil-based mix.

FERTILIZATION Do not feed until it has finished flowering. Then, use a low nitrogen, high phosphorous fertilizer every other week until leaves start to fall.

PROPAGATION Propagate from stem cuttings. Cut a nonflowering stem up to 1 foot long, and allow it to callus for a week or two before potting it up on its own.

WINNING ATTRIBUTES The flowers are absolutely gorgeous and exotically fragrant. Even as a young plant its structure and textured bark are dramatic. This tree exemplifies the tropics.

Plumeria rubra
'Bridal White'.
Photo © Global Book
Publishing Photo
Library

Polypodium aureum

RABBIT'S FOOT FERN

Polypodiaceae

Polypodium aureum is native to southern North America, Central, and South America where it may be epiphytic or terrestrial. In nature you are as likely to see it rooted to a tree trunk as rooted on the forest floor. A thick rhizome (about 1 inch in diameter) is covered with reddish-brown scales, giving it a furry appearance. Fronds grow from the top of the rhizome, emerging with a classic fiddlehead shape. Roots grow from the rhizome's underside. Fronds are blue-green, pinnate, and about 36 inches long. Spores form on the back of mature fronds, creating a geometric pattern. This fern grows exceptionally well in containers, where the furry feet are both visually appealing and easy to touch. Many ferns are difficult houseplants, since they require high humidity, but *P. aureum* is easy and adaptable. It tolerates cooler temperatures (to about 50°F [10°C]) if watering is also reduced, and looks especially fine when exhibited on a tall fern stand. If you'd like to get children interested in horticulture, a footed fern is an excellent place to start.

LIGHT Grows well in bright, indirect light; an eastern or northern window is best. In direct sun, foliage will yellow.

Polypodium aureum

WATER   This fern is surprisingly drought-tolerant. Water when the top inch of potting mix is dry.

TEMPERATURE   Grow in average household temperatures.

SOIL   Grow in either a soil-based or soilless mix.

FERTILIZATION   Feed at half strength every other week during the growing season.

PROPAGATION   Propagate from spore, from division, or by taking a cutting of the rhizome. Pin a piece of rhizome to moist potting mix and enclose in a clear plastic bag to elevate humidity. Roots and shoots should start to form in four to six weeks.

WINNING ATTRIBUTES   This fern does well in average household humidity. It is a large, impressive specimen, and its beautiful blue-green foliage adds an interesting shade to your interior landscape. The thick, furry rhizomes are an extra bonus.

Polyscias crispata

CHICKEN GIZZARD ARALIA

Polyscias fruticosa

MING ARALIA

Araliaceae

Polyscias crispata is native to Australasia where it grows in full to part sun. Trees can reach 15 feet tall with greenish-brown, gray speckled stems. Leaves are shiny, pinnate, and highly ornamental. Stems often need to be staked when they exceed 4 feet. *Polyscias crispata* is not the easiest plant to grow indoors but is definitely worth a try. It requires high light, high humidity, and precise watering. When well grown, a potted specimen is impressive with its glossy foliage and ornamental stems. Be on the lookout for aphids, which may enjoy the tender young shoots.

Polyscias fruticosa is native to Polynesia where it grows in part sun and may be 25 feet tall. Its leaves are very finely cut, pinnate to tripinnate. Leaflets resemble feathery parsley as they emerge. This tree is truly lovely: soft, graceful, and imposing when it reaches specimen size. In containers, trees rarely exceed 7 feet high, and since they are slow growers, large specimens can be expensive. Buy a medium-sized tree and help it grow; this is a plant you'll keep for years. Tall branches can be allowed to bend under their own weight, giving the plant a vase-like shape, or pruned to allow the tree to stand straight. Both polyscias grow well in containers,

Polyscias crispata

Polyscias fruticosa

especially when tightly potted. They sulk for a while after repotting; do so only when necessary. These plants require constant warmth and high humidity or they will drop leaves. In dry air, polyscias may get spider mites.

LIGHT Indoors, both grow well in bright indirect light or full or part sun.

WATER Water when the top half-inch to 1 inch of potting mix is dry to the touch. Roots should not be kept consistently wet or allowed to get overly dry between waterings. The balance is tricky but not impossible to find. Elevate humidity for both polyscias; grow on a drywell, or in a humid spot like a bathroom.

TEMPERATURE   Do not let temperatures drop below 65°F (18°C), or both polyscias will drop foliage. Cold drafts can do substantial damage, and prolonged exposure to temperatures below 50°F (10°C) may be fatal.

SOIL   Grow in a soilless mix.

FERTILIZATION   Feed both at half strength every other week during the growing season.

PROPAGATION   Propagate from stem cuttings. Remove the lower leaves before potting up the cuttings.

WINNING ATTRIBUTES   Both are beautiful trees with superb foliage. *Polyscias crispata* is bold and glossy with lovely bark and an interesting leaf shape. *Polyscias fruticosa* is equally impressive with a more delicate leaf. And here's my favorite thing about this plant: the smell. Touch the foliage to your nose and breathe deeply. It's a wonderful smell…sweet, spicy, and utterly unique.

Portulacaria afra 'Variegata'

Portulacaria afra 'Variegata'

RAINBOW BUSH

Portulacaeae

Portulacaria afra is native to southern Africa where it can reach 12 feet tall. It grows in hot, dry, sunny conditions and is an evergreen shrub with numerous twisted branches. Leaves are small (up to a half-inch in diameter), oval, smooth, succulent, and sessile. The straight species has lime green leaves; the cultivar has cream-colored variegation. Branches are segmented and a tawny reddish brown. *Portulacaria afra* 'Variegata' bears clusters of small pink flowers in nature, but doesn't usually flower indoors. It does well in containers, where it rarely grows taller than a few feet. Pinch growing tips regularly to encourage branching. Its dwarf tree shape creates a bonsai effect, without the agita. *Portulacaria afra* 'Variegata' is drought-tolerant and pest free.

LIGHT   Indoors *Portulacaria afra* 'Variegata' grows well in either part sun or bright indirect light. In high light, the foliage may be tinged with pink.

WATER   Allow the top inch of potting mix to dry out between waterings.

TEMPERATURE   Grow in regular household temperatures.

SOIL   Grow in a soilless or cactus mix.

FERTILIZATION   Feed once a month during the growing season.

PROPAGATION   Propagate from stem cuttings. Allow them to callus for a week before potting them up.

WINNING ATTRIBUTES   This succulent offers variegated foliage, lovely stem color and structure, and a tree-like shape in a tiny, manageable package. It is an excellent addition to a collection of miniatures.

Quisqualis indica

RANGOON CREEPER

Combretaceae

Quisqualis indica is native to New Guinea, the Philippines, and Malaysia where it is an evergreen vine that can grow to be 50 feet long. (Don't worry, it will be considerably smaller in your home.) Leaves are elliptical, medium green, about 6 inches long, and covered with white or brownish hairs above and below. Flowers are highly fragrant, five-petalled, trumpet-shaped, and 1 to 2 inches in diameter. They

Quisqualis indica

vary in color as they mature, opening white, turning pink, and deepening to red. Blooms are held on long peduncles (4 to 6 inches) and form a loose cluster that may show flowers of different colors at the same time. This plant grows well in containers. Young specimens have a shrubby growth habit. As they age they produce vining stems that grow to about 12 feet long. Train *Q. indica* on an upright form; use care to avoid the curved spines that grow along the vine. This plant is more fragrant at night, so put it someplace where you can appreciate its perfume.

LIGHT This is a full sun plant; give it at least six hours of sun for good bloom.

WATER Water when the top half-inch of potting mix is dry.

TEMPERATURE Grow in average household temperatures.

SOIL Grow in a soil-based mix.

FERTILIZATION Feed with a bloom-booster at half strength every other week during the growing season. Overfeeding will produce foliage at the expense of flowers.

PROPAGATION Propagate from stem cuttings or by pinning a piece of vine to moist potting mix, then separating it from the parent plant when roots have formed.

WINNING ATTRIBUTES This is an athletic vine that will give you lots of coverage very quickly. Its flowers are exceptionally lovely, varied in hue, and fragrant. *Quisqualis indica* is an excellent plant for a large, sunny window.

Rhapis excelsa

LADY PALM

Aracaceae

Rhapis excelsa is a clumping palm native to China. In nature it grows to 10 feet tall. This plant spreads by underground rhizomes; all the plants in a clump are clones. Its rough stems are covered with a dark brown fiber. They are nonbranching and bear fan-shaped fronds on stiff leaf stalks about 12 to 18 inches long. Fronds are composed of five to nine linear leaflets about 6 inches long; their blunt ends look like they've been cut with pinking shears. Foliage is an exceptionally glossy dark green, and the leaf surface is gently pleated. *Rhapis excelsa* is most attractive when grown in elevated humidity. In dry air, leaf tips turn brown and should be trimmed. Try trimming with pinking shears to maintain their original leaf shape. Indoors, *R. excelsa* does well in containers. Its unusual leaf shape and dark color make it an interesting specimen plant, perfect for a partly shaded position. Even a small plant is regal. It is a slow-growing palm, but will eventually reach 6 feet. Large specimens can be expensive.

LIGHT Grow in bright indirect light. While it will survive for a while in dim light, it will not prosper. If you have only a northern window, consider supplementing natural light with a grow bulb. Full sun will cause foliage to yellow, then brown.

WATER Water when the top half-inch of potting mix is dry. For specimens in large pots, allow the top inch of potting mix to dry out between waterings. If you give your plant a winter rest at cooler temperatures, allow the top 2 inches of mix to dry between waterings. Elevate humidity when possible.

TEMPERATURE Average household temperatures are adequate. It can tolerate temperatures as low as 45°F (7°C).

SOIL Grow in a soil-based potting mix.

FERTILIZATION Feed once a month during active growth.

PROPAGATION *Rhapis excelsa* produces suckers from its roots. Separate a sucker (with some roots attached) from the parent plant and pot it up on its own. *Rhapis excelsa* can be grown from seed, but it is a slow process, taking several months to germinate.

WINNING ATTRIBUTES The shape of this palm's fronds are unusual: graceful but with a stiff structure. It tolerates cooler temperatures and lower light than many palms, making it a useful plant for a drafty position without direct sun. A well-grown *Rhapis excelsa* of any size, with pinked leaf ends intact, is an impressive sight.

Rhapis excelsa

Rhipsalis baccifera

MISTLETOE CACTUS

Rhipsalis pilocarpa

Cactaceae

Rhipsalis species are native to Central and South America where they grow as epiphytic cacti. They have photosynthetic stems that may be smooth and tubular, or flat and spiky. Flowers are daisy-shaped and white, cream, or pink. These are followed by berries that may be white, red, or black. *Rhipsalis baccifera* is native to Sri Lanka and Africa and is the only cactus native to a location outside of the Americas. Its slim, smooth, freely branching stems form a curtain as they cascade from the pot. Small white flowers are followed by numerous, decorative, white berries that last for up to a year. *Rhipsalis baccifera* can be grown in a hanging basket or mounted to grow epiphytically. Either way, you'll want to run your fingers through its thick clusters of slim stems. *Rhipsalis pilocarpa* is native to Brazil. It is a graceful, petite species with slim, branching stems about an eighth-inch in diameter. This is the only *Rhipsalis* whose stems are covered with soft, short white hairs. White flowers are 0.5 to 1 inch wide and followed by rosy red berries, a quarter-inch in diameter. This plant is best displayed as a hanging specimen; because its stems are so delicate, you can see through them to whatever lies behind. In addition, it is perpetually either in bloom or in berry.

LIGHT   These are understory plants and grow best in bright indirect light to part sun. If light is inadequate, the plant will not flower and fruit.

WATER   *Rhipsalis* species need more frequent watering than desert cacti. Water when the top inch of potting mix is dry. They grow well in average household humidity or in the elevated humidity of a greenhouse.

TEMPERATURE   Grow in average household temperatures.

SOIL   Both rhipsalis may be bark-mounted or potted in a combination of three parts soilless mix and one part fine-grained fir bark.

FERTILIZATION   Feed with a half-strength fertilizer once a month during active growth.

PROPAGATION   Easily propagated from stem cuttings. Allow the cuttings to callus for a week before planting them.

Rhipsalis pilocarpa

This *Rhipsalis baccifera* grows mounted on an epiphyte tree.

WINNING ATTRIBUTES I never met a *Rhipsalis* I didn't like. *Rhipsalis baccifera* combines smooth, touchable stems with long-lasting white berries. *Rhipsalis pilocarpa* has showy white flowers and hairy stems. Both have a graceful growth habit, with cascading, branching stems. These plants are low maintenance and trouble free.

Rhoicissus capensis

OAK LEAF IVY

Vitaceae

Rhoicissus capensis is a vine native to southern Africa. It climbs via tendrils, has wiry stems, and is a large plant, growing to about 15 feet. Leaves are bright medium green, approximately 6 to 8 inches long, and heart-shaped, with scalloped edges similar to those of an oak leaf. New foliage is pale green and darkens gradually, creating a subtle variety of hues on a single plant. Veins are pale green, and foliage is tinged with a rust color underneath. The root system includes large nodules that store water, making the plant very drought-tolerant. Overwatering causes foliage to yellow and drop. *Rhoicissus capensis* grows very well in containers. In a hanging basket it will fill a large window. In a standard pot it requires strong support to climb; this is not a modest vine. Pinch regularly to encourage branching and promote a bushy shape. *Rhoicissus capensis* responds well to pruning. If an older plant becomes leggy, don't be afraid to cut it back hard. It may occasionally get mealybugs.

LIGHT   Grow in indirect light. In a bright eastern window it will grow rapidly; in direct sun foliage will fade.

WATER   This is a drought-tolerant plant. Allow the top inch of potting mix to dry out between waterings. In a large pot (greater than 8 inches in diameter) the plant may need water only once every two weeks.

Rhoicissus capensis

TEMPERATURE Tolerates temperatures as low as 50°F (10°C), and also does well in average household temperatures.

SOIL Grow in either a soilless or soil-based mix.

FERTILIZATION Feed at half strength every other week during the growing season.

PROPAGATION Propagate from stem cuttings with rooting hormone, bottom heat, and elevated humidity. These cuttings are slow to start, so be patient. Since it's something of a rarity in the marketplace, starting a plant from cuttings may be the only way you'll acquire one.

WINNING ATTRIBUTES *Rhoicissus capensis* is a wonderful plant—the leaves are beautifully shaped, the color is fresh and bright, and the plant grows rapidly enough to fill a window or cover a pyramid form very quickly. Because it grows well in a variety of light intensities and tolerates cool temperatures, it is a useful plant in many different growing situations.

Ricinis communis

CASTOR OIL PLANT

Euphorbiaceae

Ricinis communis is probably native to the Middle East and Eastern Africa; it has naturalized widely throughout the tropics, so pinpointing its place of origin is diffi-cult. Leaves are palmate and huge, 1 to 2 feet in diameter. Each leaf has 5 to 12 lobes and is held almost perpendicular to the plant's central stem. Foliage is green with red veins; several cultivars have spectacular, deep red foliage and bright red, spiny seeds. Flowers are small and relatively insignificant. Most people grow this plant for its outstanding foliage and seeds. When heat-treated and purified, seeds are used to produce castor oil, a laxative. All parts of this plant are extremely poi-sonous, so don't grow it if you have nibblers in your household. It grows well in containers but requires a large pot in order to reach its full height. A 17-inch pot should be adequate. Treat it as a short-lived plant. Older specimens lose their lower leaves and aren't attractive. Since *R. communis* grows so quickly from seed, start new plants periodically so you always have a prime example on hand.

LIGHT Grow in full sun. In anything less, the plant will not reach its full height, nor will it flower profusely.

WATER Don't let this plant dry out in active growth. Water when the surface of the potting mix feels dry.

Ricinis communis

TEMPERATURE Keep warm, above 65°F (18°C).

SOIL Grow in a soil-based mix.

FERTILIZATION Feed every other week at full strength. Start feeding when the young plant is about 8 inches tall.

PROPAGATION *Ricinis communis* grows easily and quickly from seed. Soak the seed for 24 hours before planting. In a single year it can grow to be 10 feet tall.

WINNING ATTRIBUTES This is a large, impressive plant; it makes a strong statement and single-handedly creates a jungle effect. The combination of size and color is perfect for a greenhouse, conservatory, or large sunroom. Dwarf cultivars (a mere 6 feet tall) are better for smaller spaces.

Ruellia makoyana

MONKEY PLANT

Acanthaceae

Ruellia makoyana is a groundcover native to Brazil where it grows in humid environments with rich soils and dappled light. This is a creeping plant; stems branch freely and can grow to be 2 feet long. It has remarkable foliage: leaves are elliptical and about 3 inches long. They are olive green with red veins and a large silvery-cream stripe down the center. This plant blooms in winter, producing pink or red flowers in the leaf axils. Flowers are trumpet-shaped, 2 inches long, and about 2.5 inches wide. After flowering finishes, give *R. makoyana* a rest by watering less frequently. Indoors, *R. makoyana* can be planted at the base of a specimen tree, as a ground cover in a terrarium, or in a hanging basket where its creeping stems will trail over the edge. It is sometimes prone to aphids, so check the tender tips of the plant each time you water.

Ruellia makoyana

LIGHT   Grow in the bright indirect light of an eastern window or under fluorescent lights.

WATER   This plant should not dry out between waterings. Water when the surface of the potting mix feels dry except during the rest period, when you should allow the top inch of potting mix to dry out. Elevated humidity is recommended; grow this plant on a drywell or in a terrarium.

TEMPERATURE   Grow above 60°F (16°C).

SOIL   Grow in a soil-based mix.

FERTILIZATION   Feed at half strength every other week while the plant is in active growth. After flowering has finished, do not feed until new leaves appear in spring.

PROPAGATION   Propagate *Ruellia makoyana* from stem cuttings or pin a trailing stem to the surface of potting mix until roots form along the stem. Then, separate from the parent plant and pot on its own.

WINNING ATTRIBUTES   This is a pretty little plant, whose bright flowers complement the highly decorative foliage. Its creeping growth habit makes it useful as a hanging basket or as a groundcover.

Russelia equisetiformis

CORAL FOUNTAIN

Scrophulariaceae

Russelia equisetiformis is native to Mexico where it grows to about 3 feet tall and 3 feet wide. Stems are slim, green, wiry, and mostly leafless; they lean gracefully as they grow taller. Its specific epithet comes from the plant's resemblance to *Equisetum* (aka horsetail). Flowers are bright red, tubular, and plentiful; each flower is about an inch long. In nature, this plant tolerates both wet and dry soils, as well as salt water environments. In containers, *R. equisetiformis* grows best on the dry side. It is not always easy to find but is sometimes sold as an annual. If you see it, buy it, and try growing it indoors. It can be planted to cascade over the side of a large standing container or be grown in a hanging basket. If you choose to summer this plant outdoors, it will attract hummingbirds.

Russelia equisetiformis

LIGHT Grow in full to part sun. Brighter sun results in more flowers.

WATER Water when the top inch of potting mix is dry.

TEMPERATURE Keep above 50°F (10°C).

SOIL Grow in a soilless mix.

FERTILIZATION *Russelia equisetiformis* grows well in poor soil; do not overfeed this plant. Fertilize at half strength once a month during the growing season.

PROPAGATION Propagate by division or from cuttings.

WINNING ATTRIBUTES The structure of this plant is quite unusual. Slim, mostly leafless stems are impressive but not massive; they add layers of depth to your interior landscape. A liberal covering of brilliant, red flowers makes this an eye-catcher for a sunny spot.

Saintpaulia optimara 'Tradition'

AFRICAN VIOLET

Gesneriaceae

Saintpaulia ionantha is the familiar African violet native to Tanzania. It is a shallow-rooted perennial that grows in high relative humidity in the shade of trees. Its stems and leaves are somewhat succulent, and the plant can tolerate moderate drought. Leaves are hairy, and must be kept dry; water on the foliage may leave spots. *Saintpaulia ionantha* is a nice beginner's plant, but *S. optimara* 'Tradition' is a knock-out hybrid, worthy of any houseplant collection. Its velvety leaves are almost entirely pink, flecked with an occasional spot of green. Flowers are also pink and blend in with the foliage. Multiple blooms are held on branching stalks, which grow from leaf axils. Saintpaulias grow best in elevated humidity. Grow them on drywells and with groups of plants. Over time, saintpaulias lose their lower leaves, exposing a leafless stem that isn't attractive. You may carefully repot your plant, burying the stem and adjusting the level at which your plant is potted. Take your saintpaulia out of its pot and remove a section from the bottom of the root ball equal to the length

Saintpaulia optimara 'Tradition'

of stem you're going to bury. (Leave at least half of the root ball intact.) Replace the plant in its container so that the bottom leaves are just above the rim of the pot. Fill in around the roots with potting mix, to just below where leaves grow from the stem. This process is more traumatic to the plant than a regular repotting, so give your saintpaulia elevated humidity by putting it in a small greenhouse or large clear plastic bag. After a few weeks, move it back into its usual spot.

LIGHT Grow in bright indirect light. It requires brighter light than green-leafed saintpaulias. In low light, the balance of pink and green variegation will shift. The plant will remain attractive, but foliage will be primarily green with pink and/or cream variegation concentrated at the edges.

WATER Water when the top half-inch of potting mix is dry. Be careful not to allow standing water to sit on the plant's leaves as this can cause spots. You can water carefully from above, or water from below, allowing water to be drawn up through the entire volume of potting mix. Pour any excess from the saucer.

TEMPERATURE Grow between 60°F and 80°F (16°C and 27°C).

SOIL Use a soilless mix or a special African violet mix.

FERTILIZATION Feed with a flowering plant food at half strength every other week during active growth.

PROPAGATION *Saintpaulia* species can be propagated by planting a leaf in soilless potting mix. See chapter 6 for instructions.

WINNING ATTRIBUTES This extraordinary hybrid looks unreal. Its leaves are so wildly variegated that the flowers, while pretty, are superfluous. A single pot makes a bold statement in the interior landscape. Don't dismiss all saintpaulias because you think they're boring; this is *not* your grandmother's African violet.

Sansevieria hyacinthoides 'Mason Congo'
Sansevieria trifasciata 'Bantel's Sensation'

Dracenaceae

Sansevieria hyacinthoides is native to southeastern Africa where it is an aggressive grower in sunny, dry conditions. In nature its leaves are 3 to 6 feet tall and up to 3 inches wide. Foliage is stiff, upright, and mottled with a gray-white pattern; leaf margins are reddish brown. Flowers are borne in spikes 2 to 3 feet tall and are quite fragrant. *Sansevieria hyacinthoides* is not an unusual plant, but S. *hyacinthoides*

'Mason Congo' is a highly coveted cultivar with leaves shaped like oars; the broadest part of the leaf may be 8 to 10 inches wide. Foliage is 2 to 3 feet tall and maintains a subtle variegation similar to that of the species. This cultivar does not flower readily indoors and grows much more slowly than the species, producing a maximum of one or two new leaves per year. A large specimen is an old specimen. It is pest free, low maintenance, and an impressive, sculptural plant. *Sansevieria trifasciata* is native to arid regions of Nigeria and is among the most ubiquitous of houseplants. In contrast, *S. trifasciata* 'Bantel's Sensation' is a rare and unusual sport of the very common *S. trifasciata* 'Laurentii'. The leaves of *S. trifasciata* 'Bantel's Sensation' grow 18 to 24 inches tall and 1 inch wide. Foliage is stiff, linear,

Sansevieria hyacinthoides 'Mason Congo'   *Sansevieria trifasciata* 'Bantel's Sensation'

pointed, and has bold, white margins with green centers. Leaves grow in tight rosettes. *Sansevieria trifasciata* 'Bantel's Sensation' is a patented plant, created by chemically treating *S. trifasciata* 'Laurentii'. As a result, it cannot be propagated by cuttings, which will not come true. (In addition, it is a reluctant bloomer, so seed is rare.) Instead, it reverts to the original, yellow-margined plant. This, combined with the fact that *S. trifasciata* 'Bantel's Sensation' is a slow grower, makes it difficult to locate. Commercial growers tend to produce what they can sell most profitably. If someone offers to part with a division of *S. trifasciata* 'Bantel's Sensation', say "yes, thank you." This is a lovely, graceful, trouble-free plant.

LIGHT   Both these sansevierias tolerate a wide range of light conditions. Grow them in bright indirect light to part sun for most attractive foliage. To initiate bloom of *Sansevieria hyacinthoides* 'Mason Congo', grow it in full sun. I have never seen *S. trifasciata* 'Bantel's Sensation' in bloom.

WATER   Both of these plants are drought-tolerant; overwatering will kill them. Water when the top inch of potting mix is dry. Average household humidity is adequate.

TEMPERATURE   Grow both in normal household temperatures.

SOIL   A soilless mix is best.

FERTILIZATION   Feed both with a half-strength fertilizer once a month during active growth.

PROPAGATION   Propagate by division.

WINNING ATTRIBUTES   Each of these plants combines the low maintenance characteristics of the most common sansevieria with unique physical beauty. *Sansevieria hyacinthoides* 'Mason Congo' is a living sculpture with unusual, paddle-shaped foliage and subtle mottling. *Sansevieria trifasciata* 'Bantel's Sensation' offers strong variegation and tight rosettes of slim, upright foliage. Both are difficult to find but worth the search.

Sarracenia leucophylla 'Tarnok'

PITCHER PLANT
Sarraceniaceae

All members of the *Sarracenia* genus are native to eastern North America; they are not tropical plants, but many of them are well suited to indoor growing. In nature these carnivorous plants grow in full sun, in moist, poor soils. Modified leaves grow in the shape of pitchers and attract insects, which slide down the pitchers' slippery sides. The insects are then digested, providing additional nutrition to the plants. In nature, the pitchers of *Sarracenia leucophylla* can be 4 feet tall. The pitcher's lid is semi-erect and has wavy margins. *Sarracenia leucophylla* is capable of trapping and digesting large bees; *S. leucophylla* 'Tarnok' is a smaller cultivar

Sarracenia leucophylla
'Tarnok'

more suitable for home growing. Its pitchers grow to be 12 to 18 inches tall. They are white with a purple, netted pattern at the top, and gradually taper to a narrow, green base. This is a slim, upright specimen plant.

LIGHT   *Sarracenia leucophylla* 'Tarnok' is a full sun plant. In low light it will lose variegation.

WATER   Keep constantly moist and elevate humidity. Sit the pot in a shallow dish of water and don't let it dry out during the growing season. Change the water once a week. This will keep the roots damp and provide adequate humidity.

TEMPERATURE   *Sarracenia leucophylla* 'Tarnok' is not a tropical plant and tolerates temperatures in the 40°F (4°C) range. You may grow it in average household temperatures or allow it to go dormant in winter. If you do this, withhold fertilizer and reduce soil moisture. Take a dormant plant out of its saucer of water, and water the potting mix when the surface feels dry.

SOIL   Plant in long grain sphagnum peat moss, or in a mixture of one part soilless mix, one part peat moss, and one part long grain sphagnum moss.

FERTILIZATION   Feed with a half strength, acid plant fertilizer once a month during active growth.

PROPAGATION   Propagate by division.

WINNING ATTRIBUTES   *Sarracenia leucophylla* 'Tarnok' is an exotic, carnivorous plant with a unique growth habit and beautiful coloring. Because it tolerates lower temperatures, this is an excellent choice for a sunny spot that may be too drafty for most houseplants.

Saxifraga stolonifera 'Tricolor'

STRAWBERRY GERANIUM

Saxifragaceae

Saxifraga stolonifera is native to China and Japan. *Saxifraga stolonifera* 'Tricolor' is smaller than the straight species, with a more delicate growth habit. Foliage grows in neat rosettes, 4 to 6 inches in diameter. Leaves are rounded, somewhat hairy, and about 1 inch across. They have green centers, white edges, and leaf margins tinged pinkish-red; the undersides are also reddish. Flowers are small and pinkish-white. They are borne in loose panicles which extend about 6 inches above the rosette of foliage. The parent plant puts out stolons that produce plantlets. These can either be allowed to trail or be potted up and grown as new plants. Stolons are very thin, and easily damaged, so hang *S. stolonifera* 'Tricolor' where it will not be disturbed. This is a slow-growing plant.

LIGHT   A few hours of direct sun is required to maintain the reddish variegation of this cultivar. Grow in part sun; full sun will be too much.

WATER   Water when the top half-inch of potting mix is dry.

TEMPERATURE   Grows well in average household temperatures. It is more sensitive to low temperatures than the species and should not be allowed to get below 60°F (16°C). Above 70°F (21°C), the elevated humidity of a drywell or greenhouse is recommended.

SOIL   Pot in a quick-draining, soil-based potting mix. Add a layer of pebbles to the pot to assure good drainage.

FERTILIZATION   During active growth, feed once a month with a half-strength fertilizer solution.

PROPAGATION   Pot up plantlets to make new plants. Provide elevated humidity while they root by enclosing newly planted offsets in a clear plastic bag for several weeks. Alternatively, you can pin a plantlet to the surface of some potting mix and

Saxifraga stolonifera 'Tricolor'

allow it to root while still attached to the parent plant. In this case, elevated humidity is not required.

WINNING ATTRIBUTES The low, mounding growth habit of *Saxifraga stolonifera* 'Tricolor' is compact and attractive, and its highly variegated foliage is outstanding. It can be grown as a hanging basket or as a ground cover in terrariums or under large specimen trees.

Schefflera elegantissima

FALSE ARALIA

Araliaceae

Schefflera elegantissima is native to New Caledonia where it grows as a shrub or small tree in partial sun. It can reach 10 to 20 feet in nature. Leaves are finely cut and palmate with widely toothed margins. Each leaf is comprised of 7 to 10 leaflets. Foliage is dark coppery green; there are also variegated cultivars with white markings on the leaves. This is a highly ornamental plant and does well in containers. Because it is somewhat tricky to grow, large specimens are rare and expensive, but with constant warmth and humidity, *S. elegantissima* makes an impressive indoor tree of about 6 feet. It has an upright growth habit and does not branch readily. The overall effect is delicate. Even a large plant appears graceful and not massive. Watch for leaf drop and spider mites under dry conditions.

LIGHT Grow in bright indirect light. An eastern window is best. A western window with a sheer curtain is also acceptable.

WATER *Schefflera elegantissima* is tricky. It must have elevated humidity; if you can't give it a greenhouse, grow it on a drywell. In dry conditions, this plant will drop its leaves. However, do not compensate for low humidity with frequent watering. Water when the top inch of potting mix feels dry to the touch.

Schefflera elegantissima

TEMPERATURE Do not let *Schefflera elegantissima* get below 60°F (16°C). Cooler temperatures result in leaf drop.

SOIL Grow in either a soil-based or soilless mix.

FERTILIZATION Feed at half strength every other week during the growing period.

PROPAGATION *Schefflera elegantissima* can be propagated from stem cuttings but requires bottom heat, rooting hormone, and elevated humidity.

WINNING ATTRIBUTES The variegation and shape of this plant's foliage are exceptional. Young plants are readily available and offer an excellent challenge to the enthusiastic indoor grower. If you can provide adequate warmth and humidity you will feel genuine pride in the result: a rare and elegant specimen tree.

Sedum morganianum

BURRO'S TAIL

Crassulaceae

Sedum morganianum is native to Mexico where it grows as a creeping groundcover in sunny, arid conditions. Thick ropes of overlapping, succulent leaves are 2 to 3 feet long. Individual leaves are 3/4 of an inch long, cylindrical with pointed tips, and pale gray-green. Pale pink, star-shaped flowers are produced in clusters at the

Sedum morganianum

end of the shoots. *Sedum morganianum* is usually grown for its foliage, but the lovely flowers are an added bonus. The stems are surprisingly fragile. Individual leaves are easily knocked off their stem by a light touch. When this happens repeatedly it leaves unattractive gaps, so handle the plant with care. Leaves will root and start new plants. In the home, *S. morganianum* is best grown in a hanging basket where its unusually shaped trailing stems can be appreciated. Place it away from heavy traffic to minimize the chances of leaves being knocked off their stems.

LIGHT Grow in full to part sun.

WATER Water when the top inch of potting mix is dry.

TEMPERATURE Can handle nighttime temperatures as low as 50°F (10°C). Average household temperatures are also fine.

SOIL Grow in a soilless mix or a special cactus mix.

FERTILIZATION *Sedum morganianum* does not require feeding. Really.

PROPAGATION Propagate from stem cuttings. Allow them to callus for a week before potting them up. Individual leaves can also be rooted by pressing the stem-end lightly onto the potting mix.

WINNING ATTRIBUTES The overlapping succulent leaves of *Sedum morganianum* are arranged in wonderfully textured ropes. This plant makes a striking hanging basket, and its light, gray-green color makes it a useful accent. Flowers are lovely and delicate, making *S. morganianum* a triple threat.

Selaginella uncinata

PEACOCK MOSS

Selaginaceae

Selaginella uncinata is native to southern China where it grows near water. This is a primitive plant, related to ferns and mosses. As such, it requires the high humidity of a waterside environment. This is an exceptionally beautiful foliage plant; leaves are initially green and acquire a pinkish-blue sheen as they age. *Selaginella uncinata* grows to about 2 inches tall and many feet long. Stems branch freely, and the overall effect is delicate and feathery. This plant grows best (and quite rapidly) in an enclosed environment such as a terrarium or bottle garden. In a very humid greenhouse it can be grown in a hanging basket or as a ground cover.

LIGHT Indirect light is best for *Selaginella uncinata*.

Selaginella uncinata

WATER Water as soon as the surface of the potting mix feels dry; this plant should not be allowed to dry out.

TEMPERATURE Keep warm, above 60°F (16°C).

SOIL Grow in a soil-based potting mix.

FERTILIZATION Feed with a balanced fertilizer at half strength every other week during active growth.

PROPAGATION This plant is classified as a fern ally. Like ferns, selaginellas produce spores rather than seeds. They may be propagated by spore, by division, or from cuttings.

WINNING ATTRIBUTES The variegation of this plant is unique and subtle. Its foliage is delicate and its low-growing habit makes it a perfect ground cover for a tropical terrarium.

Senecio haworthii

COCOON PLANT

Asteraceae

Senecio haworthii is native to the western part of South Africa where it grows as tall as 2 feet. In its native habitat, *Senecio haworthii* is endangered. However, it is a popular cultivated plant that is widely available. Leaves are cylindrical, about 2 inches long, and a striking silvery-white. They are covered with soft, felty hairs that give the plant its remarkable color. Flowers are yellow, daisy-shaped and held on long stems above the foliage. *Senecio haworthii* rarely blooms indoors, but its leaves are so bold and beautiful that it hardly matters. In containers, it grows to about 12 inches tall. Older plants lose their lower leaves and become leggy, so prune whenever the growth habit becomes unattractive, both to keep the plant compact and to provide cuttings for new plants. Plants will drop leaves if overwatered.

LIGHT   Grow in full sun to bright indirect light.

WATER   This plant is drought-tolerant. Water once a week in summer, once every two weeks in winter. If you keep the plant cool in winter, reduce watering to once a month.

Senecio haworthii

TEMPERATURE *Senecio haworthii* will grow in normal household temperatures, but also tolerates cooler temperatures than many houseplants. It can be kept at 45°F (7°C) for a winter rest if watering is also reduced.

SOIL Grow in a soilless mix or cactus mix.

FERTILIZATION Feed once a month at half strength during the growing season.

PROPAGATION Propagate from stem cuttings, which root easily. Allow them to callus for a week, then pot them up. Cuttings should root in four to six weeks.

WINNING ATTRIBUTES There's no denying the striking beauty of this plant. Its outstanding white color immediately captures your attention. It is also soft to the touch—a true "must have."

Solenostemon scutellarioides

COLEUS

Lamiaceae

Solenostemon scutellarioides is native to southeast Asia and Australasia. This has traditionally been a shade plant, but newer hybrids tolerate full sun. Still, color is

Solenostemon scutellarioides 'Religious Radish', 'Gay's Delight', and 'Kiwi Fern' (clockwise from bottom right)

most vibrant with some shade. In nature and in cultivation *S. scutellarioides* grows to 2 to 3 feet tall. Stems are four-sided. Leaf variegation is intense, being any combination of red, orange, yellow, white, purple, and green. Leaf shape may be ovate, heart-shaped, lanceolate, or lobed. Leaf margins may be toothed or ruffled. The "duck's foot" types have narrow frilly leaves and a low, mounding growth habit. The small flowers are white or lavender; they are far less significant than the foliage. Pinch out flower spikes to prevent the plant from diverting energy to flower and seed development. It's all about the foliage. Pinch growing tips throughout the season to encourage full growth. In hot, dry conditions, *S. scutellarioides* is prone to spider mites. Elevate humidity by growing on a drywell.

LIGHT   Indoors, *Solenostemon scutellarioides* should have direct sun. A western or southern window will promote bushy growth with most intense variegation. If you summer your plant outdoors, gradually acclimate it to direct sun. In low light this plant will be leggy, and foliage will be puny.

WATER   Water *Solenostemon scutellarioides* when the surface of the potting mix feels dry. Plants will wilt dramatically if the potting mix dries out.

TEMPERATURE   Average household temperatures are fine. Temperatures below 55°F (13°C) may cause leaves to drop.

SOIL   Grow in a soil-based mix.

FERTILIZATION   Feed every other week at half strength during active growth.

PROPAGATION   While *Solenostemon scutellarioides* is easily grown from seed, the plant may be different from its parent. To preserve the genotype of your chosen cultivar, propagate from cuttings. This is easily done; cuttings usually root in two to three weeks.

WINNING ATTRIBUTES   *Solenostemon scutellarioides* can be trained as a standard or pinched to promote a compact, bushy shape. Its foliage is outstanding; I can think of no plant that offers a wider range of flamboyant leaf colors.

Stapelia gigantea

CARRION FLOWER, STARFISH FLOWER

Asclepiadaceae

Stapelia gigantea is native to southern Africa, where it grows in sunny, arid conditions. It is a succulent that gets to be about 8 inches tall. The thick, four-ridged

Stapelia gigantea

stems are felted and soft to the touch. Ridges are toothed, and the tooth-like points are actually vestigial leaves; the stems themselves are photosynthetic. Flowers are huge and star-shaped, sometimes 12 inches in diameter. They look like balloons as they ripen, enlarging gradually until they pop open, then lasting for only a single day. The flowers smell like rotting meat, and their color is also meat-like: intricate patterns of brownish-red and white. Stapelias are pollinated by carrion flies that are attracted by both the smell and color of the flowers. Don't worry about a strong odor in your home; you have to stick your nose into the center of the flower to detect the scent. The root system is shallow; this plant grows well in a shallow container. Structurally this is a fascinating plant with a short but upright growth habit. It forms a clump as it ages, spreading slowly across the potting mix. Overwatering means death; *S. gigantea* will rot if the root system is kept too wet.

LIGHT   Give full to part sun. It will live in the bright indirect light of an eastern exposure, but may not flower.

WATER   Water infrequently, once every two weeks indoors, or once a week if you summer it outdoors in full sun. Watering too frequently is a fatal mistake.

TEMPERATURE   Grow in average household temperatures.

SOIL   Grow in a soilless mix.

FERTILIZATION   Feed at half strength once a month during the growing season.

PROPAGATION   Take stem cuttings from *Stapelia gigantea*. Maintain polarity and allow the cuttings to callus for several days before potting them up. Make sure the cut edges of the parent plant stay dry while they callus or rot may set in.

WINNING ATTRIBUTES   This is an unusually shaped succulent with outrageously large flowers. The star-shaped blooms can be larger than the plant itself. It is a low maintenance, pest free plant with an interesting structure, and to top it off, it's soft to the touch. No respectable succulent collection is complete without *Stapelia gigantea*.

Stephanotis floribunda

BRIDAL WREATH

Asclepiadaceae

Stephanotis floribunda is native to Madagascar where it is an evergreen climbing shrub. Foliage is glossy, dark green, oblanceolate, about 4 inches long and 1 to 2

Stephanotis floribunda

inches wide. Leaves are in opposite pairs and have a prominent, light green midrib. Flowers are bright white, tubular, five-petalled, and about 1.5 inches in diameter. They are produced in loose clusters of four to eight highly fragrant blooms. This is a classic tropical vine. It can be trained on a hoop or arbor, or around and over a bright window. This is a twining vine and may need help getting started growing around a form. Scale and mealybugs can be occasional problems.

LIGHT   Bright indirect light or part sun (a western or eastern window) is best. Foliage may be damaged by strong sun, and the plant will not bloom in inadequate light.

WATER   Water when the top inch of potting mix is dry.

TEMPERATURE   Grow in normal household temperatures. Temperature fluctuations can cause buds and foliage to drop and may prevent your plant from flowering.

SOIL Grow in a quick draining soilless or soil-based mix.

FERTILIZATION Feed with a bloom-booster fertilizer at half strength once a month during the growing season. Too much nitrogen may produce lush foliage at the expense of flowering, so do not overfeed.

PROPAGATION Propagate from stem cuttings.

WINNING ATTRIBUTES The foliage and flowers of *Stephanotis floribunda* complement each other perfectly. The glossy, dark foliage provides a backdrop for the bright, pure white flowers. The vine can be shaped according to your aesthetic preference. Not only is this plant visually appealing, but the perfume is exotic and enticing, without being overpowering.

Strelitzia reginae

BIRD OF PARADISE

Strelitziaceae

Strelitzia reginae is native to South Africa. It is an imposing plant, growing to about 7 feet tall in nature. In its native habitat it forms large clumps of stems. Leaves have long petioles (about 30 inches) and paddle shaped blades (12 to 15 inches long). The leaf bases overlap in an attractive, fan-like pattern. While its blue-green foliage is impressive, this plant is grown for its outstanding flowers. A long, red-rimmed, beak-shaped bract is held horizontally on a flower stalk about 4 feet tall. Several flowers arise from the bract over a period of weeks. Sepals are 6 inches long and bright orange, with three blue, fused petals, also about 6 inches long. The inflorescence resembles the plumed head of a large exotic bird. *Strelitzia reginae* grows well in containers; being potbound encourages blooming. Potted specimens grow to 3 to 4 feet tall. Plants usually don't bloom until they are five or six years old, so be patient. Repotting may postpone bloom for a year or two, so repot only when necessary. Since their root systems grow well when tightly enclosed, this is not a problem. If your growing space is sunny but small, try *S. reginae* 'Humilis', which grows to about 18 inches tall. *Strelitzia reginae* may get scale; check the overlapping leaf bases for insects.

LIGHT Indoors, *Strelitzia reginae* requires direct sun in order to bloom. A southern window is best.

Strelitzia reginae

WATER   Allow the top inch of potting mix to dry out between waterings.

TEMPERATURE   Grow in normal household temperatures.

SOIL   Grow in a soil-based mix.

FERTILIZATION   Feed at half strength every other week during the growing season.

PROPAGATION   You can propagate by dividing large clumps or by separating individual plantlets from the base of the parent plant and potting them up on their own.

WINNING ATTRIBUTES   The foliage of *Strelitzia reginae* is blue-green, large, impressive, and attractive, but its flowers put this plant in a league of its own. It is the quintessential tropical flower: huge and exotic with an outstanding blue and orange color combination.

Streptocarpella saxorum
FALSE AFRICAN VIOLET
Streptocarpus 'Amanda'
CAPE PRIMROSE
Gesneriaceae

Streptocarpella saxorum is native to Tanzania. Until recently, this plant was classified as *Streptocarpus saxorum*. While the flowers of *Streptocarpus* and *Streptocar-*

pella species are quite similar, most *Streptocarpus* plants are stemless. Their leaves emerge directly from the crown of the plant. In contrast, *Streptocarpella saxorum* has stems; therefore it has been moved to the genus *Streptocarpella*. You may find it labeled with either name. Its leaves and stems are slightly succulent. Foliage is ovate, fuzzy, and small, about 1.5 inches long. Leaves are grayish green and grow in whorls. Flowers are tubular, five-petalled, about an inch long, and a deep shade of violet with a white throat. They are held on wiry stems 4 inches long that originate at the base of the leaf stems. Flowers are held above the foliage, giving the appearance of a halo of bloom. As the stems of *Streptocarpella saxorum* lengthen, they begin to trail, making this an excellent candidate for a hanging basket. *Streptocarpus* 'Amanda' is a hybrid cultivar derived from South African species. Its flowers are an outstanding, electric, vibrant, purple. Blooms are trumpet shaped and 2 to 3 inches in diameter; they are held in small clusters on 4-inch stems in a central clump. Foliage is lanceolate, sessile, and hairy; it is produced in rosettes. Individual leaves are 6 to 8 inches long and about 2 inches wide.

LIGHT   Bright indirect light is best for *Streptocarpella saxorum* and *Streptocarpus* 'Amanda'; direct sun may bleach foliage. These are excellent candidates for growing

Streptocarpella saxorum

Streptocarpus 'Amanda'

under fluorescent lights, not only because of their compact size, but also because fluorescent light more closely resembles bright indirect light than direct sun.

WATER   Water when the top half-inch of potting mix is dry. Be careful not to use cold water on either of these plants. (If the water is cold enough to hurt your hands, it's cold enough to hurt the plant's roots.) The resulting damage is called *ring spot* and appears as blotches of cream-colored discoloration on the leaves. Cut back to healthy leaf tissue and use tepid water to water the plant.

TEMPERATURE   Grow both in normal household temperatures. Temperatures above 80°F (27°C) or below 60°F (16°C) may slow growth.

SOIL   Both grow best in a soilless mix.

FERTILIZATION   Feed both plants with a bloom-booster at half strength every other week during the growing period.

PROPAGATION   *Streptocarpella saxorum* is easily propagated from stem cuttings. Propagate *Streptocarpus* 'Amanda' by division or from leaf cuttings.

WINNING ATTRIBUTES   The velvety, gray green foliage of *Streptocarpella saxorum* is lovely in both texture and color. It nicely offsets the deep violet, plentiful flowers. It can be grown as a hanging plant, or as a trailing groundcover under a tree with similar water requirements. I can think of no flower with a more vibrant color than that of *Streptocarpus* 'Amanda'. It draws the eye like a magnet and is seriously gorgeous.

Strobilanthes dyerianus

PERSIAN SHIELD

Acanthaceae

Strobilanthes dyerianus is a shrub native to Myanmar. In nature it grows to about 3 feet tall. Foliage is lanceolate, toothed, and approximately 6 inches long. Leaves are purple underneath, and purple and green above, with a metallic iridescence. As

Strobilanthes dyerianus

leaves age, they fade from bright purple to silvery purple, creating a tapestry of varied hues. Flowers are small, tubular, and light blue. They pale in comparison to the foliage. Outdoors, variegation is highest in part sun; full sun can fade the colors. *Strobilanthes dyerianus* grows well in containers, where it usually tops out at about 2 feet. It can be kept smaller and compact by regular pinching. Older plants can become straggly, but since cuttings are easy to start, replace unattractive specimens with offspring from your parent stock.

LIGHT   Indoors grow in full sun for the most intense variegation. A southern or western window is best.

WATER   Water when the top half-inch of potting mix is dry.

TEMPERATURE   Grow in normal household temperatures. It will survive occasional dips to 50°F (10°C) degrees, but may drop leaves.

SOIL   Grow in a soil-based potting mix.

FERTILIZATION   Feed at half strength every other week during active growth.

PROPAGATION   Propagate from stem cuttings.

WINNING ATTRIBUTES   Gorgeous purple foliage with a metallic sheen—what's not to like? This plant adds immediate impact to any landscape. A specimen of any size provides sophistication and color.

Stromanthe sanguinea 'Trio Star'

Marantaceae

Stromanthe sanguinea is native to Brazil where it grows to 5 feet tall in warm, humid conditions and rich soils. *Stromanthe sanguinea* 'Trio Star' is a highly variegated cultivar; the undersides of its leaves are a brilliant dark magenta, and the tops are white and green. The magenta shows through the white, giving the plant a pink cast. This plant grows well in containers, although it stays quite a bit smaller than the straight species grows in nature. It rarely exceeds 12 to 18 inches. Leaves are oblong and 6 to 8 inches long. Stems are 4 to 8 inches tall and grow in a fan-shaped cluster. This show-stopper is not an easy plant to grow; it requires constant warmth and high humidity. In dry air, *S. sanguinea* 'Trio Star' is prone to spider mites, leaf margins will turn brown, and overall growth will be slow. Elevate humidity by growing it on a drywell or in a greenhouse; it is also an excellent terrarium plant. While many variegated plants lose color intensity in low light, *S. sanguinea* 'Trio Star' maintains vibrant coloring under fluorescent lights. *Stromanthe sanguinea* 'Tricolor' is a similar cultivar.

LIGHT   Tolerates a wide range of light intensities. It can be grown under fluorescent lights or in bright indirect light to part sun. Full sun may scorch leaves.

WATER   Don't let *Stromanthe sanguinea* 'Trio Star' dry out; water when the top half-inch of potting mix is dry.

Stromanthe sanguinea 'Trio Star'

TEMPERATURE This plant requires warm temperatures; keep it out of drafts and above 60°F (10°C).

SOIL Grow in either a soil-based or soilless potting mix.

FERTILIZATION Feed with a half-strength fertilizer solution every other week during active growth.

PROPAGATION Propagate by division.

WINNING ATTRIBUTES The variegation of this plant makes it an outstanding choice for a humid growing environment. It is a compact plant and provides tremendous visual impact.

Tacca integrifolia

WHITE BAT PLANT

Taccaceae

Tacca integrifolia is native to southeast Asia, India, and Indonesia where it grows in the filtered light of monsoonal rain forests. In nature it goes dormant during the dry season, but it will remain evergreen when kept consistently moist. Leaves are medium green, smooth, and 18 to 24 inches tall. They grow from a basal crown and have long petioles. The blooms are large and complex composites of bracts and true flowers. The true flowers are dark purple and grow in groups of 6 to 10 at the center of the bloom. They are topped by two large, white, upright bracts, about 2 inches tall. Below the true flowers are two white bracts about 1.5 inches long and numerous bracteoles which hang down like long whiskers. These are also white and can be 6 or 8 inches long. *Tacca integrifolia* is not an easy plant to grow. It requires high humidity, constant warmth, and can be prone to spider mites. However, if you are a connoisseur and appreciate the unusual, *T. integrifolia* is well worth a try. Congratulate yourself if you succeed.

LIGHT Bright light to part sun is best. Grow it in eastern or western light.

WATER Don't let *Tacca integrifolia* dry out between waterings. Water as soon as the surface of the potting mix feels dry. This plant requires elevated humidity. Grow it on a drywell at the very least, in a greenhouse if possible.

TEMPERATURE Keep warm; do not let temperatures drop below 60°F (16°C).

SOIL Grow in a soil-based potting mix.

FERTILIZATION Feed with a bloom-booster plant food at half strength every other week during the growing season.

Tacca integrifolia. Photo by Dennis Cathcart, Tropiflora

PROPAGATION Propagate by division.

WINNING ATTRIBUTES If you appreciate the eclectic, the extremely unusual, try *Tacca integrifolia*. You'll be rewarded with huge, composite flowers that are absolutely unique. This is an exotic eye-catcher and a remarkable specimen plant.

Tetrastigma voinierianum

CHESTNUT VINE

Vitaceae

Tetrastigma voinierianum is native to southern Asia. It is a member of the grape family, and like the grape is a large vine that climbs via spiral tendrils. This strong plant grows best in part shade with a moist, well-drained soil. Leaves are compound, with three to five leaflets, each 6 to 8 inches long. Leaf margins are serrated. The underside of the foliage is felted and white-flecked with russet. Stems are thick and jointed. In nature, *T. voinierianum* produces small, yellow-green flowers followed by grape-like bunches of fruit. The plant rarely blooms indoors. It is an excellent container plant, tolerating a wide range of conditions and quite a bit of neglect. In less than optimal circumstances, it will remain a small tabletop houseplant. When well grown, it is an impressive indoor vine that can be trained up and around a window or over an upright form. This vine is a vigorous grower and needs a strong support. If you're growing it in a greenhouse or conservatory room, train *T. voinierianum* up the sides of the house and along the rafters to create a dense, jungle covering. This plant can also be grown in a hanging basket and hung in a large window. It will quickly create a living curtain that provides privacy.

LIGHT Indoors, *Tetrastigma voinierianum* grows best in bright indirect light; an eastern or bright northern window is best. It will survive in a dim or obstructed northern window, but will not grow as large or as quickly. Try using grow-bulbs to supplement low light.

WATER Water when the top half-inch of potting mix is dry. If your plant is in a large pot (more than 8 inches in diameter) water when the top inch of mix is dry.

TEMPERATURE Grow in average household temperatures. At temperatures below 55°F (13°C), stem sections and foliage may drop off.

SOIL Grow in either a soil-based or soilless mix.

FERTILIZATION Feed at half strength every other week during the growing season.

PROPAGATION *Tetrastigma voinierianum* is easily propagated from cuttings. Each cutting should include at least one node; bottom heat will speed the process.

Tetrastigma voinierianum

WINNING ATTRIBUTES   This is a fast-growing, large vine that makes an impressive specimen plant, either trained upward or hung in a large window where its vigorous growth habit can be appreciated. Because *Tetrastigma voinierianum* tolerates lower light, it is a useful plant for difficult growing conditions.

Thelocactus bicolor

GLORY OF TEXAS

Cactaceae

Thelocactus bicolor is native to Mexico and Texas where it grows in sunny, arid conditions. In nature it may get to be 8 inches tall and wide. The cactus may be roundish or elongated with 8 to 13 ribs lined with two-toned yellow and red spines. The spiny ribs may run straight up the cactus body or curve around in a spiral. *Thelocactus bicolor* is grayish green. Flowers are showy and pink or pinkish-purple. They are trumpet shaped, about 2.5 inches long and 2 to 3 inches wide. This cactus grows very well in containers. It flowers easily indoors when given enough light. *Thelocactus bicolor* is susceptible to rot, so be sure not to overwater.

Thelocactus bicolor

In full summer sun, a small pot will probably not need watering more than once every two weeks. If you give your plant a cool winter rest, once a month watering will be sufficient. If you see signs of shriveling, decrease the interval between waterings.

LIGHT   Grow in full or part sun.

WATER   Overwatering *Thelocactus bicolor* will lead to rot and death. Water when the top 2 inches of potting mix is dry.

TEMPERATURE   Grow in average household temperatures. If possible, give it a winter rest at 45°F (7°C) to 50°F (10°C).

SOIL   Grow in a fast-draining cactus mix.

FERTILIZATION   Don't feed *Thelocactus bicolor* unless your plant is very large and old and has been in the same potting mix for four or five years.

PROPAGATION   Propagate from offsets or from seed. Seed germinates easily, but plants will take several years to reach blooming size. Offsets should be allowed to callus for a week before planting.

WINNING ATTRIBUTES   There's something fascinating about the juxtaposition of painful, threatening spines and a pretty, pink, daisy-shaped flower. *Thelocactus bicolor* blooms easily indoors. Not only are the flowers showy, but the spiral arrangement of the ribs and their two-toned spines makes this an attractive plant even when it's not in bloom.

Thunbergia grandiflora

BLUE TRUMPET VINE, SKY FLOWER

Thunbergia mysorensis

MYSORE TRUMPET VINE

Acanthaceae

Thunbergia grandiflora is a vine native to India where it can be 50 feet long, twining vigorously among tall trees. Flowers are pale, bluish purple with yellow centers, trumpet-shaped, and 4 to 5 inches in diameter. Foliage is heart shaped, toothed, and up to 8 inches long. *Thunbergia grandiflora* does well in containers where it grows to about 15 feet long. It is best displayed on a trellis or upright form so flowers are clearly visible. This vine can grow 6 to 8 feet in a single season when grown indoors. *Thunbergia mysorensis* is also native to India. It is a much bigger vine than *T.*

grandiflora. Foliage is elliptic, narrow, glossy, medium green, and about 6 inches long. Individual flowers are 1 to 2 inches long and hang in panicles that can reach 12 to 24 inches in length. Blooms are yellow and maroon and are larger at the top of the panicle, giving the cluster the tapered appearance of a bunch of grapes. While *T. mysorensis* grows well in large containers, it is not a vine for the average home; it is large and well-suited to a conservatory room or greenhouse where it can be allowed to grow among the rafters. Both vines are twiners; they do not have tendrils or aerial roots to help them climb. They may need help to start climbing, but once you've got them going, these vines will take off and grow steadily on their own.

LIGHT Grow both in full sun.

WATER Water when the top inch of potting mix is dry.

TEMPERATURE Grow in a quick-draining potting mix, either soilless or soil-based.

SOIL Grow in normal household temperatures.

FERTILIZATION Feed at full strength once every two weeks during the growing season.

PROPAGATION Propagate from cuttings, or remove suckers (with their roots) that form at the base of the plant and pot them up on their own.

Thunbergia grandiflora

WINNING ATTRIBUTES The flowers of both thunbergias are outstanding. These are fast-growing vines. They can be trained upward over trellises or topiary forms, allowing their showy flowers to hang down and providing spots of color high in your interior landscape. The flowers of *Thunbergia grandiflora* are a delicate color and hang in multiples of two to four large flowers. *Thunbergia mysorensis* is almost absurdly showy. Flowers are richly colored, huge, and dramatically pendent.

Thunbergia mysorensis

Tibouchina urvilleana

GLORY BUSH

Melastomataceae

Tibouchina urvilleana is native to Brazil, where it is an evergreen shrub and reaches 10 to 15 feet in height. It grows in full to part sun in slightly acid soil. Foliage is ovate, 2 to 4 inches long, dark green, with prominent, sunken veins. Leaf surfaces are velvety. Flowers are large, about 3 inches in diameter, and a remarkably rich, saturated purple. They are five-petalled and have prominent stamens, curved upward like fish hooks. The unopened flower buds are also ornamental, large, hairy, and reddish, as are the young stems and leaves. Individual blooms last for a day, then drop. Tibouchinas flower most heavily in late summer and fall. They bloom on new growth, so heavy pruning will not inhibit flowering and will result in a nicer plant shape. *Tibouchina urvilleana* may have a straggly growth habit and does not branch heavily in nature; conscientious pinching will encourage a bushier form. It may be trained as a standard or allowed to grow in a shrubby shape. *Tibouchina urvilleana* grows well in containers where it reaches a height of 3 to 6 feet.

Tibouchina urvilleana

LIGHT *Tibouchina urvilleana* should be grown in full sun for optimal flowering. If you summer it outdoors, overwinter it in your brightest indoor spot. If this gets less than full sun, prune weak and leggy growth before moving your plant back outside.

WATER Water when the top half-inch of potting mix feels dry. This plant will benefit from the elevated humidity of a drywell.

TEMPERATURE Grow in regular household temperatures.

SOIL Grow in a soil-based potting mix.

FERTILIZATION Feed at half strength every other week during the growing season.

PROPAGATION Propagate from stem cuttings. Use rooting hormone and provide elevated humidity while the cuttings are rooting.

WINNING ATTRIBUTES The flowers of *Tibouchina urvilleana* are outstanding: rich and velvety, their deep, saturated color becomes a focal point in any room or greenhouse. Young stems and buds are also ornamental, and the foliage is nicely patterned. It can be grown as a specimen standard or as a smaller plant.

Tillandsia capitata 'Rubra'
Tillandsia ionantha
Tillandsia stricta

AIR PLANT
Bromeliaceae

The genus *Tillandsia* is quite large and includes both epiphytic and terrestrial plants. *Tillandsia capitata* is an epiphyte native to Mexico, Honduras, and the West Indies. It grows in full to part sun, and its leaves are lanceolate and slim, about 8 inches long and a half-inch wide. Foliage grows in an open rosette, with individual leaves gracefully recurved. *Tillandsia capitata* 'Rubra' has reddish foliage year-round and maintains its variegation even in low light. In high light, variegation intensifies. Flowers are purple and emerge from between red bracts. *Tillandsia capitata* 'Rubra' can be

Tillandsia capitata 'Rubra'

Tillandsia ionantha

Tillandsia stricta

bark-mounted, placed in the crotch of an indoor tree, or potted in bark mix. Its open circular shape and unusual foliage color make it an excellent medium sized bromeliad for an indoor garden. *Tillandsia ionantha* is an epiphyte native to Mexico, Guatemala, and Nicaragua. It is much smaller than *T. capitata*; its rosette is tight and bulb-like. Outer leaves are recurved, but inner leaves grow almost straight up. The entire plant is 2 to 3 inches tall. Foliage is cylindrical, pointed, and covered with grayish scales which both protect it from the sun and absorb moisture. Flowers extend about an inch beyond the foliage and are bright purple. When *T. ionantha* is in bloom, the leaves immediately surrounding the flowers turn bright red, creating a colorful show. This miniature epiphyte tolerates lower light than many tillandsias; it grows best when bark-mounted or perched among the branches of a large plant. *Tillandsia stricta* is an epiphyte native to Venezuela and Argentina, where it grows in full sun. Its almost cylindrical leaves are covered with grayish protective scales that absorb moisture from rain and humid air. The foliage of *T. stricta* grows in a tight, upright rosette. Leaves are about 6 inches long and slightly recurved. Its inflorescence is held several inches above the foliage and is composed of bright pink bracts and purple flowers. There is also a cultivar with white bracts. *Tillandsia stricta* can be bark-mounted or grown tucked into various nooks and crannies of your indoor garden. Do not allow its base to sit in water, or foliage will rot and the plant will die.

LIGHT These tillandsias are highly adaptable to various light conditions. *Tillandsia capitata* and *T. stricta* will flower in full to part sun, and foliage remains attractive in bright indirect light. *Tillandsia ionantha* will flower in bright, indirect light and should be protected from full sun. All three grow well under fluorescent lights, although only *T. ionantha* will initiate bloom under these conditions.

WATER You may water your tillandsias in several ways. The foliage may be thoroughly drenched by spraying with a fine mist from a spray bottle or misting hose attachment. Or, dunk the entire plant in a bowl of tepid water. Once a week will probably be adequate unless your home is especially dry. Elevate humidity when possible.

TEMPERATURE Normal household temperatures are fine.

SOIL These tillandsias should not be grown in soil. *Tillandsia capitata* can be potted in bark mix, but is best grown as it grows in nature, on a tree branch. You may either bark-mount these or simply place them where you like on the limbs of indoor trees.

FERTILIZATION Tillandsias do not require frequent feeding. You can spray or soak with a fertilizer solution at half strength once a month during the growing season.

PROPAGATION Tillandsias produce offsets that may be removed from the parent plant and grown on their own.

WINNING ATTRIBUTES *Tillandsia capitata* 'Rubra' has lovely red foliage year-round, and its open rosette of leaves gives it an unusual circular shape. *Tillandsia ionantha* is easy to bloom, and as a miniature it can be tucked almost anywhere in your indoor garden. *Tillandsia stricta* is a petite novelty plant with showy flowers. When not in bloom, it provides an interesting accent for your indoor garden. All three are low maintenance and pest free.

Tweedia caerulea

BLUE MILKWEED

Asclepiadaceae

Tweedia caerulea is native to Brazil and Uruguay. Foliage is gray-green, hairy, and narrowly heart-shaped, about 3 inches long. Individual flowers are five-petalled, about an inch in diameter and borne in terminal umbels. These flowers are absurdly lovely. Buds are pinkish, and the flowers pass through several stages of coloration as they mature. Freshly opened flowers are a captivating pale blue. This watercolor shade is not quite sky blue, but neither is it teal. There's a hint of green or yellow to the hue, but just a hint. As they age, blooms turn violet, then lilac blue. Flowers are followed by long, gray-green seed pods that resemble those of the milkweed, a member of the same family. The growth habit of this plant isn't particularly outstanding. Stems are neither long and vining nor sturdy and free standing. They grow to about 3 feet tall and tend to tip and lean unless they are staked or wound around a neighbor. *Tweedia caerulea* grows well in pots. It should be pinched when young to encourage branching and can be pruned at the end of winter, right before new growth begins.

LIGHT   Grow in full sun for maximum bloom.

Tweedia caerulea

WATER Water when the top inch of potting mix is dry; this plant is fairly drought-tolerant.

TEMPERATURE Grow in normal household temperatures. A winter rest at about 55°F (13°C) is fine.

SOIL Grow in a soilless mix.

FERTILIZATION Do not overfeed, or you will get lots of foliage and few flowers. Feed once a month at half strength with a bloom-booster during the growing season.

PROPAGATION *Tweedia caerulea* is easily propagated from seed or stem cuttings.

WINNING ATTRIBUTES There is something irresistible about these flowers. They have a bewitching quality; once you see them you must possess them. The flower is so captivating that your eye will be immediately drawn to it. Use *T. caerulea* to punctuate your indoor garden with a rare and a desirable shade of blue.

Vanilla planifolia

VANILLA

Orchidaceae

Vanilla planifolia is native to Mexico and Guatemala. It is a vining epiphyte and in nature grows in dappled sun to part shade. Leaves and stems are bright green and

Vanilla planifolia

fleshy; the stem produces roots along its length that help it climb. In nature it can top 20 feet. Leaves are smooth, lanceolate, and 4 to 6 inches long. They are sessile and clasp the stem. *Vanilla planifolia* does well in containers where it will grow to about 12 feet long. This vine is not aggressive; give it vertical support and it will attach roots to any porous surface. Or, you can grow it in a hanging basket. Flowers are yellow or greenish-yellow and 2 to 3 inches in diameter. Vanilla beans are the dried fruits produced by the pollinated flowers. Flowers remain open for only a day and in captivity must be hand-pollinated. Fruit requires lengthy treatment to be edible. This is an unusual plant, and while you will probably never be able to eat the product of your labors, it produces beautiful flowers and has a graceful, unique growth habit. It is not difficult to grow, but it is difficult to find. Cuttings root easily, so if you know someone with a plant, be prepared to barter.

LIGHT Indoors grow in full to part sun. It will grow in bright indirect light but may not flower.

WATER Water when the top inch of potting mix feels dry. Leaves and stems are succulent, so this plant is fairly drought-tolerant. Elevated humidity is good, but not required.

TEMPERATURE Grow in average household temperatures.

SOIL Grow in either a fine-grained bark mix or a soilless potting mix; or, grow it as a bark mounted specimen.

FERTILIZATION Feed at half strength every other week during active growth. If your plant is bark-mounted, give it a foliar feed every other week during the growing season.

PROPAGATION Propagate from cuttings. Allow them to callus for a week before potting them in a fine-grained orchid bark or a soilless mix.

WINNING ATTRIBUTES Not only are the flowers of *Vanilla planifolia* lovely, but this orchid has an unusual growth habit. It's a versatile plant and can be allowed to trail as a hanging vine or trained on an upright form. Its bright emerald green stems and leaves stand out. It is easy to grow and pest free.

10

Extracurricular Activities

Bark-mounting Epiphytes

Growing a bark-mounted epiphyte is quite simple, and plants displayed in this manner look very cool. Caring for them is not complicated, but mounted epiphytes require more frequent watering and feeding.

Cork is my preferred mount for several reasons. It is lightweight, has an interesting surface that provides nooks and crannies for nestling root balls, and it's softer and easier to work with than wood or tree fern fiber. You'll need the following materials:

    cork slab
    epiphyte
    monofilament fishing line
    sphagnum moss
    1-inch U-staples

1. Use a hammer to gently tap a U-staple into the top of your cork slab. This will be your hanger.
2. The surface of the cork is ridged and grooved, and your plant will fit best into a hollow. Lay the cork flat and choose a place where the plant fits well. Place a small clump of sphagnum moss on the spot. The clump should be about the same size as the root system of the plant you are mounting. It will help retain moisture.

3. Place the epiphyte on top of the moss. Center the plant so roots have room to grow downward and the plant has room to grow upward.

4. Place another small clump of sphagnum moss on top of the root system. The entire root system does *not* have to be covered. The moss is there to protect the roots and provide moisture.

5. Cut a length of fishing line and tie the epiphyte in place. You should encircle the root ball several times at cross angles.

6. Soak the slab and plant for 10 to 15 minutes, and allow any extra water to drain before hanging your epiphyte in place.

7. After a few months, check your plant's roots. They will have grown into the cork, holding the epiphyte firmly in place.

A Living Curtain

My first New York apartment was dark, with a single window. Yet I yearned for greenery, a view of nature. By installing a high pressure sodium (HPS) lamp above a series of shelves, I was able to create a hanging garden; the results were exceptional.

You can construct your own combination of poles and shelves, or purchase a set of hanging plexiglass shelves built expressly for window gardening. In either case,

Cork bark with U-staple hanger

This epiphyte's roots have grown into the cork bark after several months.

clear glass or plexiglass allows for maximum light to pass through to the plants on lower shelves. A pole hung above the top of the window frame provides space for hanging plants, while shelves across the window itself are for potted specimens.

Consider the weight of your plants before placing them. Your shelves and poles must be adequately anchored to handle the load. In this situation, it's best to use smaller pots and plastic rather than terra cotta.

If your window doesn't get much light, you can supplement with fluorescents installed above or along the sides of the window frame. Or, in a really dark situation, a high intensity discharge (HID) lamp provides strong enough light to grow a wide range of plants.

Summering Plants Outdoors

Summering plants outdoors is an appealing prospect for several reasons. First of all, most plants respond to outdoor growing conditions with a flush of lush growth. Second, it's a lot easier to take care of your plants outdoors. The humidity is already high, so you can forget about the drywells, and you don't have to worry about spilling when you water. Just pour and pour until it runs out the bottom of the pot and overflow be damned.

There are a few things to consider, however. First of all, remember that full sun outdoors is not the same as full sun indoors. If you have a plant in full sun indoors, don't move it directly into a full sun exposure outside or your plant may suffer from leaf burn. When you first bring your plant outdoors, put it in a shaded position, then into dappled light, then into full sun. This way, your plant will have a chance to acclimate. A plant grown in indirect light indoors should never be given full outdoor sun.

To plunge or not to plunge? Should you submerge your potted plants into the garden beds, or arrange them above ground? Every summer I haul out the eclectic mix of plant stands I've collected over the years, and move at least half of my plants outdoors. I position some stands in sun and some in shade, but I leave the pots above ground.

Some people submerge their pots in the garden, which has both advantages and disadvantages. A pot submerged in garden soil requires less frequent watering. The cool earth surrounding the container will slow the evaporation rate, keeping the roots cooler and more moist. If you have an automatic irrigation system in place, you can position the potted specimens so the sprinklers or soaker hose water your houseplants. Your houseplants act as annuals, contributing to the beauty of your mixed border.

On the other hand, if you live in deer country (as I do), putting any valuable plant material within reach of the voracious hordes is a foolish, foolish thing to do. I would no more put one of my treasured tropical beauties where Bambi could snack on it than I would send my cat Sisko out to chase the bear away from the bird feeder. Also, plants submerged in the garden are more vulnerable to plant pests.

There are many more plant pests outdoors than there are inside your home. Do your best to prevent earthworms from getting into the pots. While they are useful garden inhabitants outdoors, in containers earthworms are a nuisance. They can damage plant roots, and their castings are so dense that soil aeration is compromised within the container. A 3-inch layer of gravel underneath your potted plant should keep earthworms away from the drainage hole.

Be sure not to submerge the lips of your pots. If you do so, the plant may send roots out beyond its pot, which will make moving the plant in fall much more difficult. As long as you can simply lift the pot and bring your plant indoors, there will be no root trauma.

Check all plants for pests before bringing them back indoors. Even if you don't see any insects, mites, or damage, consider giving your plants a preventative spraying. Ced-o-flora is an excellent, kerosene-based, insecticide-miticide. After spraying, move your plants into an isolation area for a week; reintegrate them into your interior landscape only after you're sure they are clean.

Most plants benefit from a summer vacation outdoors, and you'll appreciate the reduction in maintenance work. Summer rain does a nice job of watering your plants, and the elevated humidity of most temperate summer climates is well-suited to our houseplants. Hairy leafed plants are best kept inside, but almost anything else will thrive outdoors, if you choose the right spot and watch for pests.

Traveling with Plants

The more you love plants, the more your life revolves around them. Don't be surprised if you find yourself building vacations around visits to specialty nurseries or planning hikes to view rare rain forest orchids. It would be naïve to expect to be satisfied merely by viewing these plants. Sooner or later you will want to bring some home with you.

Always know the rules before transporting plant material. Never remove a plant from the wild. Carrying plants across international boundaries is complicated, and the rules and regulations must be respected. Often you must apply for a phytosanitary certificate, guaranteeing the health and cleanliness of your plant material. You may also need to prove that the plant was legally purchased, rather than harvested from the wild.

There are also laws governing the transportation of plants between certain states in the United States. For example, if you travel to Hawaii you can bring back all the plants you want to New York City. However, you can't bring back any soil clinging to the roots, for fear of transporting soil-borne pathogens.

Assuming you comply with the rules governing what can and cannot be transported, there are several things you can do to make moving your new plants as safe and easy as possible.

1. Bring along large zip-lock bags. Your load will be significantly lighter if you leave the pots behind and transport only the plant material. Knock each plant out of its pot, wrap the root ball in wet newspaper, and place it in a bag. Large, 2-gallon bags will often accommodate top growth as well, but even if the stems extend beyond the bag, the root ball will remain moist and protected.

2. Travel with an extra suitcase. A soft duffel bag, folded flat, can easily be packed in anticipation of filling it with plants for the return trip. Rigid cosmetic cases offer excellent protection for small, delicate specimens.

3. Check your clothes, carry on your plants. Remember that the luggage compartment is unheated, and even in the middle of summer it's very cold at 30,000 feet. If you're transporting tropicals, this may cause irreparable damage.

RESOURCES

Read! Read! Read!

It's natural that when you're passionate about something, you want to learn all you can. Read everything you can get your hands on. If you live near a botanic garden or garden center that offers classes or lectures, take advantage. I have listed a few of my favorite books, followed by other resources.

ON HOUSEPLANTS
Cruso, Thalassa. *Making Things Grow*. New York: Alfred A. Knopf, 1969.
Elbert, Virginie F., and George A. Elbert. *Fun with Growing Odd and Curious House Plants*. New York: Crown Publishers, Inc., 1975.
Everett, Thomas. *How to Grow Beautiful Houseplants*. New York: Arco Publishing Company, Inc., 1953.
Graf, Alfred Byrd. *Exotic House Plants*. East Rutherford, NJ: Roehrs Company, 1973.
Martin, Tovah. *Well-Clad Windowsills*. New York: MacMillan USA, 1994.
McDonald, Elvin. *The World Book of Houseplants*. Cleveland, OH: The World Publishing Company, 1963.

ON TERRARIUMS
Elbert, Virginie. *Fun with Terrarium Gardening*. New York: Crown Publishing Group, 1973.
Fitch, Charles Marsden. *The Complete Book of Terrariums*. New York: Hawthorn Books, Inc., 1974.
Westlane, Pamela. *Terrariums*. Secaucus, NJ: Chartwell Books, 1993.

ON BIOLOGICAL PEST CONTROL
Cherim, Michael S. *The Green Methods Manual*. Nottingham, NH: The Green Spot. Revised annually.

ON PROPAGATION
Druse, Ken. *Making More Plants*. New York: Clarkson Potter, 2000.
Hartmann, Hudson T., Dale E. Kesten, Fred T. Davies, Jr., and Robert L. Geneve.

Plant Propagation: Principles and Practices. Sixth edition. Upper Saddle River, NJ: Prentice Hall, 1997.

Nehrling, Arno, and Irene Nehrling. *Propagating House Plants*. New York: Hearthside Press Inc., 1962.

OTHER REFERENCES

Bailey, Liberty, and Ethel Bailey. *Hortus Third*. New York: Barnes & Noble Books, 1976.

Capon, Brian. *Botany for Gardeners*. Second edition. Portland, OR: Timber Press, 2005.

Chidamian, Claude. *The Book of Cacti and Other Succulents*. Garden City: Doubleday & Company, Inc., 1958.

Llamas, Kirsten Albrecht. *Tropical Flowering Plants*. Portland, OR: Timber Press, 2003.

Nobel, Park S. *Remarkable Agaves and Cacti*. New York: Oxford University Press, 1994.

Turner, R. J., Jr., and Ernie Wasson, editors. *Botanica*. Milsons Point, NSW, Australia: Random House Australia, 1997.

Zomlefer, Wendy B. *Flowering Plant Families*. Chapel Hill, NC: The University of North Carolina Press, 1994.

Clubs and Organizations

American Begonia Society
157 Monument
Rio Dell, CA 95562-1617
707.764.5407
www.begonias.org

American Gloxinia and Gesneriad
    Society
1122 East Pike Street PMP 637
Seattle, WA 98122-3916
www.aggs.org

American Ivy Society
POB 2123
Naples, FL 34106-2123
www.ivy.org

Hobby Greenhouse Association
8 Glen Terrace
Bedford, MA 01730-2048
781.275.0377
www.hobbygreenhouse.org
This association is for any avid indoor grower, even if you don't have a greenhouse.

International Hoya Association
1444 E. Taylor St.
Vista, CA 92084
www.international-hoya.org

Retail Nurseries and Mail Order Sources

Glasshouse Works
POB 97
Stewart, OH 45778-0097
800.837.2142/phone
740.662.2120/fax
www.glasshouseworks.com

Kartuz Greenhouses
1408 Sunset Dr.
Vista, CA 92085-0790
760.941.3613/phone
760.941.1123/fax
www.kartuz.com

Lake Street Garden Center
37 Lake Street
Salem, NH 03079-2243
603.893.5858

Logees
141 North St.
Danielson, CT 06239
888.330.8038/phone
888.774.9932/fax
www.logees.com

Menne Nursery and Florist
3100 Niagara Falls Blvd.
Amherst, NY 14228
716.693.4444/phone
716.695.9751/fax
www.mennenursery.com

Stokes Tropicals
4806 E. Old Spanish Tr.
Jeanerette, LA 70544
800.624.9706/phone
337.365.6991/fax
www.stokestropicals.com

Tropical World
1 Tropical World Way
Boynton Beach, FL 33436
866.949.6753/phone
561.364.8641/fax
www.tropical world.com

Tropiflora
3530 Tallevast Road
Sarasota, FL 34243
941.351.2267/phone
941.351.6985/fax
www.tropiflora.com

Hard Goods/Supplies

Charley's Greenhouse Supply
17979 State Route 536
Mount Vernon, WA 98273
800-322-4707
www.charleysgreenhouse.com

Gardener's Supply Company
128 Intervale Rd.
Burlington, VT 05401
888.833.1412/phone
800.551.6712/fax
www.gardeners.com

Indoor Window Gardening
(plexiglass, hanging shelves)
POB 335
Beverly, MA 01915
978-927-9234
www.proportionalreading.com/
plants.html

Artificial Lights and Related Equipment

Everybody's Garden Center
519 SE Main
Portland, OR 97214-3417
800.669.5483/phone
503.231.5644/fax
www.litemanu.com

Hydrofarm
(wholesaler; see website for retailers)
707.765.9990/phone
707.765.9967/fax
www.hydrofarm.com

Midwest Hydroponics
5701 W. 36th St.
Minneapolis, MN 55416
888.449.2739
www.midwesthydroponics.com

CONVERSION TABLES

TEMPERATURES: $°C = \frac{5}{9} \times (°F-32)$; $°F = (\frac{9}{5} \times °C) + 32$

INCHES	CENTIMETER		FEET	METER
$\frac{1}{10}$	0.3		1	0.3
$\frac{1}{6}$	0.4		2	0.6
$\frac{1}{4}$	0.6		3	0.9
$\frac{1}{3}$	0.8		4	1.2
$\frac{1}{2}$	1.3		5	1.5
$\frac{3}{4}$	1.9		6	1.8
1	2.5		7	2.1
2	5.1		8	2.4
3	7.6		9	2.7
4	10		10	3
5	13		20	6
6	15		30	9
7	18		40	12
8	20		50	15
9	23		60	18
10	25		70	21
20	51		80	24
30	76		90	27
			100	30

GLOSSARY

acid-loving plant: a plant that grows best when the pH of its potting mix is lower than 7.0, that is, in the acid range

acid plant fertilizer: a plant food specially formulated for plants that grow best with a pH below 7.0

angiosperm: a plant with an enclosed seed; all flowering plants are angiosperms

anther: the pollen bearing portion of the stamen; a male flower part

auxin: a plant hormone that increases root production

azalea pot: a pot three-fourths the standard depth

balanced fertilizer: a fertilizer containing equal parts nitrogen, phosphates, and potash; good for overall growth of foliage, flowers, and roots

bipinnate: twice pinnately divided; see pinnate

bloom-booster: a fertilizer containing more phosphorus than nitrogen or potassium; used to initiate bloom

bloom spike: a long stalk bearing a single flower or flowers

botrytis: a fungal disease also known as gray mold and distinguished by a fuzzy gray fungal growth

bracteole: a small bract borne on a petiole

bracts: a leaflike structure at the base of a flower

bulb pan: a pot one-half the standard depth

buttress roots: flared trunks and above-ground roots that give extra support to trees; especially common in wet environments

cachepot: a pot, bowl, or vase into which an unattractive plant container may be placed for aesthetic reasons

callus: the dried, hardened, healed end of a cutting

calyx: the outer whorl of a flower; composed of sepals

canopy: the uppermost foliage layer of a forest where many epiphytes live

caudex (pl. caudices): the woody, swollen base of a plant stem

cofactors: stimuli that act as synergists to auxins

compound: comprised of two or more distinct parts

corolla: the whorl of a flower composed of petals; immediately interior to the calyx (sepals)

cork: the spongy, absorbent layer of bark from the cork tree (*Phellodendron amurense*); frequently used as an epiphyte mount cotyledon: a seed leaf; this primary leaf is contained within the seed and provides nutrition during germination

crenate: with rounded teeth along the leaf margin

crenulate: with tiny rounded teeth along the leaf margin

crown: the central base of a plant from which new growth arises

cultivar: a specific plant grown from seed; its name is set off by single quotation marks

cultural: pertaining to the growing conditions best suited to a plant; light, humidity, and fertilization are all cultural requirements

cuticle: a thick, waxy protective covering secreted by leaves, which reduces the rate of water loss through transpiration

cyme: an inflorescence with flowers that open from the center outwards

dentate: toothed

dicot: dicotyledonous; having two seed leaves (cotyledons)

dioecious: having male and female flowers borne on separate plants

distal: toward the tip; opposite the end of attachment

dormancy: a period of rest during which a plant may die back to soil level; in nature this usually occurs during cold or dry seasons

drywell: a saucer or pan of pebbles and water, which raises the ambient humidity around the plants that sit upon it

epiphyte: a plant that grows above the ground, attached to a branch or tree trunk; it derives no nutrients from its host but gets nutrition from debris and rain

exfoliating: peeling back in layers

family: a group of related plants; families are divided into genera

filament: a male flower part; the thin stalk of the stamen that holds the anther

flat: a large, shallow pan without divisions, used for germinating quantities of seed

foliar feed: a method of feeding accomplished by spraying a mixture of fertilizer and water onto plant leaves with a spray bottle

frond: a fern's leaf equivalent

genera: plural of genus

genotype: the genetic composition of a plant or other organism

genus: a group of plants classified together due to common ancestry; can be man-made or naturally occurring

geophyte: a plant with modified underground storage tissue such as a bulb, corm, or tuber

growing point: the actively growing apical point of a plant

growing tip: see growing point

guttation: the exudation of water droplets from hydathodes; usually occurs under highly humid conditions

gymnosperm: a plant with a naked seed; all conifers and a few primitive vascular plants are gymnosperms

hardscape: landscape elements of a permanent nature other than plant material, for example, rocks, trellises, walls.

honeydew: a sugary substance excreted by sucking insects as they feed on plant juices

hybrid: offspring resulting from crossing two different species or genera

hydathodes: an opening in a leaf which exudes water; often located at the tip

inflorescence: the flowering part of a plant; a flower cluster

intergeneric: between two genera or among three or more genera

internode: the space on a stem between two nodes

keikei: a plantlet that develops on an orchid's cane or flower stalk

lanceolate: shaped like a lance-head; longer than it is wide; the wide point of the leaf is below its middle

layering: a propagation method where the stem of a plant (still attached to the parent plant) is pinned to the surface of potting mix; roots grow where the stem makes contact with the soil

leach: to remove a substance from soil by passing water through it

lenticels: a raised, corky, somewhat round spot on a stem; acts as a stomate

linear: line-shaped; long, narrow, and straight

lobed: having lobes (rounded segments) which are divided less than half way to the midrib

macronutrient: one of the six main nutrients necessary for plant growth; the three primary macronutrients are nitrogen, potassium, and phosphorus; the three secondary macronutrients are calcium, magnesium, and sulfur

meristem: undifferentiated, actively growing tissue at the growing points of stems and roots

micronutrient: one of seven nutrients required in lesser quantities than the macronutrients, sometimes called trace elements: iron, manganese, boron, zinc, copper, molybdenum, and chlorine

midrib: the central rib or vein of a leaf

monocot: monocotyledonous; having 1 seed leaf (cotyledon)

monoecious: male and female flowers borne on the same plant

monopodial: used to describe a form of orchid growth where a single shoot grows upward, for example, *Phalaenopsis* node: joint on an inflorescence or stem from which another stem, leaves, or roots may emerge

nodule: a swelling or knob-like structure

nymph: an immature insect stage

oblanceolate: inverse lanceolate, where the widest portion of the leaf is above the middle

offset: a plant shoot originating above ground from the base of another plant

ovary: the swollen base of the pistil where seeds ripen

ovate: oval-shaped

palmate: a leaf-shape resembling that of a hand with outstretched fingers

panicle: a branched inflorescence with flowers that mature from the bottom up

pedicel: a short flower stem

peduncle: a spur from which individual pedicels emerge

perlite: a lightweight, volcanic rock which is crushed, then heat-treated to make it expand; used in potting media to aerate and retain water and nutrients

petal: inner part of a flower; petals may look similar to sepals and are immediately interior to them

petiole: a leaf stalk

phylloclade: a stem that functions as a leaf, that is, it photosynthesizes

pinna (pl. pinnae): a primary division of a pinnate leaf

pinnate: a compound leaf with leaflets arranged on opposite sides of a long midrib

pistil: the female parts of a flower; composed of a stigma, style, and ovary

prothallus (pl. prothalli): the small, usually flat growth that germinates from a spore

proximal: toward the base; the end of attachment

pseudostem: a false stem; looking like a stem but not composed of xylem and phloem

recurved: curving backwards or inwards

rhizome: a root-bearing stem that grows horizontally across the potting mix and from which stems or pseudobulbs arise

scape: a leafless bloom stalk

sepal: outer parts of a flower; sepals on some flowers look similar to petals and are immediately outside them

sessile: attaching directly, without a stalk; a sessile leaf attaches to the stem without a petiole

sooty mold: a black fungus that frequently grows in honeydew

spadix: a spike covered with tiny flowers, accompanied by a spathe

spathe: a bract surrounding a spadix

species: a further division of a genus; a closely related group of plants

sport: a spontaneously occurring mutated plant with an appearance significantly different from that of the parent

spur: a slim appendage to a petal or sepal; spur-shaped

stamen: male parts of a flower composed of an anther and a filament

stigma: the portion of the pistil which receives pollen; a female flower part

stipule: a leaflike appendage at the base of a petiole; usually occur in pairs

stolon: a horizontal stem that roots at the nodes or tips and produces a new plant

stomate (pl. stomata): a leaf aperture allowing for gas exchange

style: the portion of the pistil that connects the ovary to the stigma

sucker: a shoot originating from below ground, from the original plant

sympodial: used to describe a form of orchid growth where new growth arises from the rhizome of the previous growth

tepal: when sepals and petals are indistinguishable they are called tepals

top dress: to replace the top several inches of potting mix with fresh mix

tuber: modified underground stem tissue; produces roots and stems from nodes

turgor: the plumpness of a leaf containing adequate water

umbel: an inflorescence with pedicels originating from a single point; resembles umbrella struts

underplant: to plant something underneath or surrounding another plant

understory: beneath the top layer of the forest canopy

undulate: slightly wavy leaf margins

venation: the pattern of veins on a leaf

velamen: a thick layer of spongelike material that covers the roots of epiphytic orchids and quickly absorbs water and nutrients

vermiculite: one of several minerals formed from mica, which when heated, expands to an accordion shape; it aerates soil and retains moisture and nutrients

wand attachment: a hose-end attachment for watering; wand attachments may have misting heads for soaking velamen roots and bromeliads

Wardian case: an enclosed case for growing plants, inside of which high humidity is maintained

whorl: a ringlike arrangement of parts (such as leaves, petals, stems) from a single point

PLANT NAMES INDEX

LYNBROOK PUBLIC LIBRARY

3 6646 00156 1156

635.9523 Zachos, Ellen.
Z
        Tempting tropicals.

29.95

DATE			

Withdrawn
Lynbrook Public Library

DEC   2005

LYNBROOK PUBLIC LIBRARY
CARPENTER AVENUE
LYNBROOK, NY 11563
(516) 599 – 8630

BAKER & TAYLOR